GEOGRAPHIES FOR ADVANCED STUDY

EDITED BY PROFESSOR S.H.BEAVER, M.A.

AN HISTORICAL GEOGRAPHY OF
SOUTH AFRICA

GEOGRAPHIES FOR ADVANCED STUDY

Edited by Professor S. H. Beaver, M.A.

The Tropical World
The Soviet Union
Malaya, Indonesia, Borneo and the Philippines
West Africa
The Scandinavian World
A Regional Geography of Western Europe
Central Europe
The British Isles
Geomorphology
Statistical Methods and the Geographer
Land, People and Economy in Malaya

IN PREPARATION

North America
The Polar World
Cartography
Western Mediterranean World
Eastern Mediterranean World
Human Geography

AN HISTORICAL GEOGRAPHY OF SOUTH AFRICA

BY

N. C. POLLOCK, B.A., B. LITT., M.A.

AND

SWANZIE AGNEW, M.A.

LONGMANS

LONGMANS, GREEN AND CO LTD
48 Grosvenor Street, London, W1

*Associated companies, branches and representatives
throughout the world*

PRINTED AND BOUND IN ENGLAND BY
HAZELL WATSON AND VINEY LTD
AYLESBURY, BUCKS

CONTENTS

LIST OF PLATES

For permission to reproduce photographs we are indebted to the following:
The Director of Information, South Africa House: Plates 1, 3, 4, 6, 14, 20,
21, 22, 24, 25, 26, 27, 28, 29, 30, 32, 33, 34, 41, 42, 43, 44, 45, 54, 62; Satour:
Plates 5, 9, 10, 11, 15, 16, 23, 31, 35, 36, 48, 58; South African Information
Service, Pretoria: Plate 46; South African Railways: Plates 59, 60; Africana
Museum, Johannesburg: Plate 55; Bibliothèque Nationale: Plate 8; The
Friend Newspapers, Ltd: Plates 37, 38; De Beers Consolidated Mines,
Ltd: Plates 47, 49, 51, 53, 56, 57, 61; Optima: Plates 50, 52; Paul Popper:
Plate 2; Edward Arnold (Publishers) Ltd.: Plates 39, 40 from Alice Blanche
Balfour, *Twelve Hundred Miles in a Waggon*; Henry Sotheran, Ltd: Plate
13 from J. G. Millais, *A Breath from the Veldt*. Plate 12 is from a British
official photograph, Crown copyright reserved.

FOREWORD

No historical geography of South Africa has appeared since C. P. Lucas produced his series on the Historical Geography of the British Colonies in 1898. The modern interpretation and presentation of historical geography with a critical analysis of past landscapes amplified by diagrams, maps and figures differs widely from that of sixty years ago. Judged by these criteria, this book is not a true historical geography limited in space and time in the reconstruction of the past. It is more nearly of the old genre of historical geography, where geography is called upon to give depth and fullness to historical events. This is a background book: monographs based on detailed research into the space relations of the past remain to be written.

In arrangement of material it has been thought best to devote a full chapter to the early historical setting of Africa south of the Sahara to show what influences came to bear on the southern part of the continent. Angola, Mozambique and Southern Rhodesia are treated in some detail because of the considerable influence exercised by the Portuguese and later by C. J. Rhodes in the interests of Great Britain on the Southern African scene. There is little mention of South West Africa, as for the most part it stood aloof from the main stream of historical growth and only became a mandate of the Union of South Africa after the First World War.

The book covers a period of approximately 500 years ending with the Union of South Africa in 1910. Although there are many references to events since Union we have decided not to write about this period in any detail, as it embraces too wide a field and lies more in the realm of political science than historical geography.

A broad development of South Africa is illustrated in the more general chapters. In Chapters 1, 2, 4 and 6 a picture of an expanding economy keeping pace with an expanding settlement is considered. With this essential background before the reader specific problems inherent in the political geography of South Africa are dealt with in more detail in Chapters 3, 5 and

7. It is believed that by this method the student may have the opportunity of analysing the broad principles underlying South African development along with those of more specialized studies. Because of this and the problem of reconciling different approaches to the historical geography of South Africa we apologize for any repetition that may occur and inaccuracies that may appear in a book covering such a wide field in space and time.

The spelling of African and Afrikaans names is that long current in English. The new orthography now being introduced for the African languages, has not been used. Also the prefix *ama-* which should properly precede the names of the Nguni tribes, has been disregarded for it is seldom used by English speakers. No disparagement is meant to any language or people by the omission of the new spelling or by the use of an English version of a name.

N. C. POLLOCK

S. AGNEW

September 1963

INTRODUCTION

Black Africa is commonly taken to lie south of the Sahara and Ethiopia. This separation from the Old World by desert and highland is important, for it is likely that these barriers, along with the Chad waters and Nile swamps, secured the isolation of the Negroid people. Needless to say the physical difficulties to movement never wholly excluded contact with the peoples and complex civilizations of the African and Asian shores of the Mediterranean sea. Communication with Eurasia, though tenuous south of the Sahara, and inland from the coast, nevertheless made Africa part of the Old World: a distinction that sets the Africans ahead of the Indians of the Americas, who lay outside the Eurasian heritage until the Age of Discovery.

The most important consequence of this touch with the peoples of the north is possibly the comparative ease with which the Negroid and Bantu people have withstood the diseases of the Old World on their first contact with the Europeans. Admittedly smallpox all but decimated the Hottentot clans in the Cape, while measles still proves dangerous to young children, but the Africans have shown a resilience to infection which allowed them in the nineteenth century a rapid rise in population, once tribal warfare and slavery were ended.

There has been no parallel among the Bantu people to those less able societies which, as in Tasmania and parts of America, have died out under the impact of white settlement and civilization. Indeed, it is probable that the Bushmen and Hottentots of the Cape, more akin to the Aborigines or Red Indian groups, would have been displaced as effectively, if less quickly, by the Bantu had the Bantu preceded the white settlers in the Cape. The Bantu have since shown that they were capable of absorbing a higher culture and its techniques, despite the modern fallacy of classing them among the less developed societies of the world. Indications that the Africans were capable of higher social manifestation in earlier centuries, may be counted in the great Benin culture of West Africa and the Zimbabwe culture of Southern Rhodesia, besides the military states of the

Western Sudan, which flourished in early medieval times[1] (Pl. 2.)

It can be argued that these higher cultures show Northern or Arab influence, and that south of the Limpopo there are few indications of cultural heritage save the magnificent rock paintings of the Bushmen (Pl. 1). It is true that the southern 'butt' of the continent has been a reliquary of ancient displaced floras, faunas, and peoples, and that the higher societies had only just made their appearance in the same century as the Portuguese and Dutch were rounding the Cape of Good Hope and discovering the outline of Africa.

These people were pastoralists, with agriculture considered a women's occupation of secondary importance. Their mode of life must be stressed, for pastoralism has had a profound bearing on the distribution of peoples in Africa and even on the disposition of the different racial groups, European and Indian, in South Africa. In the first place, the fact that the Bantu and Hottentots were herdsmen living a life of full sufficiency, outside a monetary or trading society, necessitated the import of labour to help in the development of the virgin country. The need for more work-hands brought slaves from Malaya to the Cape, Indians to Natal and, for a short while, Chinese to the gold mines in the Transvaal.

Moreover, since the Africans resisted absorption as a people into the new economy, they were driven into 'Reserves', where they have continued to stagnate in an outmoded economy orientated towards, and hidebound by, customs associated with unselective stock-breeding.[2] The pity of it is that Southern Africa stood outside an exchange economy by reason of the African peoples' failure to develop into settled agriculturists before the advent of the European. Had they been a settled peasantry, the impact of the European way of life might not have had such disastrous consequences; nor would race antagonism have reached the dangerous level it has at present.

H. J. Fleure[3] interprets the failure of the African people to develop a higher social organization to the inability of wheat to survive transplantation into the tropics beyond the Sahara. He comments that neither the banana nor millets, which were early introduced into Africa south of the Sahara 'brought the

---

[1] Basil Davidson has made a valuable reassessment of African civilizations in his book *Old Africa Rediscovered*, London 1961.

[2] Pl. 34.

[3] H. J. Fleure, *Some problems of Society and Environment*, The Institute of British Geographers, Pub. No. 12, London, 1947.

social organization that nearly always accompanies wheat'. Further, Fleure draws attention to the fact that the Bronze Age did not occur in Southern Africa. A misfortune, for in Europe the search for the two components of bronze did so much to foster exchange and the establishment of trade routes.

Southern Africa in her technical evolution jumped from wood and stone to poor craftsmanship in iron, just as she has today jumped from primitive iron-smelting to the complex steel age, without even serving an apprenticeship in the design and fine workmanship of wrought iron. H. J. Fleure argues that 'the early and cruder stages of iron-working acted as disintegrants socially . . . unless trade had previously existed'. So likewise, in great measure, the jump from poor iron-smelting to modern technology has been strikingly effective in African social disintegration.

Despite these arguments it is more probable that Africans remained isolated from advancement by reason of the geographical position of the southern part of the continent. Before the discovery of the route to the Indies, the tropical and southern landmass of Africa lay like a wedge between the high civilizations of the East and West. The pivotal area of South-west Asia formed the link between the peoples of temperate and Mediterranean Europe, and the civilizations of tropical and monsoonal Asia. Moreover, the nearer East is penetrated by the Red Sea and the Persian Gulf, which further reduce the land journey necessary to connect the Arabian Sea and India with the Mediterranean Sea and Europe.

Thus, able to by-pass Africa, these trade routes brought riches to the Levant, and prosperity to desert Arabia which, had the trade been wholly seaborne, might have been shared with Southern Africa. Arabian trade by land between India and Europe in fact declined after the discovery by the Portuguese of the sea route to India. It might be expected that Southern Africa would then have realized her potentialities and benefited from her position along this trade route; but before benefits could accrue from these trade relations the digging of the Suez Canal in 1869 and the Panama Canal in 1915 killed twice over the strategic position held by the Cape on the sea route between the Atlantic nations and the peoples of the Indian and Pacific shores.

It is to South Africa's lasting disadvantage that Africa and South America were so narrowly attached to the northern landmasses. Had canals not been cut across these narrow isthmuses the sea route round Africa would always have been favoured above that round Cape Horn. Though gales are strong, cross-currents treacherous and fog occasional at the meeting of the Atlantic with the Indian waters, none of these perils to navigation equals the hazards of the passage round Cape Horn, which lies 56° S.—some 21° further poleward than Cape Agulhas at 35° S. (Fig. 1).

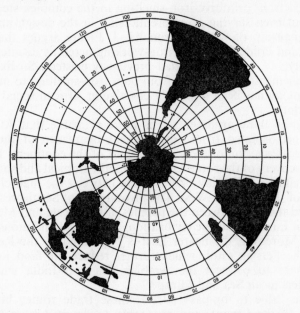

FIG. 1. Distribution of land in the Southern Hemisphere.

Deprived of the Eastern sea traffic the ports of South Africa have remained small, national enterprises rather than international emporia and entrepôts. Nevertheless, the strategic position of South Africa in the case of war between the East and the West, and the constant threat to the Suez artery even in time of peace, must influence the consideration paid to South Africa in international politics.

Since South Africa has never fully benefited from her sea position, it would appear that the country suffers yet another disadvantage by terminating at 35° S. Such a latitude precludes the development of the humid oceanic and continental temperate zones so significant in the Northern Hemisphere between latitudes 40° and 50° N. and enjoyed to some degree by the Argentine, Australia, Tasmania and New Zealand. It is those temperate humid climates that have proved themselves favourable to the full skill of European farming practices. Only New Zealand, of the southerly white settlements, approaches Western Europe in her high standards of agriculture, and obtains yields from crops and stock comparable to the records established in Europe and America.

Had South Africa been prolonged into higher latitudes with an assured maritime climate of well-distributed rainfall, it is probable that the early settlers in their dispersal towards the interior would have continued in agriculture and, for lack of a market in the early days, might have developed into a self-sufficient peasantry. Instead, once outside the confines of the better watered parts of the south-west Cape, the early pioneers turned to extensive stock herding as the only possible form of subsistence living.

Furthermore the first settlement of the Cape took place in complete isolation from other European centres, in a Mediterranean climate of which much was already of the arid type. This meant that the early colonists, on finding the environment one of difficulty, were unable to turn—as did their New England counterparts in North America—to trade and industry and deep sea fishing as a means of livelihood. From the beginning they were forced into a life of pastoralism little different from that of the indigenous peoples of the interior. (Fig. 2.)

It is logical to presume that, since South Africa was first settled by Europeans on the Atlantic side of the continent, the coast facing the European homeland would be the one to assume leadership, as was the case in the St Lawrence Lowlands in Canada and the Thirteen Colonies in North America. However, the position of the Cape Peninsula is most unfortunate. It is the first habitable area for 1,200 miles along the desert shores of the Atlantic and its further hinterland is one of stark mountain ranges and inter-montane basins; these last lying often in the rain-shadow of the mountains. Isolation has been the hallmark of South Africa from the first landing in the inhospitable Table Bay of the Cape Peninsula (Pl. 5).

Despite South Africa's great natural advantages in fronting on two oceans, there are vast empty stretches of water to the south leading to Antarctica and remote from the world's main ocean highways. The air age and the International Geophysical Year have brought Antarctica and the South Pole before the world, but in the days of sail the ocean wastes to the south of the

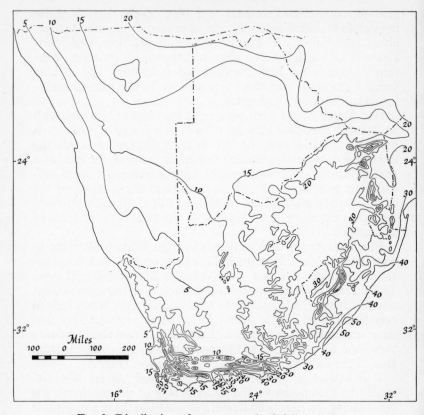

FIG. 2. Distribution of mean annual rainfall, in inches.
(After the meteorological staffs of the Royal Navy and South African Air Force, courtesy of the Government Printer, Pretoria.)
From Cole: *South Africa*, by permission of Methuen & Co. Ltd.

Cape of Good Hope were an *ultima thule* to mariners, the haunt of the Flying Dutchman. Also, to the east, between Cape Town and Adelaide, there is no landfall for 5,600 miles, while westwards across the Atlantic the volcano of Tristan da Cunha is the only island between Cape Town and Montevideo. Even so, the Portuguese would not use this shore for permanent settlement, for the coast of South Africa with its hidden shoals, conflicting currents and treacherous cross-waves, was dangerous to the clumsy sixteenth century caravels steered by the primitive Arab system of navigation. It is the Portuguese who first named

1. Bushman painting. Bushmen armed with bows and arrows and spears hunt the eland with the aid of dogs.

2. Zimbabwe—the oldest ruins date from the 11th century to about the 15th century; the conical tower and girdle wall belong to the 17th and early 18th centuries.

3. A Zulu 'Induna' or Headman Settlement. The cattle shown are the lyre-horned Zulu breed. Milking is being done mid-morning. Long-haired sheep make up the small stock. (*After a drawing by G. F. Angas, 1849*)

4. Returning from a shoot in 1801. The ox was riding animal to the Hottentots; the jerboa—a jumping rodent of arid areas—and the lack of garden enclosure around the Cape farmhouse are typical of the time. Horses as draft animals were used in the Western Cape; but oxen and mules where 'horse sickness' was a scourge.

the Cape Peninsula appropriately Cabo Tormentoso, the Cape
of Storms, though their other name Cabo de Boa Esperança
was the one finally to be adopted in translation as the Cape of
Good Hope (Pl. 6).

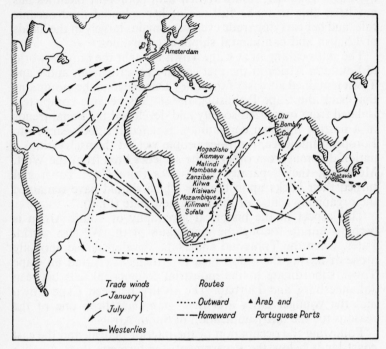

FIG. 3. Sailing Routes in relation to Wind Systems.

For these reasons the south coast of Africa remained neglected until the English and the Dutch supplanted the Portuguese and changed the emphasis of Far Eastern trading. The
Dutch concentrated on the East Indies, the English on Calcutta,
and therefore a southerly and easterly route via the Sunda
Strait was favoured to the more seasonal monsoonal route to
India via the Mozambique channel and the east coast of Africa.
To reach the Indies the English and Dutch, in their better
designed ships, beat far to the south of Madagascar in the path
of the westerlies, then in mid-ocean swung north-east to Java
and India in the full sweep of the deflected monsoonal trades
(Fig. 3).

Cape Town became the main victualling station on this new route, but despite a naturally strategic position on the route to India, the port has not been able to free itself from the function of first landfall on a lengthy ocean passage between Europe and the East. Likewise, South Africa with poor port facilities has not been able to make full use of her splendid dual oceanic role, and her carrying trade even yet remains largely in the hands of English and continental shipping companies.

The ships calling in at Cape Town brought the outside world to Southern Africa in the first century of settlement, and Cape Town remained abreast of the times. Once beyond the mountains that back the Cape Peninsula, the settlers became completely isolated from organized society and developed the social trends of a narrow ingrown community. Isolated for 200 years from European influence, the Boer people welded themselves into a nation different from other white societies bred from the West. Moreover, they separated themselves from Cape Town and turned their backs upon the city which should have remained the organizing centre of the rising new state (Pl. 4).

This aspect in the historical geography of South Africa is perhaps unique among the new states of the Western world. Later, when the Transvaal and Natal developed, the anomaly arose of having the oldest area of settlement centred on Cape Town, subordinate to the industrial commercial axis between Johannesburg and Durban. The rivalry between Cape Town and the younger cities and their states has been one of the reasons for the tardy unification of South Africa.

Following the occupation of the interior plateau and the east coast lands below the Escarpment, the farmers, Boer, English and German in origin, came into contact with the main body of the Bantu people. This contact with a culture totally unlike that of the immigrants had a profound effect on the mental pattern of the white settlers.

The shock experienced by ignorant white men when first meeting the naked Hottentots and Bushmen laid the foundation for the deep race prejudice and contempt for dark-skinned people, that is felt by the majority of white South Africans and Rhodesians. Later isolation from Europe on the part of the early white rural settlers and the association of all whites, whatever their nationality, with an indigenous people culturally inferior to themselves in technology and social organization, thereafter established the political framework of the Union of South Africa. From the first the 'native question' has never ceased to colour legislation and to bedevil the proper development of the country.

The political framework of two culturally opposed, but actually interdependent ethnic groups, is further complicated by the rise of the Coloured People in the Cape and the introduction of Indians into Natal. The relationships between these groups has profoundly affected the settlement pattern, the distribution and density of population, and also it has retarded the full economic development of the country. South Africa, with several races and a multicultural society in which the groups are antagonistic to each other, precludes an easy interpretation of the political geography of the country.

'Language exercises a decisive influence on the composition and distribution of inter-communicating social units—on who talks to whom—and thus on the activities in which men are able to participate in groups. Without linguistic communication no organized social undertaking can proceed, and without a single shared language such an undertaking becomes cumbersome and subject to misunderstanding. There are only a few nations, for example Belgium, Canada, Switzerland, where leadership is successfully shared by two speech communities or more.'[1]

Multiplication of languages and social groups with conflicting aspirations has been further complicated in the last twenty-five years by an industrial revolution which has led to the urban drift of all sections of the population and the creation of slum locations on the periphery of the rapidly expanding European cities.

The political system adopted to solve these problems is that embodied in the doctrine of apartheid, which the white electorate overwhelmingly endorsed in the elections of April 1958. The apartheid policy has come under fierce criticism, and the launching of an Afrikaner Republic in May 1961 has focused attention more closely on the Afrikaner people, who hold the destiny of the country and its diverse people in thrall to a system generally considered unjust, outdated and illiberal. An examination of the historical geography of South Africa might help in bringing the present problems into better perspective, bred of deeper understanding.

[1] P. L. Wagner, 'Remarks on the Geography of Language', *Geog. Review*, vol. xlviii, No. 1, January 1958, p. 86.

CHAPTER 1

EXPLORATION AND MIGRATION

THE coastlines of East Africa as far south as Madagascar and of West Africa as far south as Sierra Leone, were known to the Phoenicians, Greeks and Romans. The East African coast had a string of Hindu settlements hundreds of years before the Christian era, and until the fourth century A.D. the Sabaean kingdom of Southern Arabia, in a commanding position between Egypt and India, controlled the east coast. At the height of Roman power a fleet of 120 ships sailed each year to Malabar and Ceylon besides trading along the East African coast exchanging lances, daggers and other iron objects along with glass, wine and wheat for ivory, rhinoceros-horn, tortoise-shell, palm-oil, slaves and gold.

It was Roman and Greek interest in the East African and Indian trade that caused the Phoenician trade with West Africa to decay. Another major factor was the destruction by the Romans of Carthage's maritime power in the Mediterranean. For many centuries the coastal trade was abandoned and trade between the Sudan and North Africa was overland. It was not until the fifteenth century when the Portuguese probed south from Lisbon, that the west coast was again opened up for trade, first in gold and later in slaves. The shores of the great tapering southern subcontinent were probably unknown to Europe until the fifteenth century when Bartholomew Diaz first rounded the Cape, although it is possible that the Carthaginians circumnavigated Africa. Thus the whole of Africa's coastline was first charted only in the age of discovery, despite the fact that the north, east and west coasts had been known for so long.

For 1,500 years after the Phoenician withdrawal the coast of West Africa was unknown to Europe, but during the fifteenth century the Portuguese, inspired by Prince Henry the Navigator (1394–1460), began to push southwards from Morocco past the great desert bulge of the Sahara. Prince Henry provided a store-

1

house of information and fitted out maritime expeditions to explore the African coast and to develop trade links with Portugal. His great enthusiasm and leadership enabled Portuguese ships to push ever south and east from Cape Bojador, thus overcoming the formidable barrier of the Sahara.

The voyages of discovery in the fifteenth century were made possible by significant advances in ship-building, with caravel built full-rigged ships of divided sail plan replacing the one-masted cogs to be found in the North Atlantic. The divided sail plan enabled the ships to be managed more easily off treacherous and unknown shores, while longer voyages could be undertaken because of bigger ships and the fact that holds accommodated larger crews and held more stores. Improvements in the design of the mariner's compass and the use of astrolabe, back and cross staff, timepieces and mariner's charts made routes more certain, although the problem of finding the correct longitudinal position was not solved until the eighteenth century with the development of a more accurate timepiece, the chronometer.

By 1462 the Portuguese had reached the Gulf of Guinea, while Diego Cam in two voyages in 1482–4 and 1485–6 reached the mouth of the Congo river and South West Africa. In 1487 Bartholomew Diaz was the first European to sail round the southernmost point of Africa. It was not until eleven years later that Vasco da Gama was able to complete the rounding of Africa and reach India in 1498, thus proving finally that Africa projected far into the southern ocean and was not joined by a great easterly extension to India, as the ancients had supposed. The earlier voyages had kept near the coast, the Canaries or the Cape Verde Islands, each time attempting to push a little further south than previous expeditions.

Da Gama, however, armed with knowledge gained from a succession of probing voyages was able to strike straight out into the Atlantic after leaving the Cape Verde Islands and sail across the south-east trades.[1] The new full-rigged ships equipped with driving sails, sprit-sail and mizzen could be handled more easily than the single square-sail ship (Pl. 7). After tacking across the south-east trades, da Gama sailed west at about 35° S. in the zone of the westerlies which had moved north in the southern winter (Fig. 3). After three months at sea he made landfall near the Cape and reached the south-eastern coast of Africa in 1498. Having reached the Arab ports valuable help

[1] Diaz discovered the correct way of rounding the Cape on a wide seaward tack.

was given by a famous Indian pilot Mādjid, who guided the Portuguese to Calicut on the south-west coast of India. One of the greatest voyages in maritime history was completed in May 1498 when da Gama arrived in Calicut, and the successful completion of the return voyage on his arrival at Lisbon marked a new chapter in the commercial exploitation of East Africa and the Far East.[1]

Later the Portuguese captured and made use of the Arab settlements along the east coast from Sofala near the mouth of the Zambesi River to Mogadishu in the eastern Horn of Africa. It was obvious that the Portuguese would attempt to take over a ready-going concern and control the trade pattern that had been evolved by Hindus, Sabaeans, Romans, Greeks, Persians and Arabs over a very long period. In the eighth century Omani settlements were established along the east coast, followed in the tenth century by the Shirazis from Persia, who controlled the coast until the Portuguese arrival. The Arab and Portuguese settlements were fortified trading posts established on suitable island or river-mouth sites, e.g. Mombasa, Zanzibar, Mozambique and Sofala. These settlements acted as entrepôts and the hinterland was very extensive. There was no attempt at colonization of the interior of East Africa by Arabs or Portuguese.

Settlement of the interior was not undertaken partly because there were no natural routeways to the fertile and well-watered Kenya highlands or Lake Victoria basin, and also because the coastal strip in Kenya was backed by the semi-arid Nyika. Moreover, the major rivers, the Tana, Galana, Rufiji and Ruvuma draining into the Indian Ocean, rise on the edge of the plateau, have short turbulent courses to the sea, and are thus unnavigable. Livingstone found this to his cost when attempting to seek a route into the interior by way of the Ruvuma river.

Because the Zambezi is navigable in its lower reaches this river became the Portuguese gateway to Central Africa and the gold resources of Monomotapa, the latter no Spanish Eldorado, but exploited for precious metals long before the Portuguese came on the scene. Masudi, the Arab geographer of the mid-tenth century, described Sofala's hinterland as, 'a land which produces gold in abundance and other marvels'.[2] Ancient gold workings are scattered widely, gold is present over much of the

---

[1] According to E. Axelson, of the thirty-five recorded voyages made between 1419 and 1460 only eight were on Prince Henry's initiative, and the explorations were, in fact, a national and not an individual effort. *Geographical Journal*, vol. cxxvii, part 2, June 1961, pp. 148–9.

[2] Pl. 8.

plateau in the rocks associated with the Fundamental Complex, a great contrast to the vast concentration of gold-bearing conglomerates of the Witwatersrand. Stone ruins, terraces and irrigation channels testify to the vigorous Bantu culture that arose in this region from the ninth century onwards and achieved prosperity through the exploitation of gold and other resources.

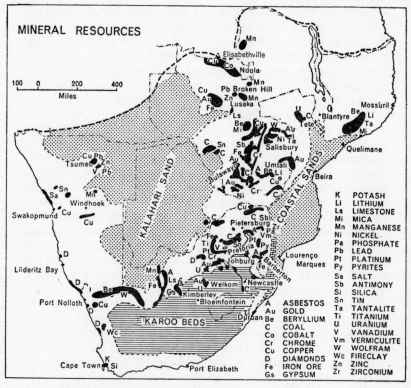

FIG. 4. Mineral Resources in Southern Africa.

From Green & Fair, *Development in Africa*, by permission of the Witwatersrand University Press.

Covilhâ, who visited Sofala in 1490, heard much about the gold in Monomotapa. King Manoel of Portugal determined to exploit these gold mines. Gold from the Gold Coast in West Africa added much to Portuguese prosperity in the sixteenth century. Control of a source of gold was vital to a small nation like Portugal. Soon after the Portuguese occupation of Sofala tribal unrest stopped the flow of gold to the coast, so Antonio Fernandes was sent to investigate the position in 1511. He found much gold being worked on the northern edge of the plateau to the south of the Zambesi river, while Joâo de Barros (1552) described alluvial gold being obtained from the Hunyani, Ruyu, Mazoe and other rivers[1] (Fig. 4).

The seat of Portuguese administration was at Mozambique, defended by the great fort of S. Sebastião (like Fort Jesus at Mombasa). There was also a Dominican convent and Portuguese town of some 2,000 inhabitants. Some 160 miles upstream on the Zambezi was Sena with its stone fort, factory and church, a prototype of Portuguese settlements in Africa. Here was based the Captain of the Rivers and some 50 Portuguese residents, mostly traders. One hundred and sixty miles further up the river was Tete also with its fort and 40 Portuguese who operated as traders in the domains of the Monomotapa. Travel to the north and west was barred by hostile tribes and cataracts,[2] so that Portuguese interest was centred in the uplands of Mashonaland with their advanced Karanga culture and gold mining. Gold was also obtained from Manicaland, reached through Sofala, the most southerly of the Portuguese settlements, although Portuguese boats were sent periodically to trade at Inhambane and at the Bahia da Lagoa. To the north Portuguese influence was slight and even their fort on Mombasa Island was only intended as a protection of their interests in the Zambezi region (Fig. 5).

At the height of their power there were never more than 400–500 Portuguese in South-east Africa, and yet their sphere of influence extended over a vast area, some 2,000 miles of coastline and a quarter of a million square miles of the Lower Zambezi and part of the Plateau. They controlled the appointment of the Monomotapa,[3] and by virtue of their supremacy in fire-power waged many successful campaigns against the Bantu. During the seventeenth century, missionaries, traders and adventurers had travelled over much of what is now Southern

[1] E. Axelson, 'Gold mining in Mashonaland in the 16th and 17th centuries', *Optima*, September 1959, p. 166.

[2] i.e. the Kebrabasa rapids, 60 miles above Tete, which prevented Livingstone from penetrating up the Zambezi. Access through the delta to the lower river was also difficult as channels were changing constantly.

[3] Despite the failure of Bareto's expedition of 1572, defeated by the fever-stricken Zambezi valley. The Monomotapa's Zimbabwe was near the Utete river, 60 miles south of the Zambezi and not to be confused with Great Zimbabwe near Fort Victoria. A Portuguese garrison was established here in the seventeenth century.

Rhodesia. Adventurers had acquired large properties and set up as feudal lords independent of Portuguese authority at Mozambique. The ivory and gold trade was of great importance, while the trade in slaves, ambergris, pearls and tortoiseshell was of considerable value and contributed much to the prosperity of Diu, Damaos and Goa in South India.

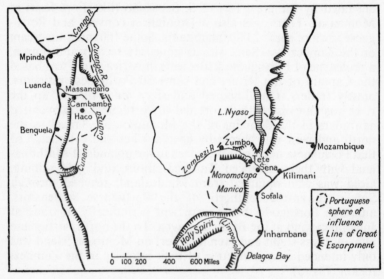

FIG. 5. Portuguese spheres of influence in Southern Africa.

European nations, particularly Holland, realized the value of Portuguese possessions in Zambezia and determined efforts were made to capture Mozambique. If these attempts had succeeded the Dutch might well have decided not to establish a refreshment station at the Cape in 1652, and the course of South African history would have been changed.

By the end of the seventeenth century, however, Portuguese commerce had declined greatly, particularly the gold trade. The Portuguese population of Sena and Tete dropped to less than half its maximum, and their centres of trade shifted to the Zambezi, as the fairs of Mashonaland were closed. The principal fair at Dambarara was overrun by a Rozwi chief, Changamira, in collusion with the Monomotapa. Despite the fertility of the Zambezi delta where rice, wheat, coconuts, cotton and sugar-cane flourished, little was done to develop the agricultural resources of the area. The Portuguese lacked capital, manpower and shipping and were further troubled by problems of administration; for Goa controlled the African interests and from such a distance Crown and local interests could not be reconciled. Another major factor was the devastating influence of disease in the Zambezi lowlands and on the coast, as the main Portuguese settlements were situated here and not on the healthy uplands of Mashonaland. The constant drain of manpower by debilitation and death did much to lower efficiency and lead to decay.

On the western side of the continent between the Cunene and Congo rivers is the large Portuguese possession of Angola, with an area of nearly half a million square miles. Most of it consists of the great southern plateau of crystalline rocks above 3,000 feet in height, partly overlain by Kalahari sands to the south and sloping down to the Congo basin in the north. As in South West Africa the plateau impinges closely on the west coast, and the descent is marked by a series of steep terraces. South of Benguela the coast becomes increasingly desert-like and is washed by the cold Benguela current. The great expanse of the high Angolan plateau is suitable for European settlement, and since 1950 the European population has doubled in size with a planned scheme of emigration from Portugal. Coffee is the major export crop, while the prospects for ranching are favourable on the tsetse-free grasslands of Central Angola. But after the first burst of colonization towards the end of the sixteenth century, Angola became subordinate to Brazil; its main importance being as a source of slaves. There was little or no gold and it has only recently become a source of industrial diamonds.

Cão discovered the mouth of the Congo on his first voyage from 1482 to 1484, and found here a wide grouping of tribes under a paramount chief, seemingly akin to a European monarch, and therefore dubbed the King of the Congo. His territory covered the southern Congo and much of Angola. A factory was established at Mpinda in 1501, and ivory, slaves and copper were traded for Portuguese goods. Journeys were made by Portuguese traders into the territory of the Congo paramount chief and later missionaries reached the domains of the Ngola which lay to the south.[1] Rumours of rich silver mines and prospects of obtaining slaves encouraged Portuguese exploitation. After 1540 slaves were obtained for the newly established sugar plantations in Brazil.

[1] The Ngola was the paramount chief of Ndongo, and the name for the territory of Angola derives from his title.

It was soon realized that Angola was suitable for white colonization and in 1574 Diaz and 400 settlers arrived at Luanda and established the first Portuguese settlement in Angola, an interesting venture as it was the pioneer of white colonization in Southern Africa. Despite its location only 9° south of the Equator Luanda has a cooler climate than Mozambique owing to the cold Benguela current. Mozambique, although 15° south, has higher temperatures and humidity primarily because of its location on the south-east coast warmed by the Mozambique current.[1] Much of Mozambique is below 1,000 feet in altitude, while along the coast the mean annual rainfall is usually above 30 inches with a summer maximum and high humidity during this period, thus creating more unsuitable climatic conditions for white settlement than in Angola. It is only on the higher parts of the crystalline plateau north of the Zambezi that cooler temperatures are more conducive to white settlement. The highlands of Angola were climatically suited to white settlement in the sixteenth and seventeenth centuries, but they were never occupied, the main reasons being lack of manpower, capital, prior concern with the slave-trade rather than settlement and the subordination of Angolan interests to those of Brazil. The Boers, with none of these concerns in seeking a healthy habitat, were able to benefit from the high plateau of Southern Africa which the Portuguese had failed to appreciate or utilize.

Diaz established fortified posts to control the route to the reportedly rich silver mines of Cambambe. Forts were built at Massangano and Cambambe in 1604, where it was found that the deposits of silver were insufficient to justify exploitation. The Cuanza river, 30 miles south of Luanda, was a useful avenue to the interior, Luanda being sited within easy access of the river. Ships could proceed upstream for 150 miles before the plateau edge was reached as in the case of the Zambezi.

A fort was built at São Felippe da Benguela in 1617, 250 miles to the south of Luanda, providing access to the highlands of the Bihé Plateau, which attains a maximum height of over 8,500 feet, the highest part of the Angolan plateau, and its resources of cattle, slaves and ivory. As in Mozambique, fairs were opened in Haco and Bango and fifty years after the first Portuguese settlement at Luanda a considerable degree of de-

[1] Mozambique with a mean annual temperature of 79° F. is a little warmer than Mombasa 800 miles nearer the equator, while Luanda has a mean annual temperature of 74° F.

velopment had occurred. The Portuguese sphere of influence extended for 800 miles along the coast from Kabinda to south of Benguela and for over 200 miles inland along the left bank of the Cuango river, tributary to the Congo.

For a long period after the end of the seventeenth century Portuguese interest and civilizing influence in Angola and Mozambique decayed for a variety of reasons bound up with Portugal's own decline as a first-rate power and competition from England, Holland and France. Arab revival in the second half of the seventeenth and eighteenth centuries caused a collapse of Portuguese power on the east coast with the loss of Mombasa, Kilwa, Zanzibar and other trading posts and their retreat south of Cape Delgado. So insecure did the Portuguese hold become that at times their bases, Mozambique, and Sofala on the south-east coast, were threatened by Bantu attacks.[1] The initial period of Portuguese colonization was one of great endeavour which achieved little of permanent value. Successful settlement of the subcontinent was to be achieved by the Dutch only during the eighteenth and nineteenth centuries and by the British in the nineteenth century in the vast, unexploited, yet healthy region to the south of Angola and Mozambique.

Between the Portuguese possessions in south-east and south-west Africa was the great South and East African Plateau, and to the south lay the curving 3,000-mile coastline of South Africa. To the Portuguese this vast interior territory was of no value; there appeared to be no exploitable resources, and their energies were fully occupied in developing the trade of the Zambezi and Angola. This great region was therefore largely *terra incognita* to Europe until the Dutch occupied the Cape in 1652 and expanded slowly into the interior during the eighteenth century.

By the mid-nineteenth century the journeys of exploration undertaken by traders, missionaries and hunters had added considerably to the geographical knowledge of the interior of Southern Africa. But until the nineteenth century maps of Africa left blank most of the interior in the south and east, or pictured it imaginatively with fabulous animals, peoples and cities. Little was known of the Bantu tribes inhabiting the interior except for those states such as Congo, Ndongo, Monomotapa and others which had come into contact with the Portuguese on the east and west coasts of Southern Africa.

The map (Fig. 6) shows the location of some of the Bantu states in East and Central Africa from the fifteenth to the nine-

[1] That is, the tribes inhabiting east and southern Africa.

teenth centuries, and possible routes taken by the Southern Bantu in their migrations southwards from the Congo and Lake Victoria basins. Powerful Bantu states developed on the southern fringe of the Congo basin, the plateau to the south

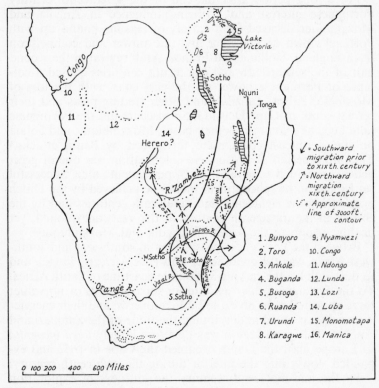

FIG. 6. Migration Routes of the Bantu prior to the mid-nineteenth century.

of the Zambezi and on the northern and western shores and highlands of the Lake Victoria region. Physical conditions would appear to be more congenial here than elsewhere in South and East Africa for the growth of a vigorous Bantu society. Eight small states have grown up round lake Victoria whose great area, 200 miles by 150 miles on an average, is of major climatic significance. This inland sea on the equator with its wide expanse of fresh water is crossed by the south-east trades which cause a heavy rainfall on the northern and western shores of the lake (Fig. 7).

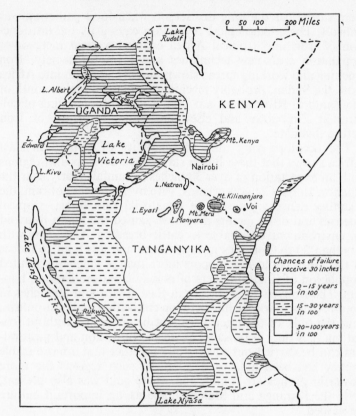

FIG. 7. Rainfall reliability in East Africa.

The gently undulating landscape near the lake, with flat-topped hills and broad valleys forming part of the miocene peneplane, rich, deep, red soils and the evenly distributed rainfall of 50 to 70 inches encouraged a dense population of Negro cultivators, on which has been superimposed an Hamitic pastoral aristocracy who have intermingled with the Negroid peoples and created these Bantu states.

A factor of the utmost significance in savanna regions, where Stone Age man in small groups carried on a precarious hunting and collecting existence, was the remarkable spread of the knowledge of iron working about 2,000 years ago. With iron implements man was then able to slash and burn the bush and clear plots for the cultivation of millet and other food crops, which were stored for the long dry season when food gathering was difficult. The technological revolution caused by the introduction of iron into tropical Africa enabled a great increase of population with new techniques and forms of society. Iron smelting and working spread slowly across and south into Africa from the Sudan, probably reaching the plateau region south of the Zambezi River about A.D. 300. Radio carbon dating of cultures at Zimbabwe and elsewhere shows no trace of iron before this date.

The accompanying map of reliability of rainfall in East Africa shows that these Bantu states have developed in regions with an expectation of over 30 inches of rainfall yearly near the equator. In the Congo lowlands, with over 60 inches of rain, the resulting dense vegetation of equatorial rain forest, tropical diseases and other factors may have caused the Bantu to avoid an environment unsuitable to cattle breeding. The areas with less than 20 to 25 inches in East Africa and less than 15 inches in the south could not support more than a widely distributed population of small numbers of nomadic pastoralists and hunters. The isohyets of 30 inches in East Africa and 20 inches in South Africa mark the line between cultivation and pastoralism, thus the bulk of the interior cannot be cultivated without irrigation. It is only in those areas where cultivation and pastoralism can be carried out successfully together that a more stable society has been able to develop. In such regions the more powerful groups are found, and where gold was also present, as in the Karanga and Manica domains, an important culture developed.

The high altitude of the great South and East African Plateau tended to reduce the incidence of debilitating tropical diseases such as malaria, yellow fever, trypanosomiasis (sleeping sickness), etc. Buchanan writes: 'Disease, malnutrition and low agricultural production forms in fact a vicious circle in Nigeria as in the remainder of tropical Africa.'[1] The great variety of tropical diseases reduces the energy of the peasant and makes him an inefficient cultivator with a low output. On the higher plateaux these diseases are less prevalent and the incidence of tsetse and thus trypanosomiasis is lower (Fig. 8).

Annual and seasonal amounts of rainfall over much of Africa are low and highly variable, the maximum occurring in summer except for a small area with an equatorial regime. Evaporation

[1] K. M. Buchanan and J. C. Pugh, *Land and People in Nigeria*, London, 1955, p. 56.

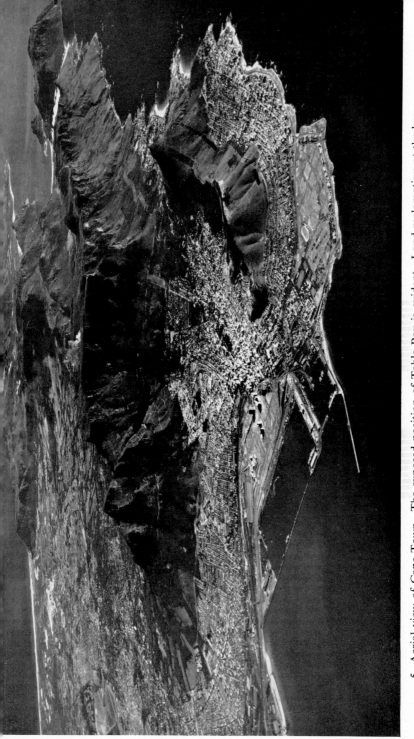

5. Aerial view of Cape Town. The exposed position of Table Bay is evident. Land reclamation at the bay-head, creation of docks behind sea-walls, and the help of a breakwater have given modern harbour facilities. The amphitheatre gave the initial settlement shelter from the south-easterly gales; the piedmont slopes proved suitable for vines.

6. A Portuguese map based on Ptolemy's outline of Africa, showing all newly nam[ed] headlands and bays discovered in rounding the Cape of Good Hope.

7. Portuguese caravel.

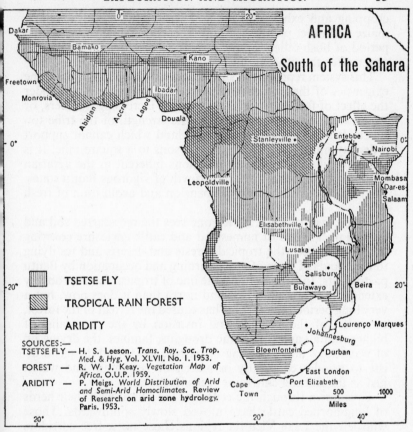

FIG. 8. Major Environmental Handicaps in Economic Development in Africa.

From Green & Fair, *Development in Africa*, by permission of the Witwatersrand University Press.

is intense in the plateau regions with dry air and cloudless skies. Soils over much of tropical Africa are poor; tropical red soils are considerably leached and have a low organic and mineral content. Finer sand particles are washed down leaving a thirsty, sandy, surface layer overlying a hard pan. These soils are easily exhausted and have a fragile crumb structure. The prevailing agricultural response to the poor soils and variable rainfall of the tropics has been one of shifting cultivation or bush fallowing. This necessitates constant movement after a few years of

A.H.G.S.A.—3

cropping and exhausting the soil with yams, cassava, millet, maize and other plants. The soil regenerates slowly over a long period of bush fallow by the growth of a secondary vegetation cover after the peasant cultivator has moved on.

This system represents a simple and sensible adaptation to the exigencies of the tropical environment, but breaks down under the effect of factors, such as pressure of increasing numbers, or when warfare and famine reduce the strength of the tribe too much. It also needs large areas of land which cannot support a density much higher than 100 persons to a square mile. It is therefore likely that these limitations inherent in the agrarian economy militated against the growth of vigorous Bantu states. They could survive only by expansion and acquisition of fresh land.

Flying over savanna Africa one sees the red scarred soil and layered pockmarks of homestead and cattle enclosure covering the land between the tropical forests and deserts and testifying to thousands of years of grass burning and occupation by Bantu pastoralists. In Roman times the line of tropical forest probably extended much further east and north than it does now, but a very long period of grass fires has caused the retreat of the forest, extension of the savanna and invasion by the pastoralist of higher rainfall areas. Periodic droughts, famines, the drying up of waterholes and withering of pasture has forced the pastoralists to wander constantly in search of new grass and water, just as the shifting cultivator seeks fresh soil.

Thus down through the centuries the Bantu with their herds of long-horned cattle have moved slowly southwards. Those who left the Lake Victoria regions chose tsetse-free corridors across the Tanganyika plateau.[1] Then, either passing round the head of Lake Nyasa, they crossed the uplands of what is now the Rhodesias and, skirting the waterless Kalahari, entered the High Veld of South Africa from the west; or driving their herds to the east of Lake Nyasa followed the line of the plateau edge and entered South Africa from the north-east (Fig. 6).

The word 'Bantu' really means 'the people' and is a linguistic term to designate the great groups, now numbering sixty million, of Negro-Hamitic people inhabiting East and South Africa. They are by far the most important ethnic group in this region; the Hottentots and Bushmen, formerly ranging

---

[1] H. Ingrams, *Uganda*, London, 1960, p. 165, says that sleeping sickness and animal trypanosomiasis have only spread into East Africa from West Africa and the Rhodesias in the lasty eighty years.

far and wide over Southern Africa, have now been driven into the wastes of South West Africa and the Kalahari and are very few in number. Tropical Africa's indigenous peoples were formerly divided according to physical characteristics into Bushmen, Negro and Hamite, but successive migrations, splitting up of tribes and conquest have caused such an inextricable intermingling of ethnic groups that this criterion has proved difficult to accept. The major criterion for Seligman's classification into Bantu, Negroes, Hamites, Bushmen and Hottentots, was thus language and not physical type. Because of these migrations the Bantu can be divided into three great groups, the Western, Northern and Southern Bantu, the last group numbering some 15 million. Hailey divides the Southern Bantu into two main groups; the south-eastern consisting of the Nguni and Thonga clusters and the south-central consisting of the Venda and Sotho.[1] According to Schapera there are four main clusters; Rhodesian (Shona), South-eastern (Zulu–Xhosa), South-central (Sotho–Tswana) and South-western (Ovambo–Herero).[2]

Routes taken by the migrating Bantu and their dates of entry into Southern Africa are highly conjectural, as there is little or no historical evidence before the nineteenth century, apart from the accounts of shipwrecked mariners who managed to struggle back to the Portuguese possessions in the sixteenth and seventeenth centuries and the Dutch settlements at the Cape in the eighteen century. Some assistance can be obtained from oral tribal traditions, and physical, anthropological, archaeological and linguistic evidence. Interpretation of this evidence is made very difficult by the constant tendency of tribes to split up into small units. There was also the widespread disorganization of tribal life and structure caused by the Zulu wars of the early nineteenth century and the struggles against the European. The latter caused further widespread migrations, while contact with the European exchange economy promoted wholesale detribalization.

The Bantu, it is believed, entered Southern Africa in a series of movements over a long period. They may well have acquired their technique in agriculture, metal working and tribal organization by the beginning of the Christian era, after which, combined with increasing numbers, they proved sufficiently power-

[1] Lord Hailey, *An African Survey*, Revised 1956, Oxford, 1957, p. 40.
[2] I. Schapera, *The Cambridge History of the British Empire*, Cambridge, 1936, Vol. VIII, p. 35.

ful and organized to press southwards.[1] The first invaders of Southern Africa may well have been the ancestors of the Shona of Southern Rhodesia, who developed the advanced Zimbabwe culture from the ninth century on. The Karanga Kingdom was bolstered up by the Portuguese, but was conquered at the end of the seventeenth century by the Rozwi, whose control was broken in turn by the desperate Ndebele during the 1830s in their flight northward from Shaka's onslaught in Zululand. An offshoot of the Rozwi established a state in the upper reaches of the Zambezi which was also destroyed by the Kololo, Sotho refugees from Shaka's wars.

After the Karanga came the progenitors of the Sotho and Tswana people who pressed through the plateau gap between lakes Tanganyika and Nyasa, crossed the Zambezi and finally settled on the eastern edge of the Kalahari north of the Orange–Vaal confluence. Here they established a Sotho tribal group and absorbed much Bushman blood. During the sixteenth and seventeenth centuries the main body of Sotho and Tswana advanced into the Transvaal where they expanded across the High Veld and into Basutoland. Anthropological and air photographic evidence of pre-European hut and kraal clusters on the High Veld indicates that this region had a considerable population before the arrival of the Boers. The Rev. J. Bennie writing in 1837 refers to the fact that, 'The remnants of the former populous tribes have left their fortresses and reside in the glens under the protection of the emigrants [Boers] who found the country a desert.'[2]

As in East Africa it is the map of rainfall distribution that is of paramount importance in studying the pattern of Bantu movements into Southern Africa. Two-thirds of South Africa has less than 15 inches of rainfall yearly, the critical limit for Bantu pastoralists. It was the better watered eastern third of South Africa and its grasslands that were to be contested by Boer and Bantu during the late eighteenth century and much of the nineteenth century. The 15-inch isohyet also determined the route of hunter, trader and missionary into Central Africa and to the east of this line lay the vital Missionaries' Road to the north (Fig. 2).

The plateau lies in the trade wind belt, and maximum rainfall for most of South Africa occurs in summer, when air masses from the Indian Ocean are drawn into the southward extension

[1] See page 10.
[2] D. *Williams, An Account of a Journey—1843*, Rev. J. Bennie, p. 13.

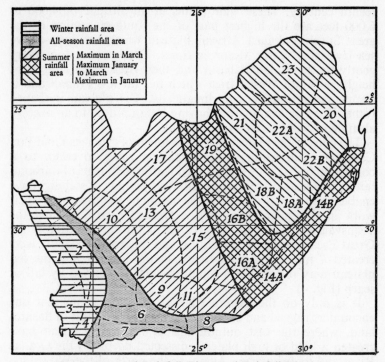

FIG. 9. Seasonal Rainfall Zones and Rainfall Districts.
From Wellington, *Southern Africa*, II, by permission of the author,
the Government Printer, Pretoria and Cambridge University Press.

of the tropical low pressure system. The heaviest falls occur
to the east especially along the line of the Great Escarpment,
but rainfall decreases rapidly to the west. Rainfall is highly
variable in amount and seasonal incidence; the onset of plough-
ing rains may vary considerably and in marginal areas with a
rainfall of less than 20 inches drought may cause a failure of
the maize harvest in two or more successive years. Drought
has been a major cause of pastoral movement, and the struggle
between Boers and Bantu for possession of good grazing was
closely bound up with the irregular rainfall regime characteristic
of tropical and sub-tropical Africa (Fig. 9).

The Sotho and Tswana pastoralists were able to range freely
unhampered and unchallenged across the wide treeless, temperate grasslands of the High Veld, until the Matabele and
Mantati depredations and Zulu invasions during the early nine-

teenth century. These wide plains at an altitude of 4,000 to 6,000 feet are the highest part of the southern section of the great South and East African Plateau which has been above sea level since early Mesozoic times. The interior slopes very gently to the Kalahari basin and then rises to an equivalent height in South West Africa which has far less rainfall and is steppe vegetationally and climatically. The plateau is shaped rather like a saucer, its rims having been uplifted to an average altitude of 5,000 to 6,000 feet (Pl. 9).

The core of the plateau is the basement of Archaean and Pre-Cambrian sedimentary and crystalline rocks, overlain to a considerable extent by undisturbed Karoo sediments of Carboniferous to Jurassic age. Long continued periods of stability have enabled erosion cycles to leave monumental traces of their work in the great plains of the Orange Free State and the Transvaal and the giant terraces below the eastern edge of the Great Escarpment. Pediplanation and horizontal bedding have created a monotonous landscape in the interior and the flat plateau may roll on for a hundred miles unrelieved by hill or scarp (Fig. 4).

It is only on the eastern edge of this high plain that one encounters rugged and broken terrain, as for example in Basutoland, where the vast outpourings of Stormberg basalt have created a kind of high plateau, dissected deeply by the Orange River and its tributaries. Again, to the north of the Witwatersrand, vigorous headward erosion by the Limpopo, Sabie, Komati and other rivers has stripped off the Karoo cover to give a broken surface (Pl. 10). Along the eastern flank of the plateau the Great Escarpment is fretted into a maze of ridges and dissected hill lands by the erosion of swift coastal rivers, such as the Tugela, Umzimkulu and Umzimvubu (Pl. 11). It was in regions like this that the tribes, fleeing from the marauding bands of warriors in the time of the Lifaqane or wars of despoliation in the 1820s, sought refuge and it was in the Stormberg basalt bastion of Basutoland that Moshesh was able to withstand Bantu, Boer and British attacks and forge the Basuto nation of today.

There is little tree growth on the plateau owing to centuries of veld burning, dry cold winters and strong winds. *Themeda triandra* or red grass is the climax over most of the plateau. It is one of South Africa's best pasture grasses, the grazing value being highest in the early stages of growth, but after three months the protein and mineral content declines rapidly. To the west the *Eragrostis, Sporobulus, Aristida* and other grasses become dominant and are less luxuriant, tougher and more widely spaced. Man has affected drastically the vegetation pattern of South Africa. In the sixteenth century when the first Bantu pastoralists invaded the area the High Veld consisted of waving grasslands of *Themeda triandra*, green in summer and coppery brown in winter. Early nineteenth-century pictures show good stands of red grass where now Karoid vegetation holds sway. Desert encroachment has carried the forerunner, the Karoo type of vegetation, east to the sea and into Basutoland to an alarming degree.[1] Bitter Karoo (*Chrysocoma tenuifolia*) and some of the pioneer karoo vegetation of little nutritious value have invaded the Basutoland mountain pastures of red grass (Fig. 10).

Prior to contact with the Europeans in South Africa the Bantu occupied most of the region except for the arid and semi-arid Karoo and Kalahari wastes and the winter rainfall region of the south-western Cape. Their distribution corresponded fairly closely with the line of 15 inches summer rainfall which runs north–south in line with the 26° east longitude. Their social organization was more elaborate than the Hottentots and they were divided up into a large number of tribes, the size varying from less than 1,000 to over 50,000. The size and importance of the tribe varied considerably according to the power of the chief, the effects of conquest and natural factors such as disease and famine. Various tribes occupied specific areas, and the tribal territory was generally well defined.

The institution of chieftainship among the Southern Bantu was of major importance; the chief was the tribal leader, the fount of government and arbiter of disputes, the trustee of tribal land and benefactor in times of famine. The chief was also responsible for performing tribal ceremonies, such as the ritual eating of the first fruits still practised by the Swazi. Tribute, fees and fines went to the chief who was also the repository of the tribal wealth and was expected to succour the weak and reward the faithful. A council of tribal elders or headmen helped the chief in tribal government and usually acted as a salutary check on a would-be autocratic chief. As the tribal organization became more elaborate and the tribe larger, a paramount chief might rule through a hierarchy of subchiefs and headmen, appointments usually being hereditary in certain

[1] J. P. H. Acocks, *Veld Types of South Africa*, Memoir of the Union Botanical Survey, No. 28, 1953.

families, for example, the family of Moshesh in Basutoland. The present position of the chief has been undermined by growing detribalization in contact with the European economy, although the present South African government is attempting to revive the traditional pattern of chieftainship in Bantu areas.

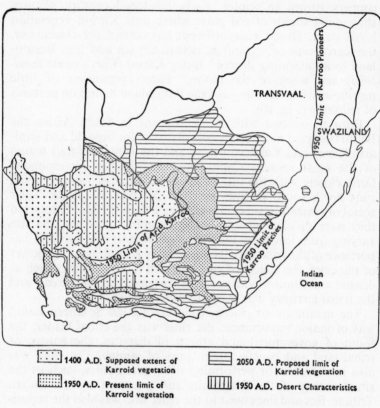

FIG. 10. Desert Encroachment in South Africa.
(After Acocks.)

At the other end of the scale the basic social grouping was the family and homestead, sometimes in single units, or as in Basutoland and the Transvaal in groups of ten to fifty households forming a kind of village. In an extreme form, where springs cause a concentration of population as in semi-arid Bechuanaland, agricultural towns of a large size are found. Nevertheless, even amongst the *stads* of Bechuanaland the most important unit is still the family cluster. Each homestead was an independent unit and these units or kraals were scattered indiscriminately over the tribal territory. Siting of individual homesteads was based as much on the chief's or individual's whim and human factors such as necessity for defence, as on access to natural resources of water, grazing land and thatching grass (Pl. 12).

The chief was the custodian of tribal land, which belonged in theory to the chief, who allocated lands to heads of families. Plots or strips of cultivable land and hut sites were granted under a form of individual tenure, the head of the family having the use of these lands during his lifetime. During the autumn and winter when the maize or millet harvest had been garnered, the stover on individual strips was declared common pasturage. Pasture and waste were likewise common property and held under communal tenure; not unlike the feudal system in parts of Europe. In contrast the European farmer regarded a landholding as his personal property, a view quite different from the Bantu concept of land belonging to the tribe and not the individual. These diametrically opposed views naturally led to continuous friction in relationships between Boer and Bantu landholders.

As the Southern Bantu were predominantly a cattle-keeping people, the kraal or cattle enclosure usually formed the focal point of the homestead or group of homesteads ringed around by the huts. Men looked after the cattle which played a very important part in the life of the tribe, being used as currency, in the marriage arrangements, and for religious ceremonies. They were symbols of prestige and wealth, little attention being paid to quality. They also provided milk and occasional meat; the skins were used for clothing, horns as receptacles, the dung for fuel and mortar, and oxen were useful for transport. Game, however, provided most of the meat (Pl. 3).

The savanna of Africa was the home of vast herds of antelope of many different varieties and the availability of meat played an important part in the diet of Bantu and Boer. Animals were snared and trapped or slaughtered in great numbers during large hunting expeditions. Captain Harris who visited South Africa in 1836 writes of the large herds of game encountered near the Maritzani river: 'We soon perceived large herds of Quaggas and Brindled Gnoos which continued to join each other until the whole plain seemed alive. . . . I could not estimate the accumulated numbers at less than fifteen thousand, a great extent of country being actually chequered black and white with their congregated masses'[1] (Pls. 13, 14). There were few commissariat problems for the white hunter, missionary, trader and farmer who lived off the country and could subsist for long periods on a diet of little other than dried meat called biltong,[2] if fresh game was not available.

The women cultivated the fields and produced food crops of maize, millet and vegetables such as pumpkins and beans. Each wife usually had her own plot and cultivated it with a simple hoe after her husband had cleared it of vegetation. Methods were primitive, rotational practices were imperfectly applied in the form of bush fallowing, manuring was unknown and irrigation rare. The staple diet consisted of a stiff maize meal or porridge, assisted by vegetable or wild plant relishes and a sour beer made from grain. Each household was almost completely self-sufficient, and there was little trade except for the barter of iron objects and occasionally clay pots. Iron smelting was in the hands of itinerant smiths who were believed to have magical powers and who were greatly respected by all tribesmen (Pl. 15).

The Sotho have now split up into three main groups, the Western Sotho or Tswana in Bechuanaland, the Eastern Sotho in the Transvaal and Southern Sotho whose focus is in Basutoland. The Tswana consist of a number of tribes, such as the Tlaping, Rolong, Hurutshe, Kwena, Ngwaketse, Ngwato and Tawana. They tended to settle on the eastern edge of the Kalahari with a mean annual rainfall of over 15 inches. To the west lack of surface water restricts grazing, while the northern bush lands and Okavango delta were affected by tsetse fly and, therefore, not suitable. The scarcity of water in the cattle area itself has necessitated a concentration of population on available water holes and springs, particularly those of strong source east of the Dolomitic Limestone and Basement Complex. The Tswana 'town' is an atypical aspect of Southern Bantu settlement, which is usually scattered haphazardly. Over half the population now lives in villages of over 1,000 inhabitants, while Kanye, Serowe, Molepolole and Mochudi each have more than 10,000.

Burchell who visited the Tlaping at Litakon in 1812 describes

---

[1] Captain W. C. Harris, *Narrative of an Expedition into South Africa*, Bombay, 1838, pp. 74–75.
[2] Similar to pemmican or jerked beef.

it in detail.[1] It spread out over a large area on a plain and its present site had been occupied for only six years. There were no streets and the houses were scattered haphazardly, being grouped in clusters, each containing about 150 people and under their own chieftain. Each homestead was bounded by a strong elipsoidal fence. The main hut was in the middle of the enclosure and was circular with a thatch roof projecting some four feet beyond the outer wall, the eaves supported by wooden posts set in a low wall and forming a kind of veranda. There were no windows or apertures, except for the door. Sometimes a small room was built inside the hut and used for sleeping quarters in winter (Fig. 11).

FIG. 11. Tlaping hut type and plan. (After Burchell)

As with the Dutch 'stoep' the veranda was the focus of activity and had a shallow fire hole at one end. Transverse walls divided the inner court into a yard used for storage, particularly of grain, behind the hut, and a forecourt in front. The floors of hut and court were of clay and cattle dung mixed and beaten smooth. Burchell was impressed by the neatness and cleanliness of the huts and enclosures.

[1] W. J. Burchell, *Travels into the Interior of Southern Africa*, 1822–4 (Reprint 1953, Glasgow), Vol. II, ch. 17.

One or more cattle enclosures were attached to each division of the town, although most of the cattle were kept at posts some distance away, and sour milk was sent into the town once or twice a week. Agricultural lands benefiting from the proximity of subsurface water were scattered round the town and it was the work of the women to plant crops of corn, beans and water melons. They also built and looked after the huts.[1]

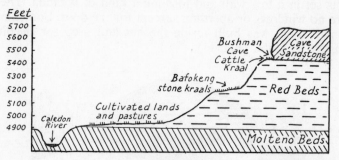

FIG. 12. Land utilization and village site among Bafokeng (Basutoland).

Basutoland is a great contrast to the semi-arid plains of Bechuanaland. Here vast outpourings of Stormberg basalt have built up additional layers on the Karoo sediments to a height of over 11,000 feet in places.[2] The basaltic highlands of Basutoland are South Africa's main watershed and are highly dissected by the Orange and its tributaries. Numerous mesas and buttes at the edge of the highlands offered refuge to scattered tribes fleeing from the Lifaqane of the 1820s.[3] Prior to this, at some time during the eighteenth century, the first Bantu inhabitants of Basutoland were probably the Fokeng who intermarried with the Bushmen, and used their Cave Sandstone shelters, although their circular settlements were usually located lower down the slope (Fig. 12). Competition for the rich lands of the eastern Orange Free State between Boers and Sotho in the period from 1840 to 1870 gradually drove the Sotho back to the east of the Caledon river, leaving the bulk of the southern High Veld to the Boers.

[1] I. Schapera in his book, *Western Civilization and the Natives of South Africa*, London, 1934, p. 14, says that the men did the woodwork and erected the roof, and the women built the walls, thatched the roof and smeared on mural decorations.

[2] Pl. 11.   [3] Pl. 16.

Homesteads were often built on the sides of mesas and buttes on an intermediate terrace or slope between the cultivated lands below and pastures on the mesa top. When danger threatened the population could retreat to the flat top of the mesa, well protected by a rock palisade of cave sandstone or basalt skirting the top of the mesa. Dolerite dykes cutting through the sandstone and weathered into straight-sided channels often afforded easy routes to the summit, but the narrow gulley could be blocked by stone works in time of war. Huts are generally placed to catch the morning sun in a country where radiation brings the temperatures well below freezing point in winter, and to the point of frost even during summer in the higher valleys. Inversion of temperature keeps the huts to the mid-valley slopes away from the frost hollows of the cold valley bottoms. Mid-slope, near a reliable spring and preferably directly in the rays of the rising sun are the most favoured sites for huts.

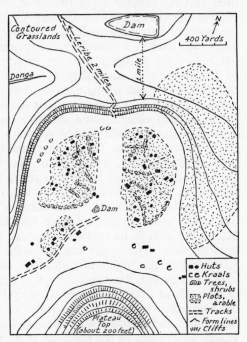

FIG. 13. Distribution of huts and arable land in a Sotho settlement.

In pre-European days settlements were circular in form with the chief's homestead, cattle kraal and *khotla*[1] in the middle and the rest of the huts grouped around it, the whole enclosed by a circular fence. Settlements are no longer circular in plan, but tend now to be haphazard, scattered or strung out in a line below a mesa scarp or along a slope (Fig. 13).

The huts were ovoid or circular in form with mud or sod walls and thatch roofs connected by a palisade or screen

[1] Tribal meeting place.

where cooking was carried on. An ovoid or calabash form of hut is depicted in Figure 14. It had a narrow, low, elongated entrance leading into the usual circular type of hut. The use of this type of doorway may have been as a protection against wild animals.

In the second half of the nineteenth century with missionary influence, stone, especially the soft Cave Sandstone, began to be used and rectangular types of hut to be built, not unlike the 1820 settler cottages of the Eastern Cape. As in Bechuanaland the floors of huts were made of a mixture of clay and cow dung. There was usually a raised terrace forming a veranda. Individual huts were grouped together to form a cluster, the head of the household occupying the main hut, subsidiary huts being used for subordinate wives, older children and stores. Several cattle kraals of stone, either square or circular, are to be found in each village. Some of these kraals are linked.

Huts in Basutoland reflected very closely the influence of the physical environment. Timber was scarce, so that walls were of mud or grass turves, and roofs of thatching grass. Since adequate roofing material is hard to come by stands of thatching grass were highly prized and protected. Later, when settlement was extended up into the mountains towards the end of the nineteenth century, lack of deep turf and absence of timber caused the huts to be smaller and more primitive with dolerite boulder walls. The upper limit of settlement is now at about 8,000 feet in the highlands, although cattle posts are located above this height. Transhumance was practised extensively and great herds of livestock would wind up from the lowlands into the mountain pastures where nutritious grasses appeared in September and October with the onset of summer.[1] The herds would then return to the lowlands in autumn before the winter cold. The extent of transhumance has now diminished greatly and most of the livestock are retained in the highlands throughout the year. Wool has long been the major export from Basutoland.

The Nguni-Tonga groups followed a more easterly route along the eastern edge of the high plateau, or through the Low Veld into Natal and the Eastern Cape. By the sixteenth century the Nguni had probably reached the eastern plateau slopes,

---

[1] The main pastures of Basutoland are seboku and letsiri grassland approximating to sweet and sour grass veld and consisting of *Themeda triandra*, *Festuca rubra*, *Danthonia disticha* and other grasses. See *An Ecological Survey of the Mountain Area of Basutoland*, Crown Agents, 1938, pp. 13 and 16.

EARLY TYPES OF SOTHO HUTS

MODERN TYPES OF SOTHO HUTS

A HOUSEHOLD, TEBETEBENG VALLEY   TAUNG STYLE OF HUT

FIG. 14. Sotho hut types.

from where they spread south and east towards the Eastern
Hottentots, with whom they intermarried and from whom they
acquired the Hottentot click, now a distinctive feature of the
Xhosa language. By the beginning of the eighteenth century
they had come into contact with Dutch hunters from Stellenbosch and in the second half of the century with the Boer pastoralists with whom ensued a hundred years of Border warfare.

By the eighteenth century they had split up into a number of separate tribes, the most southerly being the Xhosa. Now the Xhosa, Tembu, Pondo, Pondomisi, Xesibe, Bhomvana and other tribes live in the Eastern Cape and Transkei with scattered remnants of the Fingoes, who formerly lived in Natal, but were broken up by the Zulu wars (Fig. 6).

In Natal, Zululand and Swaziland the most important tribes are the Zulu, Tetwa, Ngwani and Swazi, while the Tonga have moved into the north-eastern Transvaal and Mozambique. It was in this region below the Great Escarpment that the impact of the Zulu wars was most seriously felt. Rebel Zulu hordes broke away from Shaka and fought their way west and north to found independent states, such as the Matabele under Mzilikazi who shattered the Shona tribes of Southern Rhodesia; the Shangana who conquered the Tonga and formed the Gaza Kingdom; and the Nguni groups who raided as far north as Lake Nyasa and settled on both sides of the Lake.

The Nguni tribes found a fertile region on the lower terraces of the eastern plateau, well watered, and with reasonably fertile Natal loam soils. It is irregular, rolling country deeply scored by many rivers such as the Pongola, Tugela and Umzimvubu, whose valleys, gorge and basin alternately, are warm with deep alluvial soil and were well-wooded in the seventeenth century. It was a favourable environment for the Nguni who were hoe-cultivators and cattle people, the valleys and woods were cut into and used for tillage, while the rolling grasslands pastured their cattle. Limited transhumance was practised, and in winter cattle were taken from the sour grasslands on the higher terraces, now called the Mountain Grass Veld, to the lower regions and the more nutritious sweet grass veld. It is probable that the Nguni tended to concentrate on the lower warmer regions below 4,000 feet, and especially below 2,000 feet in the coastal region where frost is rare and a wide range of subtropical and tropical crops can be grown. This is known as the palm belt, and north of Durban sugar cane is now the most important crop.

Writing of the Zulu, A. T. Bryant,[1] maintains that they came originally from the Nyanza–Kenya region. Their kraals were situated on ridge tops, hill slopes and grassy interfluves and consisted of concentric rings of outer palisade, huts, which were dome-shaped and grass thatched, and a central cattle enclosure (see Fig. 15). Each family had its own *umuzi* or cluster

[1] *The Zulu People*, Pietermaritzburg, 1949.

8. Portuguese map of the Zambesi Basin. The approximate position of forts and trading posts is shown. The 'corte de monomotape' at 'Zimbaue' is of interest.

9. The High Interior Plains or High Veld—at an altitude of 4,000 feet to 6,000 feet—have been above sea-level since Mesozoic times. Residual buttes and mesas stand along the Basutoland border. Young Afrikaner oxen in the foreground—these travel well on the hoof.

10. Swaziland. Palaeozoic metamorphics finely dissected where Karoo sedimentaries have been stripped from them along the escarpment edge.

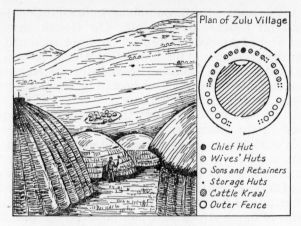

Plan of Zulu Village

● Chief Hut
⊘ Wives' Huts
○ Sons and Retainers
· Storage Huts
⊘ Cattle Kraal
○ Outer Fence

FIG. 15. Plan of Zulu village and hut type.

of huts. The outer fence might be a hedge of thorny bitter-apple or a wooden stockade. Huts were of a bee-hive shape, a hemisphere of thatch, bound firmly over a wattle framework.[1] A dim light filtered through the framework and partially lit the interior to show the clay cowdung floor, the firehole, the semi-circular pot, and a calabash shelf, piles of sleeping mats, assegais on racks, various oddments, and perhaps grain stuck into the thatch. The Zulu did not build in stone, the wattle domed hut being constructed in a well-wooded region.[2] These bee-hive huts are characteristic of much of Africa from the Fulani of Northern Nigeria to the Chagga of Mount Kilimanjaro. Apparently the *rondavel* type of hut is of nineteenth-century origin, the early Xhosa huts also being beehive in type. Every kraal was self-sufficient and division of labour was marked; the men built the framework of the huts, erected and repaired fences, cut bush and long grass, and looked after the cattle. The women toiled in the fields, each woman having her own plot; they thatched huts, made sleeping mats, hauled firewood and water and performed a variety of other tasks.

Another offshoot of the Southern Bantu, the Herero and Ambo appear to have left their homes on the south-eastern edge of the Congo basin during the sixteenth century and migrated west into the semi-arid regions of southern Angola and South West Africa. The Ambo cultivators reached the sandy white plains of Amboland with a rainfall of 20 inches and stayed

[1] Pl. 3. [2] Pl. 11.

there, as this was a more favourable agricultural region than the dry pastoral regions to the south. The Herero pastoralists trekked west of Amboland, through the Kaokoveld and south into the dry grasslands of the South West African plateau. They were halted near the Khomas Highlands by the Nama in the mid-nineteenth century and later broken by the Germans after the region became German territory.

In the mid-seventeenth century the south-western Cape was occupied by the Hottentots and Bushmen, the latter hunters living in small groups amongst the greater numbers of pastoral Hottentots (Pl. 1). Rather similar in physical type, their separate identity was not generally realized by early travellers and the Dutch settlers. The Hottentots probably originated from the admixture of Bushmen and Hamitic stock. The earliest inhabitants of South Africa were not, however, the Bushmen as Stow[1] and others may have thought, as pre-Bushmen cultures flourished over much of the country. There are a number of widely separated cultures at centres such as the Cape Peninsula, Middledrift, and along the banks of the Vaal. Boskop man lived in South Africa from ten to twenty thousand years ago.

Hottentots were nomadic pastoralists and hunters who were driven south by Bantu pressure from the region of the Great Lakes, and trekking north-west and south via Angola, or perhaps down the east coast, arrived at the Cape in the thirteenth and fourteenth centuries. In the mid-seventeenth century they were scattered in small tribal groups of 300 to 2,000 people each along the south and west coasts. The clan was the most significant unit, the tribe merely being a loose collection of clans. Each tribe had its own territory, the focal point generally being a spring or water supply, a factor of great importance in the semi-arid interior of the Cape. Their economy was based on long-horned cattle and fat-tailed sheep, in contrast to the Bushmen who were hunters and collectors. The main item of diet was milk, supplemented by hunting and collecting. Oxen were used, as among the Southern Bantu, for draught and riding animals (Pl. 4).

They lived in portable beehive-shaped huts grouped in a circle round the central cattle kraal. An interesting description of the Hottentots comes from Thomas Kitchen's Atlas of 1782: 'They remove their dwellings frequently for the conveniency of water and fresh pasture and encamp in a circle form'd by 20 or 30 tents or rather Huts made with slender poles covered with

[1] *The Native Races of South Africa*, London, 1910, ch. II.

mats or skins. They are looked on as the laziest Generation under the sun—Hottentots Women as in Guinea work and have the care of making the provisions for the Family. . . . They have little Traffick among themselves.' An early nine-teenth-century picture shows an encampment of the Hottentots on the banks of the Garieb (Orange) River, and the method of erecting these huts which could be taken to pieces and carried by the oxen on trekking from one centre to another (Pl. 19).

The Hottentot clans soon disintegrated under the influence of European and Bantu contact. The ravages of European diseases such as smallpox greatly reduced their numbers,[1] and occupation of their land and waterholes by Boer pastoralists forced them to trek to Little and Great Namaqualand, the semi-desert region to the south and north of the lower Orange river. Half-caste clans such as the Afrikanders and Griqua established themselves along the Orange River. The Afrikanders were free-booters who trekked into Great Namaqualand at the beginning of the nineteenth century, joined the Nama Hottentots and fought against the Hereros for possession of what was to be-come German South West Africa. The Griqua occupied the potentially valuable diamondiferous ground near the junction of the Orange and Vaal Rivers, and subsequently trekked to a region in the Eastern Cape, below the Great Escarpment, now known as East Griqualand. In the south-eastern coastal area between the Sundays and Great Fish rivers lived the most easterly branch, the Eastern Hottentots who came into contact with the Xhosa and because of conquest and intermarriage lost their identity. There are very few pure Hottentots left now. The Cape Coloured population has largely absorbed them. Lady Duff Gordon writing a hundred years ago exclaims with great surprise at seeing the supposed last Hottentot survivor at Genadendal.

The Cape Coloured population has considerable admixtures of European, Malay and Bantu strains, as well as Hottentot. Whereas in the U.S.A. a Negro is a Coloured man, in South Africa the Coloured person is one of mixed blood. They have increased rapidly in numbers, for at the end of the eighteenth century Hottentots, Bushmen and mixed breeds numbered only twenty thousand, and from less than one million in 1946 they had increased to one and a half million by 1960. Their main area

[1] G. M. Theal's *History of South Africa*, London, 1897, Vol. I, p. 428 describes the ravages of smallpox and says it caused such havoc among the Hottentots that they practically disappeared.

of settlement is in the south-western Cape. They have tradition-
ally supplied the farms of the south-western Cape with labour,
but increasingly they are becoming urbanized and engage in
factory and domestic work. They tend to form the working and
lower middle classes in the towns, but their advancement is
hindered by social and economic barriers.

The Malays tend to form a tiny distinctive group descended
from slaves imported from the East Indies in the seventeenth
and eighteenth centuries and united by their Muslim faith. They
formed the artisan class at the Cape in the late eighteenth and
early nineteenth centuries and contributed considerably to the
fine Cape Dutch furniture and buildings of the early nineteenth
century. Lady Duff Gordon was very taken by their fine
manners and industrious sober character. She says, '. . . the
men wear conical hats and are the chief artisans', and 'Malay
here seems equivalent to Mohammedan'.[1] They have now been
identified for census purposes as a separate racial group,
although forming part of the Cape Coloured population.

As with the Hottentots, the Bushmen were pushed southwards
by the pressure of Negro and Hamitic invaders and, following
the great herds of game in the savanna zone that encircles the
Congo basin, they entered South Africa at some period before
the Hottentots. In pre-European days the Bushmen occupied
the whole of Southern Africa south of the Zambezi. They were
a more serious opposition than the Hottentots to the extension
of Dutch settlement at the Cape. They were hunters and collectors requiring extensive territory for their use, and having no
knowledge of pastoralism or cultivation. Peaceful co-existence
with white and black pastoralists appeared to be impossible and
competition for land between Bushmen hunters and invading
pastoralists was ruthless. The Bushmen were forced to retire
to the Cape mountains during the eighteenth century emerging
periodically to kill and raid cattle. Boer commandos winkled
them out only with considerable trouble and dealt with them
harshly. Later they were hunted down by the Bantu in the
Highlands of Basutoland and along the edge of the Great
Escarpment and exterminated there too. The survivors retreated
to the arid fastnesses of the Kalahari where they still pursue
their hunting existence comparatively undisturbed. On the
fringes of the desert Bushmen like the Masarwa have been influenced greatly by the Tswana.

[1] Lady Duff Gordon, *Letters from the Cape*, ed. by John Purves, London,
1921, pp. 24 and 31.

The Bushmen's organization was far weaker than that of the Hottentots. Hunting bands of fifteen or more families occupied certain areas whose bounds were defined by waterholes. They were most skilful hunters and trackers; animals were hunted with bows and arrows, throwing sticks and spears, and trapped in snares and pits by the men. The women had the task of collecting wild vegetables, wood and water. Within their defined hunting zones the Bushmen wandered constantly; their shelters in the plains being rough erections of bushes and in the mountains caves and rock overhangs which were freely decorated with representations of the hunt, dance and other activities. Some of these Bushman paintings are extremely naturalistic and artistic, the leaping and bounding forms of animals and hunters being executed with great accuracy (Pl. 1). Bushman drawings are often superimposed on earlier pre-Bushman drawings of a different style.

Southern Africa projects wedge-like into the southern seas, the Cape of Good Hope and Agulhas being the ultimate object of maritime exploration, while the ultimate goal of African landward migration is reached in the south-western Cape. Of the three main ethnic migrations to the south, it was only the Bantu who did not reach the winter rainfall region of the south-western Cape. The Bushmen and Hottentots had been driven south by Bantu pressure and, wedged in historical times between the advancing Boer and Bantu pastoralists, were almost eliminated

A. Watering Place
B. Slaughter House
C. Wall
D. Lodging House   F. Entertaining House
E. Companyes Garden   G. Stall for Cattle

FIG. 16. Van Riebeeck's settlement at Table Bay.

as separate ethnic strains by processes of extermination, disease and absorption. By the end of the fifteenth century the coasts of Africa had finally been explored and plotted, and a hundred years later the Portuguese were firmly established in Angola and Mozambique leaving the seemingly valueless and wild coastline of South Africa between these Portuguese possessions unoccupied and unexploited. It was left to the Dutch to establish a refreshment station at the Cape of Good Hope in 1652, and so to begin the historical period after the long pre-history of man's occupation of Southern Africa (Fig. 16).

The high interior plateau was the scene of Bantu migrations which spilled over the edge of the Great Escarpment on to the warmer coastal terraces of South-east Africa here to meet the Portuguese, who were attracted by the gold of Karanga and Manicaland and the trade of the rivers, and who were concerned with the African guardianship of their commerce with the Indies. Farther south it was only towards the end of the eighteenth century that sufficient pressure had been built up in the quest for land that trekkers and Bantu contested the ownership of land and ushered in a century of border warfare.

CHAPTER 2

EARLY DAYS AT THE CAPE

THE Portuguese were well established in Angola and Mozambique by the mid-sixteenth century and have maintained their hold over the coasts of south-central Africa since then, despite attempts by the Dutch to occupy both territories. The Portuguese used ports on the south-east coast such as Sofala, Mozambique and Mombasa as revictualling stations for their caravels that hugged the coast before sailing across to India, but neglected the long stretches of arid and dangerous coastline between Angola and Mozambique. The Dutch had become firmly established in the East Indies with headquarters at Batavia, and therefore tended to use the more easterly route to Java, also followed by the English until their trading interests became more concentrated on India. Both the English and Dutch used St Helena as a stopping place to and from the Far East, but by the mid-seventeenth century the resources of the island, such as pigs, were rapidly being used up. Also it was far out in the South Atlantic and on the last lap of the homeward voyage, whereas the Cape was roughly equidistant between Europe and the Indies.

The long regular coastline; noticeable lack of harbours embayments and peninsulas; the gleaming desert coast of the south-west, aptly termed the Skeleton Coast north of Walvis Bay; the lack of a coastal plain and sand-barred river mouths restrict maritime traffic to a few widely spaced points of contact. Saldanha Bay 60 miles north of Table Bay, is the only good harbour south of Angola and has a five-mile-wide deepwater entrance and sheltered position behind granitic hills. Like Angra Pequena in South West Africa it, however, lacked a water supply and so a port was not developed. Modern ports such as Walvis Bay and Swakopmund on the Namib Desert coast have only become established in the last fifty years with the aid of present-day technical skills in obtaining water, since European

35

exploitation of South West Africa has occurred. It was Table Bay that became the site of the first permanent European settlement in South Africa. It had a good permanent spring and was therefore much used as a temporary halting place by Dutch and English ships in the first half of the seventeenth century (Fig. 17).

By the beginning of the seventeenth century the Portuguese had lost their supremacy in the Indian Ocean to the Dutch. Portuguese energies had been exhausted by their great colonial expansion. At home, factors such as the growth of big estates, disappearance of the peasant, and in 1580 annexation by Spain (after the annihilation of the Portuguese army in Morocco in 1578) had contributed further to Portugal's decline. Lisbon, from where the Dutch had previously obtained their supplies of spices and other tropical products, was closed by King Philip, and the Dutch had perforce to seek their own supplies in the Far East. Eric Walker says that 'Geography made the Dutch a nation of middlemen, set at the crossing of the sea, rivers and roadways of Western Europe. . . .'[1] Several Dutch companies were speedily formed to trade with the East and these were amalgamated in 1602 to form the Dutch East India Company, which soon became the most powerful and profitable trading company of the time. Expansion in the East was rapid and from 1602 to 1604 the Dutch captured Bantam, the Moluccas and Java. In 1619 the council of India was established at Batavia, the eastern headquarters of the Company, which later controlled the settlement at the Cape. By 1620 Holland was a thriving union of seven provinces with a prosperous population, and had become the greatest middleman in Europe owning nearly half Europe's shipping.

Increasing numbers of ships in well-organized fleets made the long voyage to and from the Far East. Voyages were uncomfortable and monotonous, there was a scarcity of water, a lack of fresh vegetables and a diet composed almost entirely of salt meat and biscuits. If the voyage were long and delayed by equatorial calms or contrary winds scurvy might kill half or more than half the crew. In November 1695, for example, a fleet of eleven ships arrived at the Cape with 678 men unable to walk, a further 228 having died on the way out.[2] There are numerous other instances of frightful mortality on the voyage

[1] *A History of Southern Africa*, London, 1959, p. 25.
[2] G. M. Theal, *History of South Africa, 1625–1795*, London, 1897, Vol. I, p. 372.

and of ships unable to leave the Cape as the majority of the crew had succumbed to scurvy. It was thus essential to establish a revictualling station somewhere on the route to the Indies, as loss of valuable man-power was so high, a loss that could be diminished greatly if fresh food and water could be supplied to ships' crews half-way through the long voyage.

The advantages of Table Bay were obvious, and it is somewhat surprising that it was only occupied permanently in the second half of the seventeenth century. Edward Terry described it in 1615, '. . . for besides a most delectable brook of pure water, arising hard by out of a mighty hill (called from its form the Table) there are good store of cattle and sheep. . . .' Backed by its impressive table-topped mountain, whose steep precipices of grey sandstone on a granitic base facing north were often obscured by a plunging waterfall of white mist pushed over by the turbulent south-easter, and known as the tablecloth, Table Bay became a temporary port of call to many an East Indiaman. Hottentots could often be induced to barter cattle and sheep, while good water could be obtained from two streams that tumbled down from Platteklip gorge to the sea. For many years before the first permanent settlement there were abortive attempts at annexation. In 1619 a joint project by the Dutch and English East India Companies for settlement at the Cape was suggested, but came to nothing. In 1620 Captains Shilling and FitzHerbert of the English East India Company annexed Table Bay for England, but their offer was declined by King James I (Pl. 20).

Projecting far enough into the southern ocean to tap the region of the westerly wind belts and winter rainfall of Mediterranean type, the Cape Peninsula had sufficient rainfall for the cultivation of vegetables, fruit and wheat. In 1647 the *Haarlem* was wrecked in the Bay and most of the crew were saved, but had to spend a year marooned at the Cape before being picked up by passing ships. They grew vegetables successfully, although their attempts to grow corn were unfruitful. On returning to Holland a memorandum was drawn up urging the establishment of a port and vegetable garden at the Cape. After due consideration the Council of Seventeen decided to proceed with this plan, and on 6 April 1652 Jan Van Riebeeck arrived in Table Bay with a small fleet of three ships to found the first permanent European settlement in South Africa. He was given instructions by the Council to build a fort to protect the water supply and accommodate a garrison and sick sailors; to lay out gardens and orchards, and barter cattle and sheep with the Hottentots, so as to ensure an adequate supply of food for the Company's passing ships.

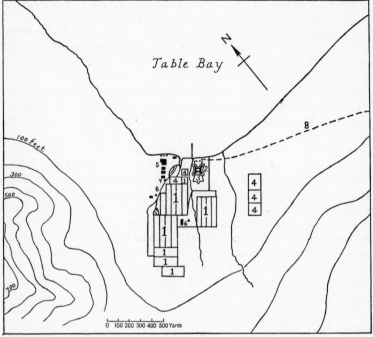

1. *Gardens of Netherlands East India Co.,45·7 acres* 2. *Fort Goede Hoop*
3. *Cattle and sheep kraal* 4. *Private gardens* 5. *Burghers' houses*
6. *Brick works* 7. *Company's corn mill* 8. *Wagon road to forest and valley farms*

FIG. 17. The importance of water in siting the settlement at Table Bay, 1662.

The ground rose gradually from the curving line of the bay to the encircling hills and mountains, which rise by steep scarps to 3,000 feet in Table Mountain and the Windberg (Devil's Peak), and the butte of Lion's Head perched on the couchant sprawl of Signal Hill. It was on this crescentic belt of land some two miles long and one mile wide, below the 500-foot contour, that the little settlement grew up (Fig. 17).

Van Riebeeck chose the site for the new settlement approximately 200 yards from the beach, and on the banks of the Fresh

River, the perennial stream draining into Rogge Bay. A fort of earth and timber approximately 50 feet square was built and water from the Fresh River flowed into the moat. Workshops, storerooms, hospital, stables and a kraal were soon built, and a vital task was the laying out of a vegetable garden and orchards near the fort. Vegetables, such as cabbages, radishes, onions, cress and beetroot, were a success, but the strong wind and poor soil proved too much for corn. There had been a long drought before 1652 and this caused pasture to wither and Hottentots to scatter.

Van Riebeeck's first grant of land was on Green Point Common which proved too dry and windy for cultivation. Later he was granted a farm of 202 acres at Boscheuvel on the slopes of Wynberg Hill, where he grew wheat, planted orchards and 1,200 vines on 50 acres and produced the Cape's first wine. There are many references in Van Riebeeck's journal to the strength and gusty nature of the south-easters in Table Bay.[1] As physical conditions were not favourable for the production of corn in Table Valley, wheat, oats and barley were tried experimentally in a more sheltered area on the eastern slopes of the Windberg at Rondebosch and did well in the loamy soils of the Liesbeeck Valley. The success of the venture is intimated by the fact that a large barn, the 'Groote Schuur', was erected and a number of discharged company officials were settled as small farmers on the banks of the Liesbeeck.

Official farming by the Company had proved too expensive, so the Council of Seventeen decided to experiment with a type of small-scale family farming producing corn, vegetables and meat for the Company's ships. Van Riebeeck's estimate of the amount of land available for settlement was exaggerated.[2] In 1657 the first nine land grants, each of 30 acres with freehold tenure, were given along the banks of the Liesbeeck River. The soil, a deep loam, was among the most fertile in the Peninsula; there was a good perennial flow of water in the Liesbeeck; the mountain slopes were well timbered; it was more sheltered than in the Table Valley and cattle could be pastured in the sandy areas

[1] D. Moodie, *The Record Papers on the Native Tribes of South Africa*, Cape Town, 1838, p. 61, 'And though we have formerly reported that corn would not succeed, that must be understood to apply to this Table Valley in consequence of the S.E. gales over Table Mountain.'

[2] Moodie, *Records*, p. 61. op. cit., Despatch from Van Riebeeck to Chamber 17, 28 April 1655, '. . . as we have much closer at hand, about the forest whence we fetch our timber, and 2 to 4 mylen from the Fort, land enough for a thousand families.'

adjoining the Cape Flats. Farming was greatly restricted by Company policy, for example, vegetables could only be sold to ships some days after their arrival and after the Company had sold their own supplies. But soon enough food was being produced in a normal year to supply the ships.

By 1662 there were 39 plotholders, who with wives, families and white servants (knechts) formed a farming community of about 150. But of the original nine pioneer farmers of 1657 only two remained, most of the discharged Company servants proving unsatisfactory farmers. The first houses were primitive, rectangular structures of wattle and daub, with thatched roofs, and floors of mud and cowdung, a type of habitation that was to be the basic form in the subsequent settlement of South Africa. It was only at the end of the century that more substantial burger dwellings were put up.

For over ten miles to the south of the Windberg and Table Mountains there stretches a continuation of the mountain backbone of the Peninsula, dominated by the Constantiaberg (3,048 feet) and enclosing the Constantia Valley, the only other large area in the Peninsula suitable for settlement. Farmers settled in the Constantia Valley in the 1670s; the most energetic farmer being Governor Simon Van der Stel, who developed the well-known Constantia estate and vineyards. A break occurs in the sandy Fish Hoek gap, and the mountain chain continues lower and more broken for some 15 miles to Cape Point, a region where the land was too rocky for farming. But a sheltered bay, Simon's Bay, within the larger False Bay, was used later by the Company as a winter anchorage for their ships and this region only became of importance towards the second half of the eighteenth century (Pl. 5).

The Cape Peninsula, therefore, was almost like an island in its effect on the first twenty years of settlement. To the east this rock girt promontory is bound to the mainland of Africa by the tombolo of the Cape Flats, a difficult barrier to overcome in the later years of the expanding settlement. The Peninsula was like many another island site off the coasts of Africa—Gorée, Luanda, Mozambique, Kilwa and Mombasa. There was serious talk of digging a canal across the sandy isthmus and so completing its natural strategic value. However, this project proved far too expensive and soon the risk of a Hottentot attack from the interior became more remote. Nevertheless, in order to contain the settlement and protect it from Hottentot attacks, Van Riebeeck was instructed to enclose the colony by a

palisade, redoubts and a hedge of wild almonds.[1] This first
frontier stretched from the mouth of the Salt River in Table
Bay along the line of the Liesbeeck River to Boschheuvel. But,
as happened at successive stages, this frontier was unable to
keep the colonists in, and they soon spread out across the Flats
and towards the first range of folded mountains (Fig. 18).

FIG. 18. First settlements beyond the Cape Flats,
1675-95.

Besides agricultural developments a start was made with
whaling, sealing and fishing, particularly at Saldanha Bay. The
cold Benguela current which flows northward up the coast of
South West Africa encouraged a great variety of fish—steen-
braas, harders, hottentots, crayfish, etc.—which formed a useful
addition to the diet of the settlement; seal and whale meat were
used for the slaves. Van Riebeeck was impressed by the forests
growing on the slopes of Table Mountain to the south and east
where the rainfall was heavier. Generally, however, the vegetation is of the Mediterranean maquis type composed of evergreen
shrubs with smaller woody plants and a wide variety of bulbs
and perennials. A wagon road, the first in South Africa, was
made from the fort to the forests on the eastern and southern

[1] A small section can still be seen on Wynberg Hill and is now preserved as a
national monument.

slopes of the Windberg. Hout Bay (Wood Bay) was exploited later, but soon the fine stands of yellowwood, Camdeboo and Cape stinkwood, wild olive, almond and other trees had been cut down. The records contain frequent complaints about the lack of exploitable timber in this treeless region o Mediterranean climate. It was only much later in the eighteenth century that the Tsitsikama and Knysna forests were exploited. Much timber had therefore to be imported from the Far East.

After twenty years, however, the settlement, which had now become a colony and confined to the northern half of the Peninsula, had used up all the available grazing. New land for grazing and cultivation had to be sought. Expeditions had been sent to explore the interior, barter cattle with the Hottentots, prospect for minerals and even try to contact the kingdom of Monomotapa. In 1671 permission was given to occupy and cultivate some 4,000 acres of land on the western flanks of the Hottentots Holland mountains, the first range beyond the Cape Flats.

Little more was done to extend the settlement until the arrival as Commander in 1679 of Simon van der Stel, who was sent out to accelerate the rate of settlement and encourage immigration to the Cape. The Company were anxious to develop the Cape as a strong colonial possession because of the fear of a French attack and the uncertainty of obtaining cattle from the Hottentots. From 1680 to the early years of the eighteenth century the Company tried to encourage people to settle and farm at the Cape, but without much success. A reply from the Council of Seventeen to van der Stel reads '. . . but we see very little chance of being able to provide you, from this quarter, with industrious farmers, because people who will work can at present earn a very good livelihood here, and there is no want of land to work upon'.[1]

Van Riebeeck left the Cape in 1662 (Fig. 17). By this time it was in a thriving state. The population had increased to nearly 400, of whom about 100 were Company servants. The Company gardens of over 40 acres lay to the south of the Fort, and west of the Fresh river, and grew a wide variety of vegetables and fruit. There were a few private gardens and a cluster of burger houses in the little village near the Fort, in addition to the brickworks and Company's corn mill.

The next stage in the growth of the colony was marked by the long and energetic governorship of the van der Stels, father and son, which lasted for nearly thirty years. One of Simon

[1] Moodie, *Records*, op. cit., p. 376.

van der Stel's first acts was to visit the Hottentots Holland. In the Eerste River Valley he found good arable land and perennial water. He founded the village of Stellenbosch in 1679 and by 1680 there were nine families. A company official, the landdrost, was appointed to superintend Company farms and cattle stations at Klapmuts, De Kuylen, Tygerberg, Bommelhoek, Boerenboom, Diepe River, Hendrik Visser's and Riet Valley and act as Company agent in the vlak or village of Stellenbosch. To assist him a court of four heemraaden was appointed, composed of local farmers. The court settled civil disputes, maintained streets, paths and bridges, distributed land and allotted water rights. In many respects their duties were analogous to those of a district council now.

The nucleus of the village on the banks of the Eerste River was provided by the *drostdy* (landdrost's house), church and *pastorie* (parsonage). Round these were grouped a few houses with large gardens watered by irrigation channels, led off from the Eerste River, and running down the wide oak-lined streets. Many of these oaks survive today in the attractive university town of Stellenbosch, a fitting testimony to the vigour with which the van der Stels pressed forward with their afforestation programme, despite opposition from the burgers. Stellenbosch was to draw favourable comment from many a traveller in the eighteenth and nineteenth centuries. It was strategically located at first to act as the headquarters of the new district of Stellenbosch, and lay on the route of expansion over the Hottentots Holland to the east. To the east and north easy routes led round the Simonsberg to the settlements in the upper Berg River valley. The village had no more than a dozen houses by 1690, but was the centre of a large district embracing Drakenstein, the Land of Waveren, Fransch Hoek and Paarl. It set a pattern for future settlement in South Africa; villages that grew round church and *drostdy* (Fig. 19).

Mackenzie, writing much later, says, 'The Colonial villages or towns—as some of them may now be properly termed—have usually grown up round the Dutch church as a nucleus'.[1] There was usually a large open space near the church where farmers could outspan every quarter for communion or *nachtmaal*. On these occasions farmers who might have travelled for long distances would replenish their stores; a brisk trade would be carried on and the village would come to life for a short period (Pl. 21).

[1] J. Mackenzie, *Ten years North of the Orange River*, Edinburgh, 1871, p. 18.

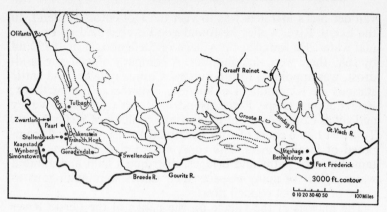

FIG. 19. Early urban settlements in the Cape.

By 1681 the population of the settlement had increased to 600, the burgers owning 9,000 sheep and goats and 1,100 oxen, while the Company had 5,000 sheep and goats and 1,200 cattle.

By the 1680s increasing numbers of Dutch and Germans had come out from Europe and settled in the Upper Berg River Valley. In 1687 23 colonists were given land in the Great Berg River Valley. Of great importance to the little colony was the arrival of about 150 French Huguenots. A despatch was sent by the Council of Seventeen to van der Stel in 1687, '. . . and we have now to apprise you that we are about to send you, among other freemen, some French and Piedmontaie fugitives . . . Among those persons you will find wine farmers and brandy distillers . . .'[1] The Huguenots did not form more than one-sixth of the total burgher population, but in order to ensure that their identity would merge they were interspersed among the Dutch and German settlers at Drakenstein and Fransch Hoek. The farms they were granted on freehold tenure were 125 acres and therefore much larger than the original grants on the Liesbeeck River.

The Huguenots had a considerable social and economic influence on the burger community. They introduced better methods of viticulture, and being ardent Calvinists, who had suffered much for their faith, they helped to strengthen the religious life of the colony. Although initially dispersed they managed to acquire farms in close proximity and the area in which they settled is now known as Fransch Hoek. Many well-

[1] Moodie, *Records*, p. 422.

11. The Drakensberg with Mount aux Sources. A basalt capped front of the Nata Escarpment and watershed, here fretted into bastions 11,000 feet high and into spurs and outliers. Zulu storage hut and fold in foreground.

12. *Stad* of Bechuanaland. Agglomerated settlements around water-points in the semi-arid margin of the Kalahari. Some settlements have 1,000 or more inhabitants. The Protectorate has a population of 300,000 in an area of 275,000 square miles.

13. Trophies of the hunt, 1899. Slaughter of game quickly cleared the veld of wild-life.

14. Quaggas (now extinct), wildebeest and blesbuck, being hunted near the Vaal River.
(Oil painting by Thomas Bain)

known Afrikaans surnames of today can be traced to this Huguenot origin, names such as du Toit, de Villiers and Malan.

Farms extended down the Berg River valley to Drakenstein and by the end of the seventeenth century had reached the Land of Waveren.[1] A definite settlement pattern emerged with the small town of De Kaap (Cape Town) and the farms of the Liesbeeck and Constantia Valleys in the Peninsula separated by the Cape Flats from the bulk of the corn and wine farms. These extended in a belt along the slopes of the Hottentots Holland mountains in sheltered valleys such as the Berg and Eerste River, or round the base of isolated hills and mountains such as the Tygerberg and Paarl Mountain.[2] In addition to the more settled districts of the south-west Cape nomadic pastoralists had already begun to move away from the Cape by the beginning of the eighteenth century, a trek that was to lead them in little more than a hundred years on to the High Veld and the Zoutpansberg, a thousand miles to the north.

Several hundred colonists settled at the Cape by the end of the seventeenth century and, in contrast to the discharged Company servants, proved better farmers and good colonists, content to settle down at the Cape and form a stable element of the population. It is from this small farming nucleus at the Cape at the end of the seventeenth century that the majority of the Afrikaans population has grown.

Thus, after fifty years, the Dutch settlement at the Cape was firmly established and from an experimental refreshment station it had become a real colony. Simon van der Stel travelled 300 miles to the north and discovered the copper mountains in Namaqualand, whose isolation delayed exploitation until the mid-nineteenth century. By the end of the seventeenth century cattle farmers were grazing stock in the Little Karoo and cattle raiders had reached the Fish River. Settlement at first expanded down the Berg River Valley until the gap of the Little Berg River was reached and a way found through the Cape ranges into the Tulbagh basin and so to the Breede River Valley. This wide faulted depression between the Hottentots Holland and Hex River mountains was an easy route to the east. Gaps through the Upper Breede gorge and the Hex River led on to the Great Karoo.

Increasing aridity to the north of the Olifants River with less than ten inches of rainfall caused the northward expansion to halt. Trekking continued to the east once the obstacles of the

[1] Pl. 22.   [2] Fig. 18.

Hottentots Holland Kloof and Houw Hoek pass had been overcome. Cattle farmers coming down the long valley of the River Zonder Eind joined those migrating along the Breede River valley, the main stream of pastoralists going east between the Langeberg and the sea towards the summer rainfall region of the south-east Cape.

Geographical factors greatly aided the outward movement. Although the Cape mountains, trending north and south in the Hottentots Holland, Olifants River mountains and other ranges, and east-west with the Langeberg and Swarteberg, appear a formidable barrier from the seaward side to which they present their steep sides, there are many easy gaps and passes through the mountains leading into the interior. Once away from the main river valleys, springs and water holes were far apart and necessitated long treks, particularly at times when a highly variable rainfall might cause drying up of waterholes. The poor quality of the grass and its low carrying capacity for livestock, coupled with low standards of farming, meant that only an ultra-extensive form of pastoralism could be carried out.

Three distinct classes had evolved at the Cape by this time:[1] the inhabitants of the small town of De Kaap; the wine and corn farmers of the south-west; and the nomadic trekboers, or cattle farmers, who were pressing on into the interior and along the east coast, despite attempts by the Dutch governors and the Company to control their unruly burgers and consolidate the boundaries of the Cape.

At the beginning of the eighteenth century the settlement which had grown round the castle had become a small town housing Company officials and townspeople. The latter were largely traders, canteen keepers and lodging house owners catering for the fleets calling at the Cape and the small farming population. The town had two principal streets, the Heerengracht (now Adderley Street) and Keizersgracht (now Darling Street) with canals down the side. The size of the Company's gardens gradually diminished as more crops were grown on the free burgers' farms and the land used for the expanding town. Most of the buildings lay to the west of the fort and the Fresh River. Besides the Castle, rebuilt in stone from 1665 to 1679 under the threat of French attacks, the other public buildings were the

---

[1] O. F. Mentzel in his 'Description of the Cape' Van Riebeeck Society, Cape Town, 1944, Part III, ch. 7, distinguished four classes of farmers: (1) Free burgers in the city with one or more farms in the country; (2) Resident farmers; (3) Industrious farmers; (4) Cattle herdsmen.

new hospital completed in 1699 to cater for 500 patients, the Church, the Slave Lodge (now the Old Supreme Court Building) and a house for distinguished visitors. The area between the Castle and the town was cleared and the old Fort levelled, the cleared space serving as parade ground and storage space; it is still known as the Grand Parade and used now as a car park and market. Rustenburg was the country residence of the Governors, while above the town were built such houses as Orangezicht and Leeuwenhof (Pl. 20).

Dampier describes the town in 1691 '. . . there is a small Dutch town in which I told 50 or 60 houses; low but well built with stone-walls; there being plenty of stone, drawn out of a quarry close by'.[1] In 1693 Ovington overestimated the size of the town, he talks of 100 houses, and grossly overstated the burger population as four to five thousand planters.[2] In 1707 Maxwell wrote, 'Besides their principal town in Table Valley . . . where they have a Fort, a Hospital, a supply'd Church with about 300 families, they have two other small towns in the country called Dragenstein and Stellambuss, inhabited for the most part by French Protestants, who make most of the wine the place produces . . .'[3]

Soon after the successful development of arable farming at the Cape an individual and distinctive style of Cape Dutch architecture developed. The first houses were primitive structures of wattle and daub, but at the turn of the century a number of gracious houses had been built. These buildings reflected European and Eastern styles of architecture, the effects of climate and local materials and the type of local labour that was available to the colonists. Some of the early Cape gables reflect the influence of Holland and Flanders, while the steeply pitched roof from Holland is reproduced in thatch at the Cape. The influence of Batavia is seen in the raised terrace or stoep with pillars at the front of the house. The shuttered windows and lofty rooms, vine covered verandahs and the lack of fireplaces in the houses bespeak the equable temperature and warmth of the Cape climate, with its dry summer heat and moist mild winters (Pls. 22, 23).

Cape Dutch houses and their furniture illustrate as well the great skill of Malay artisans and later the architectural ability and skill in carving of men like Thibault and Anreith.[4] It was only in a stable, peaceful region, such as the south-western

[1] Van Riebeeck Society, *Collectanea*, Cape Town, 1924, p. 123.
[2] Ibid., p. 107.   [3] Ibid., p. 53.   [4] Pl. 24.

Cape, away from the nomadic pastoralists of a troubled frontier zone where the fortified farmstead was developed in the nineteenth century, that a distinct and regional architectural style could develop, such as that of the Cape Dutch.

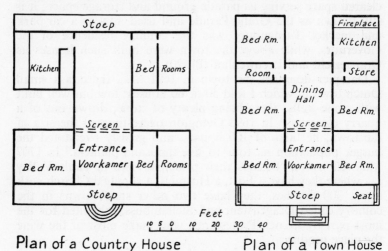

FIG. 20. Plans of Cape Dutch houses.

There are two main types of Cape Dutch houses, the first group being found mainly in the country, with steep, thatched roofs and gables and in plan either like an ⊥ on its side or an inverted ⊥ shape; the second group were mainly urban and consisted of square, flat-roofed houses with a decorated cornice in front (Fig. 20). Dorothea Fairbridge suggests that the form of the common, prone H-shaped house may be due to the lack of long roof planks, as the house resembled two barns joined together by a long room in the middle.[1] James Walton suggests that it grew out of additions to the original rectangular form, the kitchen being removed to the rear giving the inverted ⊥ shape, which with further additions grew into the ⊥-shaped house.[2] (Pl. 22).

Local materials were used as extensively as possible; reeds for thatching came from *vleis* on the Cape Flats or rivers like the Palmiet and Berg; yellowwood and stinkwood from the kloofs of the Cape mountains were used for flooring, joists and

[1] D. Fairbridge, *Historic Houses of South Africa*, London, 1922, p. 17.
[2] J. Walton, *Homesteads and Villages of South Africa*, Pretoria, 1952, p. 8.

furniture. Bricks were made at De Kaap; stone came from quarries on Signal Hill or Robben Island, while lime was obtained from seashells collected as far away as Saldanha Bay. Bricks and paving materials were also imported from Holland and Batavia, and teak for shutters, window frames and staircases came from the Far East.

Houses in the country were usually single storeyed, the attics being used for store rooms, but by the nineteenth century they were being converted into additional bedrooms, as noted by Lady Duff Gordon when she stayed at Caledon in the 1860s.[1] However, at the end of the eighteenth century Lady Anne Barnard noted that the upper part of the Cape Dutch house in which she stayed was only a store room. She described the plan of the house '. . . but the division of every Dutch house in the Colony is the same, namely a hall, a square room on either hand, and another family eating-room behind, with two bedchambers'.[2] The 'family eating-room' formed part of the central long room which was usually divided off from the *voorhuis* or *voorkamer* by a great armoire, chest or screen (Fig. 20). The floor of the rooms and stoeps was usually of red tiles, the ceilings of yellow-wood. Large sash windows were common, and the glass was imported from Holland. There were many distinctive types of gables, some being simple curves, others more ebullient and rococo in design with intricate plasterwork. Gables were erected over the front entrance, while the ends of the house were also gabled (Pls. 22, 23).

Many of the Cape Dutch farmhouses were built at the turn of the century when prosperity came to the Cape farmers during the governorship of the van der Stels. The wealthiest farmer of this period was Henning Huysing the meat contractor, who received grants of over a thousand acres of land on the Eerste River; owned grazing rights at Groen Kloof; possessed more than 20,000 sheep and 1,000 cattle; owned property in the town at the Cape and built a great house at Meerlust. Meerlust had many rooms and was unlike the usual H type of house. It had a large entrance hall with rooms on either side and the dining hall was a low room immediately behind this. Building was started at the beginning of the eighteenth century. As at Groot Constantia there are fine outbuildings with elaborate plaster decorations, e.g. the pigeon house, wine cellar and other store rooms (Pl. 23).

[1] *Letters from the Cape*, ed by John Purves, London, 1921, p. 65.
[2] *South Africa a Century Ago*, ed by W. H. Wilkins, London, 1901, p. 111.

The second type of flat-roofed, square town house developed partly because of the ease with which thatched roofs caught fire. The flames fanned by strong winds in a crowded street would soon destroy large numbers of buildings, as for example at Stellenbosch in 1710 when the church, all the company property and twelve houses were burnt down. The Council of Policy, therefore, recommended flat tile or cement roofed houses for De Kaap. By the mid-eighteenth century nearly all the houses in the town were tiled and not thatched. Mentzel mentions the tailor Muller who pulled down his old house and built a three-storey building with a flat roof in the new Italian style. The ground plan of the town house differs in shape from the country house, but the general lay-out of the rooms was somewhat similar. Instead of gables over the front of the house a low wall or parapet with a triangular pediment hid the view of the roof. The regular arrangement of sash windows and large fan-ornamented doorways of the town house had something of the English Georgian serenity and balance (Pls. 24, 25).

One of the earliest and largest houses in Table Valley at the beginning of the eighteenth century was Leeuwenhof, the home of Johannes Blesius, fiscal at the Cape in the time of the van der Stels. It is characteristic of some of the best Cape Dutch architecture of the eighteenth century. Latrobe described it in 1815 as a good Dutch building which was delightfully situated among shady groves of various trees. It had a portico or gallery running along the front of the building with an espalier roof covered with vines. The woodwork was of teak, with a carved teak staircase probably constructed by Malay slaves. The wide hall running the length of the house was paved with red tiles, while the steps were built with small bricks brought from Batavia. The house was square and flat roofed with wide sash windows and shutters.

The stoep was a characteristic feature of both town and country houses, initially porticoed and vine covered, it later acquired a verandah roof. It formed a centre of social activity, particularly at the end of a summer's day. Equable Cape winters and warm dry summers meant that fireplaces were unnecessary and as a result chimneys were rare.

On a smaller scale single-storeyed houses with flat roofs and curving or flat parapets, in terrace form, housed the freed slaves in a small community which grew up on the slopes of Signal Hill. Some of these houses in the Malay Quarter have been repaired and preserved by the Cape Town Municipality.

Similar, simply planned houses were built during the nineteenth century in many a Cape village and are now inhabited by the Coloured people.

The heyday of Cape Dutch architecture was towards the end of the eighteenth century when many houses were altered and new ones built. There was temporary prosperity in the 1780s and 1790s with increasing numbers of ships calling at the Cape, and with the French and British wartime occupation. The architects Schutte and Thibault and the sculptor Anton Anreith achieved some fine work, for example the house at Papenboom and the pulpit of the Groote Kerk. By the 1780s the town had expanded from its core between the sea front and Groote Kerk on to the lower slopes of Signal Hill and Table Mountain encroaching on to the Company's gardens. There were a number of regularly spaced, wide streets and over a thousand houses. The Heerengracht, oak and canal bordered, was still the main street with some of the finest houses. Typical of the houses of the period are the Martin Melck and Koopman's de Wet houses in Strand Street. De Kaap probably had a population of about 6,000 people including over a thousand Company servants who tended to form a distinct section of the community. As a result of the French occupation from 1784 and the cosmopolitan atmosphere created, De Kaap became known as 'Little Paris' in the 1780s. However, the number of taverns that flourished because of the large garrison would suggest that its alternative title of 'Tavern of the Seas' was more appropriate.

The second group living at the Cape was composed of the wheat and wine farmers, whose farms lay within a 50-mile radius of the town. High transport costs, slow speed of cumbersome ox wagons and execrable communications made arable farming uneconomic farther than three days' travel from the Cape. The maximum distance an ox wagon could travel was 15 to 20 miles a day. Mentzel, who lived at the Cape from 1732 to 1740, praised the industrious class of arable farmer, who was always busy and could supervise and perform all the farming operations.[1] He contrasted him with the cattle herdsman, his fourth class of farmer, who even with a superabundance of cattle, eked out a miserable existence, cut off from human society. The standard of agriculture was, however, fairly low, the outlook of the farmer parochial, and more akin to that of the nomadic pastoralist or cattle farmer than to the commercial

[1] Mentzel wrote his *Description* some 40 years later, and some of his remarks are more applicable to the Cape in the 1770s than in the 1730s.

community at De Kaap. Heavy wooden ploughs were used, and although drawn by teams of eight oxen, barely scratched the surface of the ground. Little manure was used on the fields; in a country where timber was scarce cowdung was used for fuel and also mixed with mud and straw for flooring farm houses. The sandy Cape Flats were a difficult physical barrier and took two to three days to cross with an ox wagon loaded with farm produce. Each farmer thus tended to be more or less self-sufficient and a cash economy was poorly developed. There was also the initial difficulty of clearing the ground of vegetation before cultivation could begin, the Mediterranean scrub being difficult to clear with primitive implements.

The typical farm of the south-west Cape formed a distinct community with its attractive gabled and thatched farmhouse flanked by oaks with a *jonkheer's* (farm manager's) house nearby, slave quarters, stables and storehouses and, according to whether it was a wine or wheat farm, wine cellars or barns. In fact it was far more akin to the plantations of the southern states of North America than the small farms of Europe.

Van Riebeeck had hoped to establish a peasant farming community on European lines, but soon after the first farms were granted along the Liesbeeck river a shipment of slaves arrived and the burgers came to rely on slave rather than on free white labour. By the mid-eighteenth century slaves outnumbered the burgers. Much has been written about the effect of slavery on the white society that developed at the Cape in the eighteenth century. In 1717, in a reply from the Council of Policy to the Council of Seventeen's enquiry into economic conditions at the Cape, de Chavonnes was the only official to speak out against slavery and advocate the advantages of white labour.

The historian and geographer might well speculate as to what the future of South Africa might have been if extensive white immigration had been encouraged during the eighteenth century and the economy based on European labour, as occurred later in Australia and New Zealand, rather than on slave labour. Climatically there was no reason why farm labour could not be performed vigorously by white workers. The Cape has a climate akin to that of the Mediterranean lands, while over half South Africa is from three to five thousand feet in altitude, the dry atmosphere and altitude tempering the heat of summer. And although away from the winter rainfall region of the south-west Cape much of the rest of the Cape is only suited to extensive pastoralism, physical factors were sufficiently favourable to support a far denser population. Unfavourable economic conditions rather than physical conditions were the main limiting factor to a larger white population and more effective economic exploitation of the Cape.

The Cape's economic basis was precarious and was affected by factors such as the Company's policy of restricting any trade by the burgers that might be detrimental to their own interests, the small size of the local market, and difficulties of exporting surplus products. Internal communications were very bad, South Africa had no navigable waterways in contrast to North America. There were no roads, only rough wagon tracks, and away from the Western Province only the cattle and sheep herder could overcome the hazards of bad communications and great distances to markets. It was only the mineral discoveries of diamonds and gold in the latter half of the nineteenth century that placed South Africa on a firm economic basis.

The Company sent out three fleets each year amounting to 60 to 70 ships in all. A large Dutch East Indiaman needed about 300 soldiers and sailors to man her, so that a fleet of 15 to 20 ships might have three to four thousand men aboard requiring 300 to 400 cattle and a thousand sheep. As the eighteenth century wore on the number of sails on the Company ships increased and they were made smaller, thereby reducing the number of sailors required. In addition the number of ships grew less as the fortunes of Holland and the Company declined. As a result, the market for corn, wine, vegetables and fruit was often oversupplied, but there was a constant demand for livestock products. Poor crop years in 1712 and 1713 were followed by a bumper harvest in 1714 which caused a glut on the market. The surplus was shipped to Batavia which complained of poor quality.

The Company had close control of commerce and trade by means of monopolies and leases. The corn, wine and meat leases were the most valuable, and over half the Cape revenue was derived from them. An attempt by Governor Adriaan van der Stel and other Company officials to corner the market in these commodities by producing large quantities of crops on their farms, which eventually covered one-third of the arable area of the Cape, was defeated by burger opposition, and the governor was recalled.

From the early days of the settlement attempts were made to grow a wide variety of tropical and sub-tropical crops such as indigo, flax, rice and tobacco, but they were a failure, mainly for climatic reasons. Failure also attended the venture to start a wool industry at the Cape, despite vigorous efforts by Adriaan van der Stel and the introduction of pedigree merino rams. The burgers were not interested in and knew nothing about the production of wool; their main concern was to rear sheep for sale to passing ships. Large numbers of the hairy fat-tailed sheep were obtained from the Hottentots and soon the few pedigree stock were lost in the large flocks of hairy sheep. From 1662 to 1707 the number of sheep increased from over 800 to 80,000 and by the end of the eighteenth century there were nearly half a million sheep (Pl. 18).

The main farming area of the south-west Cape was on the western slopes of the Hottentots Holland, and in sheltered valleys such as the Eerste and Berg rivers, or the slopes of isolated hills and mountains such as Tygerberg and Paarl Mountain between the Peninsula and the Cape Ranges. The map (Fig. 18) shows the location of these farms and the main concentration in the Eerste and Berg River valleys.

Vineyards were situated in the Constantia Valley, where location near the sea and higher atmospheric humidity helped to produce a better quality grape; on the slopes of granite hills such as Paardeberg and the Table Mountain sandstone slopes of Piketberg and Riebeeck Kasteel; in valleys at the western foot of the folded mountains, and also in a number of valleys such as the Eerste and Berg rivers. The best soils for vineyards were derived from granites, while the east-facing vineyards on the slopes of Paarl mountain ripened earlier than elsewhere owing to a favourable aspect. Vineyards were generally located in sheltered valleys away from the south-easters, and on well drained slopes that could be irrigated. Cape wines were mostly of the *vin ordinaire* type and of poor quality. The high degree of sunshine at the Cape produced a sweeter, heavier and less acid type of wine than in Europe. There was a wide range in quality from the European-known Constantia wines to the ordinary variety sold in the taverns of De Kaap. Batavia complained of the poor quality of the wines exported from the Cape. Mentzel, however, praised the quality of Cape wine, although he does say, 'For the Abbé de La Caille is quite justified in saying that the inhabitants of the Cape do not yet know how to treat their wines properly'.[1] Brandy was also produced and was a valuable item of trade. Production of wine had reached three-quarters of a million gallons by the end of the eighteenth cen-

[1] Op. cit., Part III, ch. 7, p. 181.

tury. Wheat farming, in contrast to viticulture, was on a very extensive basis. Seed was sown broadcast over a large area and yields were low. The main area of wheat farming was in the Swartland on the coastal plain to the north of De Kaap. The early colonists called it the Swart or black land because of the colour of the vegetation. Later wheat production spread to the higher but more undulating lowlands known as the Ruêns between the Langeberg and the coast. Rainfall near De Kaap was between 15 and 20 inches, but 50 miles or so to the north it was below 15 inches.[1] Over three-quarters of the annual rainfall occurs in winter, the growing season for wheat.[2] Rainfall is also more dependable than elsewhere in South Africa. Fairly high winter temperatures favoured spring wheat. Although climatic conditions were favourable soils were poor, particularly the shallow sandy soils derived from Malmesbury shales, and both these soils and the more fertile granitic soils lacked nitrogen and phosphates.

The south-west Cape is still one of the major wheat growing areas of South Africa. Wheat is a profitable crop because of the high subsidies paid to wheat farmers. The rotation in early days was wheat for two to three years, with oats for one year, followed by a fallow period of from one to seven years which provided pasture for livestock. This system broke down in the twentieth century when high prices paid during the two world wars encouraged continuous cultivation. Yields, initially low, have declined, and the Swartland suffers from extensive erosion. The problem is to find a suitable grass for the dry summer, so as to increase the extent of mixed farming.

The arable farmers of the south-west Cape invested a great deal of capital in their estates, on buildings, equipment and slave labour, but the returns were low, and in fact a loss was often incurred on the year's working. Slave labour was used prodigally, especially on wheat farms, and proved profitable in a region where land was abundant, capital was scarce and implements primitive.

The African slaves did the heavy work in the fields, Malays were artisans and craftsmen, while the half-castes became household servants. On every farm were to be seen the slave quarters and often a slave bell. The main farmhouse, with its dark rich coloured thatch and teak windows and shutters offset by the gleaming white of curved gables and plaster of the exterior and the graceful green of vine covered stoeps, usually lay on a

[1] Fig. 2.   [2] Fig. 9.

hill slope looking out over serried acres of vineyards. The house was flanked by oaks and camphor trees, often backed by the towering purple and gold of a Cape mountain. The great wine cellar was also one of the most important buildings on the farm, the lovely wine cellar at Groot Constantia being built in 1791 by Hendrik Cloete and decorated by Anton Anreith the sculptor.

After the first attempt at encouraging white settlement at the Cape during the period of the van der Stel's governorship, the Company decided to restrict further immigration. Possibilities of extending and improving arable farming seemed remote, the problems of surplus production were difficult to solve; yields were low and fluctuating, partly because of natural factors, while quality was poor. There were no alternatives to the hazards of agriculture; no exploitable minerals had yet been found. The Company also forbade the development of manufactures which might have absorbed some of the surplus agricultural labour. Disease, particularly smallpox,[1] caused havoc periodically, despite the apparent healthiness of the climate. Prosperity in Holland at the beginning of the eighteenth century also militated against emigration.

The burger population thus grew slowly and was not much more than 5,000 by mid-century. This growth was due almost entirely to natural increase and not immigration. In 1751 the Stellenbosch Heemraaden regarded the white population as too large, and complained of people trekking away because springs were drying up, and grasslands were being invaded by karoid shrubs, a very early reference to the deterioration in the vegetation cover of South Africa.[2] In 1773 the population consisted of 1,490 Company servants and 8,465 burgers of whom 2,300 were men, 1,578 women, 2,318 boys and 2,269 girls. By 1795 the burger population had increased to about 15,000. There was a preponderance of men throughout the eighteenth century, a preponderance particularly marked in the slave population of whom nearly three-quarters were adult males.

The third section of the white population at the Cape consisted of the nomadic pastoralists or the trekboers who, at the beginning of the eighteenth century, were already trekking away to the north and east, around or through the kloofs and passes of the Cape folded mountains. The Land of Waveren was occu-

[1] 1712 burger rolls give the population as nearly 2,000, whereas after the 1713 smallpox epidemic the burger population decreased to about 1,700 in 1716.
[2] G. M. Theal, *Chronicles of Cape Commanders*, Cape Town, 1882, p. 347.

pied by 1700, and it was not long before the cattle farmer had pushed south and east along the Breede and Zonder Eind River valleys. The frontier was extended rapidly towards the southward moving Bantu. The first permit to graze east of the Hottentots Holland mountains seems to have been granted in 1709 to Appel, whose cattle station at Boontjie's Kraal Willem van Putten visited when he travelled to the hot springs at the future site of Caledon in about 1710.

Expansion to the north was defeated by aridity, so that the main movement occurred to the east and the summer rainfall region. By 1730 the Olifants River to the north and the Great Brak River to the east had been reached; and by 1770 the Roggeveld and Nieuveld mountains had been settled and the mouth of the Gamtoos River reached. The Great Karoo, with an average rainfall of only five to ten inches, acted as a considerable barrier to the trekboers who skirted it. Some moved to the north below the Great Escarpment; the majority to the south between the Zwarteberge and Langeberg, or down the Lang Kloof to the Sundays River, or along the coastal lowlands between the Langeberg and the sea.

The long mountain chains of the Cape parallel to the coast are more of a barrier than the Great Escarpment to the rain-bearing winds, causing a marked rain shadow in the Little and Great Karoo basins. The Nieuveld stretch of escarpment north of these ranges is an additional barrier in excluding moisture from the Upper Karoo or interior plateau of the Cape. Nearly a half of the Republic has less than ten inches of rainfall, decreasing to less than five inches in the desert areas along the Atlantic coast, as also in the rain shadow areas of the Karoo. Despite adverse rainfall conditions the sclerophytic and succulent vegetation is so well suited to merino sheep and angora goats that the farmers of today in this area are wealthy. They are aided by wind pumps, known as windmills in South Africa, whose galvanized iron sails creaking in the breeze, and set over a borehole, are one of the most familiar features of the South African landscape. But in the eighteenth century the lack of water was a major handicap to exploitation of the area and settlement had to be concentrated in the highland rims or along the edges of this great arid basin.

Towards the end of the century, as the trekkers pushed on over the Gamtoos River they came to the fringe of South Africa's summer rainfall region, a sub-humid region with 15 to 20 inches average annual rainfall, transitional in climate and vegetation to the better watered south and east. Environmentally the semi-arid areas are more difficult than the truly arid areas. Settlement has caused a disturbance of the natural vegetation which had evolved in delicate equilibrium with the natural environment. It is in these belts that there is now an invasion of Karoid scrub in the western section and unpalatable bush in the Transvaal Low Veld. Invasion by these unwanted plants is termed the 'march of the desert', marking a steady deterioration in the carrying capacity of the natural pasture, which has led to the belief that South Africa is drying up. The same ecological phenomenon is occurring in the Saharan belt of North Africa where through man's misuse of the soil the desert appears to be encroaching and the rainfall decreasing (Fig. 10).

The semi-arid belts are characterized by mixed Karoid grass veld and bush veld. The disposition of these vegetation types coincides with a change in the rainfall régime between the Cape and the summer monsoon east of 26° E. In the west this belt extends north–south, and stretches from the western Transvaal through the western Orange Free State to the eastern Cape between the Great Fish and Kei Rivers. In the Cape this transitional belt corresponds to the old frontier between Boer, Briton and Bantu. In every essential, orographically, climatically, historically and politically these belts of climatic change mark the frontier land, particularly in the eastern Cape and western and northern Transvaal.

One of South Africa's best watered areas, where summer and winter rainfall influences mingle and cause well-distributed rainfall, is in the Outeniqua Mountains between George and Plettenberg Bay. One of the few remnants of warm temperate evergreen forest in South Africa, similar to the forests Van Riebeeck saw on the southern slopes of Table Mountain, is to be found here. During the eighteenth century the forests of stinkwood, yellowwood and other valuable woods were more extensive than now and with the increasing demand for wood at the Cape began to be exploited extensively towards the end of the eighteenth century.

But over most of the wide region into which the trekkers moved the lack of water was a major handicap to exploitation. In the Eastern Cape and Karoo physical conditions necessitated a limited form of transhumance from the higher and colder mountain regions in winter to the lower and warmer Karoo with its meagre winter rainfall, and a return to the better grass of the uplands in summer when rainfall was at its maximum. The sour veld of the Eastern Cape becomes tough and unpalatable in winter and lacks proteins and phosphorus, and there was a parallel movement to the sweet veld at lower altitudes. This nomadic life meant that most farmers had to have two farms, usually of great extent, but on an average each of 6,000 acres. The size of the farm was usually measured by walking for half an hour from the central position, the area thus enclosed being about 3,000 morgen.[1]

When a trekboer found a suitable fountain or watering hole he applied to the Company for a loan farm or *leenings plaatsen*, which was then granted on payment of an annual fee at De Kaap. Loan tenure was the prevailing method of holding land in the pastoral regions, its insecurity and the ease with which it could be obtained were particularly important in causing the spread of the trekboers. An attempt to reduce this insecurity by a form of loan freehold with permanent tenure and security over 60 morgen, not 3,000, was unsuccessful, as pastoralists needed far larger farms than those of 60 morgen. The usual practice was to seek out springs already occupied by the Hottentots, dispossess them and occupy their grazing land.[2]

The fact that grazing fees had to be paid once a year at De Kaap, that marriages had to be arranged through the Matrimonial Court there, coupled with the necessity of visiting De Kaap for supplies of gunpowder, clothes and coffee, were the only links binding the trekboers with the townspeople and the administration. De Mist on his travels to the Eastern Cape at the beginning of the nineteenth century saw what appeared to be the whole of the border pastoralists on the move. These migrations usually occurred in the early spring when the pastures were good. Regulations concerning attendance at the Matrimonial Court were soon changed and local landdrosts were empowered to make the necessary arrangements. With the gradual growth of settlement at Swellendam and later Graaf Reinet, the need for trekking to De Kaap decreased greatly. Life was often dangerous, with attacks by wild animals on the stock, and raids by Bushmen and later Bantu, which made the pastoralist reluctant to leave family and livestock untended for long.

[1] One morgen equals 2·116 acres.
[2] J. Campbell in *Travels in South Africa*, London, 1815, p. 66, describes how a Boer, who had bought the neighbouring farm, turned away a number of Hottentots who were occupying the Zuur Bron or Sour Well.

Compared to arable farming in the south-west, returns from pastoralism were far greater, and capital needed at the outset far less. Thompson discusses the economics of setting up as a stock farmer; for 2,200 rix-dollars or £165 a man could buy a wagon, a span of ten oxen, three horses, 50 cattle and 500 sheep, and with a gun, wagon chests, churn, and large iron pot was fully equipped as a trekboer.[1] Barrow says at the end of the eighteenth century, 'He begins the world without any property, the usual practice being that of the wife's friends giving him a certain number of cattle and sheep to manage, half the yearly produce of which he is to restore to the owner, as interest for the capital placed in his hands'.[2] This was somewhat like the loan or *mafisa* system of placing cattle, common among the Bantu. In fact the trekboer's system of extensive pastoralism was little different from that of the Bantu invaders from the north. The carrying capacity of the veld was low, capital and labour were scarce, and land was the only commodity that was cheap and abundant, so that extensive ranching was a sensible and economic way of using it.

There was an increasing demand for meat at De Kaap, the basis of the livestock trade being fat-tailed sheep (see Pl. 18) producing good mutton, and goats which throve on the scanty pasturage of the Karoo and rain-shadow valleys of the Cape mountains. During the eighteenth and nineteenth centuries sheep were the main concern of pastoralism rather than cattle which were to be found in the better watered areas of the Eastern Cape and later on the High Veld. Life was at a subsistence level and there was little in the way of a cash economy. Boers and their Hottentot servants became expert hunters. Hunting became complementary to stock-breeding, the meat from wild animals playing an important part in the diet of the trekboers, particularly the poorer pastoralists who were reluctant to slaughter stock for domestic use. Extensive hunting expeditions could be undertaken on horseback with a very limited supply of dried meat in the form of *biltong*. The products of livestock and hunting—sheep, cattle, hides and skins, soap, beeswax, ivory, etc. were taken long distances to market by ox wagon.[3] Sheep were commonly sold on the farms to wandering butchers' agents, the *slagter's knechts*. The pro-

[1] G. Thompson, *Travels and Adventures in Southern Africa*, London 1827, p. 325.
[2] J. Barrow, *Travels into the Interior of Southern Africa*, London, 1806, Vol. II, p. 123.
[3] *Scenes and Occurrences in Albany and Cafferland*, London 1827, p. 13.

15. Bavenda women of the Northern Transvaal. These people have a marked artistic tradition.

16. Basuto hut in the making, with a cave sandstone mesa in the background.

17. Portrait of Moshesh, Chief of the Basuto, who welded a new people from the broken remnants of tribes, surviving the Mantati depredations.

18. Fat-tailed sheep. In an economy of self-sufficiency the fat-tailed sheep was much prized. (*From Burchell 'Travels in the Interior of South Africa' 1822*)

duction of soap was important in the economy of the frontier regions. It was made from sheep's fat and an alkali obtained from the gannabos which grows well in arid areas. Later when the supply of gannabos had been exhausted another species of Salsola was used instead'.[1]

Society was very loosely organized, the unit being the family. Farms were often a great distance apart, the average farm being of 6,000 acres would mean four to five miles between farm houses even in a well-populated district. Swellendam and Graaf Reinet were the nearest settlements for most of the pastoralists at the end of the eighteenth century and even these might well be over a hundred miles away. Lady Anne Barnard describes the country beyond Swellendam, 'After dinner we drove 20 miles without seeing a house, cornfield or human creature'.[2]

The trekboers lived in a variety of structures, some temporary, some more elaborate and permanent. The temporary structures were the ubiquitous ox wagon and the 'hartebeest' hut. As so much of their lives was spent in migrating slowly from winter to summer pasture or in search of fresh pasture and water, the ox wagon was of great importance.[3] The hartebeest hut, erroneously named after the hartebeest buck, was really a long curved hut made with hard reeds or *hardebiesies*, covered with mud, and not from the skins of the buck. These huts should thus be termed *hardebieshuise*. The curved walls were roofed with thatch and there was only one doorway and no other light penetrating the interior, the cooking being done outside (Fig. 21). The cottages or cabins were rather more substantial and were not unlike the medieval peasant's cottage or the houses belonging to Coloured people that can still be seen in the older Cape villages today. They were usually two-roomed dwellings with mud or stone walls, floors of mud and cowdung and roofed with thatch (Fig. 21, Pl. 27).

Le Vaillant describes a primitive frontier house, 'They are merely a barn, consisting of a single room, without any division, in which the whole family live together, without separating, either day or night'.[4] Burchell refers to the Hottentot huts at Genadendal which were a crude imitation of the colonists, and had reed and mud walls and thatch roof.[5] Lady Duff Gordon

[1] W. J. Burchell, *Travels in the Interior of Southern Africa*, London, 1824, Vol. II, p. 113.
[2] Lady Anne Barnard, ibid., p. 172.   [3] Pl. 26.
[4] *Travels in Africa*, London, 1796, Vol I, p. 54.
[5] *Travels in the Interior of Southern Africa*, Vol. I, Reprinted from 1822 edition, London, 1953, p. 82.

stayed in one of the Genadendal mission cottages and described them as with 'mud walls daintily washed over with fresh cow dung, a ceiling of big rafters, just as they had grown, on which rested bamboo canes close together across the rafters'.[1]

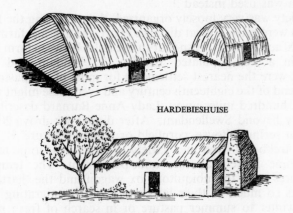

HARDEBIESHUISE

EARLY HOMES OF THE VOORTREKKERS

FIG. 21. Early Trekboer house types.

Sometimes the houses were more elaborate as in the Sneeuw-berg and had four to five rooms. G. M. Thompson, writing in 1823, described one of these houses. 'The house resembles a large barn divided into two or three apartments. One of these is the kitchen which also serves for the sitting and eating apart-ment. In the others the family sleep; while in the outer one already mentioned visitors and travellers are accommodated. . . . The more wealthy and long settled families, however, usually have the kitchen separate from their sitting room . . . but the poorer classes are content with a few thong-bottomed chairs and stools, two or three wagon chests and a couple of deal tables . . . The houses being without any ceiling are open to the thatch; and the rafters are generally hung full of the ears of Indian corn, leaves or rolls of tobacco, slices of dried meat called bill tongue . . .'[2]

Until the middle of the eighteenth century there were only three settlements at the Cape, the little town near the Castle and the villages of Stellenbosch and Drakenstein. In 1743

[1] M. Masson, *Birds of Passage*, London, 1950, p. 150.
[2] Op. cit., p. 46.

Baron van Imhoff found only three churches at these settlements, and so ordered two new churches to be built, the sites
forming the future villages of Tulbagh and Malmesbury. The
first church site was chosen in the Tulbagh Basin near the entrance to the Roodezand Pass and on a tributary of the Little
Berg River, so that water could be led off to irrigate the gardens.
It was a convenient meeting place for farmers in the Tulbagh
Basin, the Hex and Breede River valleys and the Warm Bokkeveld. There was also access to the Great Karoo via the Upper
Breede River valley. A church and parsonage were built and
between them a small village grew up, known as Roodezands
Kerk. At the beginning of the nineteenth century the drostdy
was built two miles to the north and formed the nucleus of a
separate village. The tiny settlement did not prosper as it was
too isolated and off the main route to the more populous south-
east Cape. It only served as a church centre for surrounding
farms and when the drostdy was built later it proved too far
from the village to aid its growth. Burchell describes it in 1823,
'The town, at this time, was nothing more than half a score
of neat white houses placed in a row . . . at the back of which
were as many more of an inferior size'.[1]

There was considerable difficulty in choosing the second site
which had to be accessible to the Swartland wheat farmers.
The site selected was thirty miles south-west of Roodezand
Kerk and just to the north of the Paardeberg. It was unsatisfactory, as it lacked a good water supply away from the main
range of the Cape mountains. As at the first site, a small village
grew up round the church, and was known as Zwartland Kerk
until it was named Malmesbury during the time of Sir Lowry
Cole's governorship.

Another small settlement developed in Simon's Bay which
the Company finally selected in 1742 as their main winter
anchorage in place of Table Bay, which was dangerous owing
to the prevalence of north-westerly gales which caused great
havoc to shipping.

By the mid-eighteenth century the trek of farmers to the east
had been so rapid that it proved necessary to establish a new
administrative district to the east of Stellenbosch. In 1745 the
district of Swellendam was separated from Stellenbosch, and
at first comprised all the land between the Langeberg and the
sea, from the Breede River in the west to the Bushman's River
in the east. In 1746 the site for the new drostdy was chosen on a

[1] Op. cit., Vol. I, p. 92.

small tributary of the Breede River, about ten miles east of the junction of the Breede and Zonder Eind River valleys and tapping the traffic moving down both valleys and converging here. It was also situated almost midway between two passes, Kogman's Kloof and Tradouw's Pass leading over the Langeberg to the intermontane basins of the southern Cape mountains and to the Great Karoo. The site was favourable, backed by the mountains and with good supplies of water and timber. The drostdy and a few other buildings were quickly erected, but until the end of the eighteenth century it was only a hamlet. Campbell describes Swellendam, 'It is a small town, lying in a valley surrounded by hills . . . The houses of Zwellendam are handsome and have a fine appearance in the middle of a desert', a reference to the very sparse distribution of population in the district[1] (Fig. 19).

Various attempts were made throughout the eighteenth century by governors, from the van der Stels to Tulbagh and van Plettenberg, to stem the eastward movement of the trekboers and control cattle bartering and trade with the Hottentots and Bantu. Farmers living in the Lang Kloof went on long trading trips, known as *togts*, to obtain salt from the Swartkops River and to trade with the Bantu and Hottentots. A proclamation from Governor Ryk Tulbagh dated 26 April 1770 states, 'that henceforward no one shall be at liberty to settle beyond the Gamtoos River'.[2] A somewhat similar order by Governor van Plettenberg in 1774 says, 'that henceforth no one shall proceed with any goods or merchandise, conveyed on wagons, cars, horses or pack oxen, into the interior, or ride about with the same for sale to inhabitants whether for cattle or any other article . . .'[3] In 1775 thirteen trekkers petitioned the governor to be allowed to remain beyond De Bruyns Hoogte.[4] In the same year the Landdrost of Swellendam also asked for the good pasture lands beyond Bruintjies Hoogte and stretching to the Fish river, to be added to the Swellendam district. He stated 'that unless this district spreads further to the east and northerly, the inhabitants will not be able to provide for themselves or children any more farms . . .'[5].

In order to investigate conditions on the troubled frontier, where the trekboers had met the Gunukwebe (half Xhosa, half Hottentot) and Xhosa in force, Governor van Plettenberg

[1] J. Campbell, *Travels in South Africa*, London, 1815, pp. 28–29.
[2] Moodie, *Records*, Part III, p. 6.
[3] Ibid., p. 24.   [4] Ibid., p. 39.   [5] Ibid., p. 47.

travelled extensively in the Eastern Cape. In 1778 he planted a beacon on the Zeekoe River, near the future site of Colesberg, to mark the north-eastern limit of the colony. The eastern boundary was along the Great Fish River. An additional district was created at Graaf Reinet towards the end of the eighteenth century to cater for the many farmers living in the Sneeuwberg. A drostdy was built forming the nucleus of the settlement which at first consisted of only a few mud huts, which did not impress Barrow. The site was excellent on an easily defensible meander of the upper Sundays River and at the mouth of a *poort* or gap where it emerges from the Great Escarpment. It commanded three routes over the Escarpment, one over the Koudeveld mountains at Zuurpoort, the second via the Bloukrans River and the Sneeuwberg, and the third via the headwaters of the Sundays River north to the Orange River and Botha's Drift. It also lay on the east-west road below the Great Escarpment. At the beginning of the nineteenth century Graaf Reinet became the most important settlement on the Eastern Frontier (Fig. 22).

By the 1740s there were over 400 loan farms, and by the 1780s the trekboers had fanned out in an arc stretching nearly 500 miles from De Kaap and had reached the Groot or Orange River at Pella in the north, and the Zeekoe River draining into the Orange River in the north-east. They had penetrated the southerly edge of the Great Plateau and reached the Great Escarpment in a number of places, from the Nieuwveld to the Sneeuwberg and the upper Fish River valley. Advance further to the east was held up by the southern and westerly advance of the Bantu. The trekboers had occupied a vast semi-arid region before the Bantu arrived, and in so doing they halted the Bantu invasion, which otherwise might well have reached the south-western Cape by the nineteenth century. Although the white pastoralists had taken possession of a great stretch of country in a hundred years, their rate of advance was far slower and the distance covered much less than in Canada, the United States of America and Australia in the nineteenth century.

The trekkers lost contact with the administration and the church at the Cape and leading an independent isolated sort of life became somewhat contemptuous of authority. The separatist republican instinct which found expression in the Boer republics of the nineteenth century and in a republican South Africa in 1961 was fostered by their nomadic life in a thinly populated region. They developed a distinctive way of life

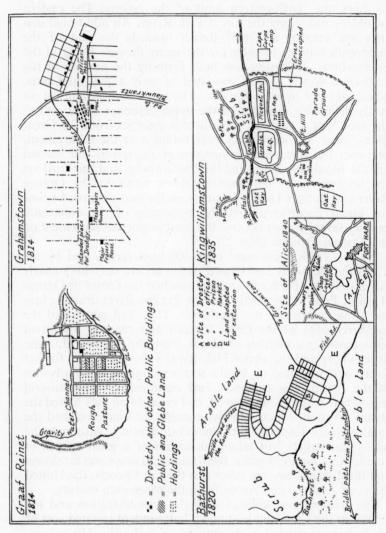

FIG. 22. Plans of early 'urban' settlements in the Eastern Cape.

rather different from the settled arable farmers of the Cape and the town of De Kaap.[1] Mentzel paints a somewhat gloomy picture of the pastoralists and tends to exaggerate the ill effects of isolation. Lichtenstein says, 'The total seclusion of the colonists from general intercourse with the world, and with civilised life, their confinement to the little circle of their own families, the easy manner in which the first necessities of our nature are satisfied, are very disadvantageous to them under many points of view'.[2] The following comment comes from Lady Anne Barnard who was more friendly towards the Dutch at the Cape than many writers, 'Their stoep was covered with a set of large idle Boers in their blue jackets, some of the family, men who did hardly anything beyond eating and smoking, scarcely superintending the work of the farm, which is carried on by slaves'.[3]

Although independent and obstinate in their dealings with authority the trekboers were courageous, courteous and hospitable. Travellers made frequent use of the scattered farm houses in journeying through the Cape in the eighteenth century and early nineteenth century, as there were very few inns and none beyond the settlements. There are frequent reports of the warmth of hospitality received in lonely places. Le Vaillant writes, 'What proves still further the extreme goodness and benevolence of these people is, that a stranger, the moment he is received by the master of the house, becomes in a manner a member of the family'.[4] The title *Oom* or Uncle is a common one amongst the Afrikaners now.

An important influence in their isolated and nomadic lives was the Calvinist religion which helped to unify them and yet make them intolerant towards their non-white labour and the coloured races with whom they came into contact. These independent white pastoralists, embittered by their harsh pioneering life and struggles with man and nature, cut off from the flood of reason and later humanitarianism that invaded Europe, reinforced by strong religious beliefs and resentful of authority, evolved a racial philosophy based on the superiority of the white man, a philosophy that has become the ruling force of

---

[1] Professor Gie in the *Cambridge History of the British Empire*, Vol. 8, p. 165, does not agree with this and suggests that the differences between the pastoralists of the interior and agriculturalists of the south-west should not be over accentuated.

[2] *Travels in Southern Africa*, Van Riebeeck Society, Cape Town, 1928, Vol. I, p. 463.

[3] Op. cit., p. 177.   [4] Op. cit., p. 63.

Afrikaner nationalism. By the end of the eighteenth century the trekboers differed considerably in temperament and customs from their forebears in Holland, Germany and France. The seeds of modern South Africa's racial strife were sown in the eighteenth century with the eastward trek of the boers and their clash with man and nature along the frontiers of the eastern Cape.

CHAPTER 3

THE EASTERN FRONTIER

THE frontier in the Eastern Cape is no longer shown as a fixed boundary line. With the incorporation of the Transkei territory, long known as Kaffraria, into the Cape Province in 1884, the boundary line was erased—the frontier had officially ceased to exist. Nor is the name 'frontier' preserved in local speech; it has been replaced by the term, 'The Border'. Thus the weather forecast for the area is announced under the heading: The Cape, Midlands and Border.

Within the border area there is a three-fold territorial division: the character of each part is the outcome of the long conflict between Europeans and Africans for the exclusive right to occupy the land. To the west of the Great Fish River and its tributary the Kat, lies land known then as the Colony which was occupied by the Dutch stockfarmers in the years preceding 1780 (Fig. 23).

To the east of the Colony between the Great Fish and Great Kei Rivers, and hemmed in largely by the Katberg and Amatola Escarpment, lies the Ciskei. This much disputed territory marks the spasmodic withdrawal of the African tribes before the pressure of better armed white peoples. Parts of this territory have been variously known in the historical period as the Neutral Zone, the Ceded Territory, Queen Adelaide Province, and British Kaffraria. These names illustrate very well the constant change and state of flux experienced in a borderland. This belt remains today an area of heavily populated black reserves and large, virtually empty, white farms; the two so intermingled that the Group Areas Act of 1956 includes a map of the Ciskei to show how further movements of population and exchange of land between black and white must be implemented if apartheid is to be achieved.

The last of the three border divisions is the Transkei, which lies to the east of the Great Kei River, and its tributary the

FIG. 23. The Eastern Frontier.

PLATEAU

SCARP

White Kei R.

·6107

·5239

·8430 ·7583

①③ Indwe

1858
1858

5010

GRIQUALAND
(1879)

①③Maclear

·4918 ·4854

·5625

·5290

PONDOLAND

①③ Umtata
(1894)

TEMBULAND
(1886)

Umtata

·B ⑨Queenstown

K A F F R A R I A

·251

Indwe R.

1848

⑨Cathcast

·4461

F I N G O L A N D
(1879)

① Idutywa

(1884)

X H O S A

Bashee

⑨Seymour

·B ⑧Alice

Royal
Forest Reserve

① Stutterheim

1848

Great Kei R.

Kingwilliams
-town

⑦

① Berlin

+B
+B

Buffalo

Keiskama

1838

1780

Bathurst
④

④Port
Alfred

Great Fish R.

CEDED TERRITORY

⑨ East London

	Cape Fold Belt Ridges
〰	Escarpments by size
- - -	Successive Boundaries with dates
·····	Administrative Districts in 1848
①	Towns in order of Foundation
◯	Royal Forest Reserve
▥	British Kaffraria (Dependency 1848-1866)
········	Final distribution of tribes with dates of annexation
■ ▪	Sites of Forts and Military Posts
•	Sites of Planned Villages
▲	Distribution of German Settlements
+B +H	Missions to Bantu and Hottentots
▨	Areas covered by Br. Settlements 1820
➤	Boer penetration of Interior

White Kei. This African territory has few enclaves of European held land, and it is the most densely and closely settled land of any rural area in the Union. Between the Drakensberg and the Indian Ocean the Transkei covers ridge, valley, coastal belt and favoured interior plateau; it is not limited, as often happens to a reserve in a white area, to cover only the less desirable land.

Mid-sixteenth-century Portuguese records of shipwrecks along the eastern coast of South Africa show occupation of the 2,000-foot plateau, ten miles inland from the coast. By 1686 the various Xhosa-speaking tribes can be identified by the names mentioned in the records, and it is now reasonably certain that the land was in use as far south as the Buffalo River at East London.[1] Professor Wilson shows that in this area also, and indeed extending beyond the Buffalo onwards to the Cape Peninsula, lived the Khoikhoi or Hottentots, who, though pastoralists, supplemented their diet by fruit gathering in the coastal and riverine bush and shell-fish collecting from the rocky shoreline.

Inland, particularly within the semi-arid basins behind the Winterberg-Amatola escarpment, lived the hunting Bushmen. Thus in the lands which came to include the Eastern Frontier, between the Bushmen of the Escarpment margin, who moved in company with the game they preyed on, and the Khoikhoi of the coastal belt, lived the more advanced Bantu people of Nguni stock.

Each group, it will be noticed, represented a different cultural and organizational level of society. Their way of life was determined by the environment and therefore each culture sought the environment best suited to its needs. But it is important to realize that although the arrangement between the groups was zonal, nevertheless they lived side by side. Displacement of the weaker groups by the Nguni was certainly taking place and it is clear they occupied in general the best land; but there are examples of a kind of symbiosis between the groups, e.g. Bushmen acting as rainmakers to an Nguni tribe; or Xhosa accepting Khoikhoi as clansmen after aid in war, e.g. the coastal Gqunukwebe clan of the Xhosa.[2]

For a long period, at least until the mid-nineteenth century, the frontier lay between the notched front of the Winterberg-Amatola plateau and the sea. The borderland spatially occu-

---

[1] M. Wilson, 'The Early History of the Transkei and Ciskei', *African Studies*, Johannesburg, 1959, Vol. 18, No. 4, pp. 167–80.
[2] Ibid., p. 176.

pied a triangle of land of which two sides were firmly fixed. The immovable base of the triangle was the sea coast, which beginning at the Great Fish River mouth changed trend just beyond that river to strike north-east in a remarkably straight coastline. At the Great Kei River, set diagonally to the coast, is the other constant leg of the triangle; there was never any dispute that beyond this deeply entrenched and thicket-choked valley lay 'Kaffir-land'. The third side was the frontier itself; this shifted progressively eastwards, as the force of the white advance pushed the Xhosa peoples back on their tracks.

The frontier war of 1779 was the first of nine to follow in the next hundred years.[1] The original trouble arose because not all the grazing in the Zuurveld was sour and unnutritious. On the coastal marine abraided foreland, good sweet grazing occurred on the outliers and outcrops of tertiary limestone. This grazing was used to interchange with the acid grasslands of the uplands, otherwise transhumance was practised between the sour veld of the Grahamstown heights, best grazed in the spring and early summer, and the winter bush-covered pastures of the coastal lowlands, with their greater variety of edible plants.

Cattle rearing in the Eastern Cape demanded 10 to 20 acres of land for each head of stock, besides the necessity of practising transhumance between sweet and sour veld. In a country of no fences and vast spaces the flocks and herds, either of white farmers or of the tribes, were continuously on the move between upland and lowland according to season, to vary grazing, and between ridgeland and valley floor each day to seek water.

Once the burgers had entered Algoa Bay lowlands and the Zuurveld, it was inevitable that conflict should arise between them and the Gqunukwebe pastoralists. Had the European system of cattle farming been on a co-operative basis friendly adjustments might have been made by the tribe; but the European demand to the exclusive ownership of the land could not be understood by people following a system of shared commonage.

Since 1770 the lower Gamtoos had been the line dividing the opposing pastoralists. Once across the river the burgers tried to enforce the recognition of the division between black and white claims. The heights known as the Bruintjies Hoogte

---

[1] A. E. du Toit, 'The Cape Frontier: A Study of Native Policy with special Reference to the years 1847–1866', *Archives Year Book for South African History*, 1951, Vol. I. This definitive text has been used as a framework for the geographical interpretation to follow.

were proclaimed as the boundary in 1774, and the country to west and south of these uplands was to be kept free from encroaching tribesmen. The Riet River emphasizes the line of these heights, which from a distance look a well-defined scarp, but are in a state of advanced dissection and therefore little of a barrier.

Now that Boer expansion by the coastal route had reached Algoa Bay lowlands the indecisive nature of the Bruintjies Hoogte–Gamtoos line was abandoned in favour of the Great Fish and Bushmans Rivers. The new line had the advantage of running south from the Great Escarpment itself and not from the Sneeuwberg spur, of which the Bruintjies Heights were part. The new boundary abandoned the Fish River where it enters the longitudinal reach and passed over a low col, to continue along the line of the Bushmans River. Save for the col, thought to be the abandoned valley of the Great Fish River itself, this boundary formed an almost continuous and easily recognized river line, in the lower part of which the deeply entrenched river offered a serious barrier to movement. By this frontier, the greater part of the Zuurveld to the west of the lower Great Fish River remained in possession of the tribes.

Here in 1779 the first serious skirmish took place. Armed with throwing spear and hide shield, the tribesmen were easy targets for the guns of the horsed and mobile Boers. Reprisals were demanded and the Zuurveld, if in name only, was wrested from the clans. The boundary along the Bushmans River was moved east, by which action in 1780 the Great Fish River became the limit of the Colony throughout its length.[1]

The halting of their coastal advance was for the European a bitter disappointment: within reach and almost within sight was a promised land of waving grassland, or so it seemed to those pioneers who had crossed the unpropitious and forbidding Karoo. A human barrier to further movement eastwards thus presenting itself, the coastal Boers turned north to swell the ranks of those who were already passing on to the interior plateau. To canalize this northern movement and to keep some control on the tenuous threads that bound the borderland to the mother colony, the hamlet of Graaf Reinet was given prominence and permanence by the appointment of a landdrost or magistrate at that station in 1785. Placed within a meander scroll of the Sundays River where it leaves the escarpment,

[1] du Toit, op. cit., p. 2.

Graaf Reinet controlled the routes to the interior in what has been called the First Trek before 1836 (Fig. 22).

The African migration now halted could not so easily swing away and be funnelled off elsewhere. Crowded between the insurmountable Drakensberg Escarpment on one flank and the sea on the other, the coastal tribes could no longer obtain fresh land nor continue to expand their tribal lands except by war.

After the next serious clash of 1793 certain measures were brought into effect by the Cape Government. Following the principle of a forward 'capital'[1] or strongpoint on the frontier most sensitive to foreign encroachment, a new border march was declared, called the district of Uitenhage with the seat of a drostdy or magistracy at the settlement of that name.

Uitenhage district was carved out of the great territory of Graaf Reinet to form in 1804 the sixth administrative district of white settlement in Southern Africa.[2] The inland boundary of the new district can be seen to separate the north–south consequent reaches of the eastern Cape rivers from their longi-tudinal better-watered lower courses. Indeed the new district was an expression of the slowly dawning regionalism which was beginning to emerge in South Africa. The district of Uitenhage is transitional in climate and relief between the Cape Fold belt and the plateaux and terraces of the Transkei. Swellendam, to the west of it, commanded the vale and ridge landscape of the southern Cape; the drostdy of Graaf Reinet controlled the farmers sheltered in the great pedimented basins of the Karoo. Thus each district was associated with a geographical complex which was characteristic of it and gave to it a nascent personality (see Fig. 23).

The site of Uitenhage settlement was that of an abandoned farm burnt out in the frontier war of 1799. It lay inland from the coast not on but near the tidal head of the small Swartkops river where the route, skirting the Great Winterhook spur, passed north to Graaf Reinet and other frontier posts. In the creation of Uitenhage as a frontier town one has an example of the land tradition of the Afrikaner people, in contrast to the maritime tradition of the British. Uitenhage bears the same relationship to British Port Elizabeth as does the Boer 'covenant' town of Pietermaritzburg to the British port at Durban.

[1] Vaughan Cornish, *The Great Capitals*, Methuen, London, 1923.
[2] G. M. Theal, *History of South Africa since 1795*, London, 1908, Vol. I, p. 114.

In the new district of Uitenhage the presence of large numbers of Xhosa, separated from the main body of the Nguni peoples by the lower Fish River, was a constant source of irritation to the white men, eager to take possession of land over which tribal stock grazed. In 1812 to put an end to cattle theft and skirmishes between the groups, the Cape Governor ordered all 'Kaffirs' to be removed from the Zuurveld. By March 1812 a combined force of troops and burghers had driven 20,000 Ndlambes and Gqunukwebe tribesmen and their cattle across the Fish River.[1]

These homeless people were driven back into the territory of their kinsmen, with whom they had quarrelled and from whom they had removed themselves to safety beyond the thickets of the Fish River valley. Crowded in among hostile kinsmen, unease grew to desperation, and in 1818 the Ndlambe chief attacked the people of Chief Gaika (whom the Europeans wrongfully considered paramount among the tribes). Gaika was defeated in the battle of Amalinde near Debe Nek. Escaping death, Gaika, the favoured chief of the Colonial Government, appealed for help, and with the aid of mounted British troops and burghers some 23,000 head of Ndlambe's cattle were retrieved from the victors (Pl. 28).

In revenge Ndlambe and his people, inspired by the prophet Makanna, swept westward to attack Grahamstown in 1819. The outcome of this frightening attack was the determination of the Colonial Government to place an empty quarter between the opposing white and black pioneers from which all settlement was to be excluded. To achieve this the frontier was now moved east to the Keiskama River, while the land between the Keiskama and the Fish as far as the Baviaans River junction was cleared of its population. The land to be emptied was that held by the Gqunukwebe tribe and the Ndlambe people. These were the tribes who had lost the Zuurveld in 1812 when 17,000 people had been evicted; now eight years later they were to be thrust, along with those previously resident in the territory, back into lands occupied by other tribes. In this total evacuation one important exception was granted to Gaika and his people. It was agreed that the eastern boundary should not follow the Keiskama to its headwaters in the Amatola Mountains, but should exclude the sheltered mountain-girt valleys of the upper Keiskama and Tyumie Rivers which formed the heartland of the Gaika territory (Fig. 23).

[1] du Toit, op. cit., p. 6.

19. Hottentots on the banks of the Orange River, with portable huts transported on the backs of oxen. *(From Burchell 'Travels in the Interior of South Africa' 1822)*

20. Cape Town, 1782, with Dutch warships in Table Bay. Enclosed fields on the piedmont slopes.

21. Pretoria, founded in 1855, and named after Andries Pretorius the Voortrekker leader. This is Church Square during 'nacht-maal', or Quarterly Communion when farmers gathered for the service.

22. Bien Donne, Groot-Drakenstein. The farm was originally granted to Pierre Lombard in 1699; gable restored, 1800.

23. Mierlust is representative of the dissem-inated farming settlements in the piedmont valleys beyond the Cape Flats.

The Keiskama is much shorter in length than the Fish, but both rivers have at first a southerly course until they enter a structural vale within the Beaufort shales, when their valleys turn abruptly eastwards along this weak belt. The two rivers approach each other to within ten miles, then the Fish reasserts its southerly direction to the sea. This isthmus of land between the two rivers, so smoothly bevelled by the African pediplain, has considerable strategic importance. The main route leading to the Tyumie and Keiskama valleys, from either Grahamstown or from the coast, passed along this interfluve. The gap was guarded by a military post at Victoria, later superseded by Fort Wiltshire (1819), which, standing on a platform of a rock-cut terrace a little way from the Keiskama, developed for a period into one of the most important weekly trading fairs of the frontier. This promising beginning was not enough to cause the Fort to grow into a settlement and it remains today a historic monument, half obscured by euphorbia 'trees' and cactus plants.

Beaufort post to the north, guarding the exit to the Kat head valleys, had a more fortunate history. This strongpoint, established in 1823 because the Gaika chief's Great Place was in the vicinity, later sheltered a trading fair. In 1846 it was strengthened into a garrisoned fort and administrative centre, after which its permanency as the frontier town of Fort Beaufort was assured (Fig. 24).

Movement along the coastal route across the neutral territory (or what was soon called significantly 'the ceded territory') was controlled from Peddie post. This strongpoint, nearer in position to the Fish River than the Kei, is in line with two important crossings over those rivers, Trompetter's Drift and Line Drift. Fort Peddie, as it was called later, could view and control the movements of the people most troublesome to the colonists. In this coastal area, where lived the Gqunukwebe clan and the Ndlambe, there was the heaviest investment of men and stock, following the removal of all people from the Zuurveld in 1812. Now in 1820 these same people, and those amongst whom they had come to live, were ordered to move further east across the Buffalo River.

The evacuation of the ceded territory except for the Amatola mountain territory of the Gaika, caused an effective blockade to the mixed coastal clans, such as the Gqunukwebe and Ndlambe. Purer Nguni stock like the Gaika Xhosa, lying behind them were turned north along and behind the Amatola highlands, just as the Boers had been turned northwards in the frontier districts to the west of the Fish when their forward movement was blockaded.

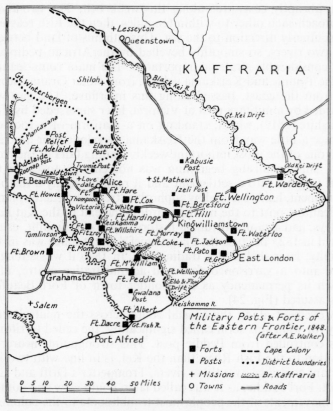

FIG. 24. Military Posts and Forts in the Eastern Frontier, 1848. (After E. A. Walker.)

An example of the movement is recorded in the appropriation by Xhosa clans of the Kat River head valleys, and of the adjacent Mancazane Valley. Xhosa entry here displaced the Tembu people who moved north-west to the Tarka River area. The newly occupied valleys lay within the terms of the Neutral or Ceded Territory and should have been clear of men and stock, but their remote position left them undisturbed for a while; however, orders for their evacuation came in 1829 following on the decision to implant here a group of 'loyal'

Hottentots under a surveyed scheme of colonization. The Hottentots to be settled in the Kat Valley were broken remnants from the Western Cape, who, with some admixture of white blood, were left landless and vagrant behind the advancing front of white colonization.

Thousands of Hottentots came forward to be settled in these deep valleys at the foot of the Katberg and only a few were given land. Watercourses working on the gravity system were laid to irrigate the arable land on the river terraces. By 1833 the settlements on the Kat River held a population of 2,185, as well as 731 tribesmen who had attached themselves to the Hottentots (Fig. 23).

Within a year of the evacuation of the Neutral Territory, families seeing little reason to abandon good land, began to drift back to their old homes. The Katberg settlement weakened the argument of holding an empty buffer zone, so in 1825 the Government allowed the coastal tribes back into the Ceded Territory. The land to the west of the Kat river remained lightly inhabited, and the Governor

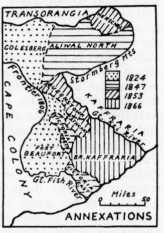

FIG. 25. Annexation of Territory by the Cape, 1824–66.

in 1831 arranged the settlement of 100 young Boers and Britons between the Konaap and the Fish Rivers, on condition they would bear arms and form a territorial unit for the defence of the frontier. It was stressed that for each grant of land of 6,000 acres, it was expected that there should be resident on the property at least four men capable of bearing arms. This new settlement scheme was never fully implemented, but because of it the Fort Beaufort district came to have a predominantly European farming stock, while that part of the Ceded Territory to the South of Fort Beaufort (later the district of Victoria East) was destined to become a very mixed racial area like that of British Kaffraria (Fig. 25).

Closer settlement with young able-bodied men and their families foreshadowed the only sizable colonization scheme of British stock in the Cape Colony. The creation of the Neutral Territory as an empty quarter was linked to the idea of a closely settled frontier behind the line of the lower Fish River. Such a policy would stop the steady enlargement of the Cape Colony by encroachment on tribal land. But when the tribes were allowed back into the coastal belt it was urged that the Zuurveld should be so closely settled that it would prove impossible for the tribesmen to take possession of any vacant land between European farms. The scheme proved attractive in Britain where unemployment and depression following the Napoleonic wars made many families eager to venture abroad (Fig. 23).

It is with the policy of planning for a dense frontier population which would in time be self-defending, and therefore cut the cost of maintaining imperial troops, that the scheme of the 1820 settlers in the Eastern Cape is associated. Of the different ethnic parties that were assembled under leaders in Britain, the Highlanders were sent to the Winterberg valleys. Occupying this rugged country (the Great Winterberg rises to over 7,000 feet) the Scots were expected to guard the Graaf Reinet area and the northern approaches to the coastal belt (Pl. 29).

The English, most of any in numbers, were directed to the Zuurveld in the district of Albany, which in 1814 had been excised from the now unwieldy district of Uitenhage. The colonists were set down in parties on previously surveyed locations, as the grants were called; the size of the location depended on the number of able-bodied men in the group, but allocations to individuals never allowed more than 100 acres of land for each man. This ensured that settlement would be close and the farming intensive. The larger parties of 50 families or more were expected to form a village and a parish centre to which the smaller parties could be attached. Twenty-five to fifty families were thus located on portions of undeveloped veld that any frontiersman would consider hardly viable for one family[1] (Pl. 30).

From a plan submitted to the Governor in 1820 it is evident that the groups of settlers south-east of Grahamstown were placed in a belt of high ground and open subsequent vales covering a quartzitic anticline and shale filled synclines (Fig. 26). The area was also a watershed and, therefore, remnants of an earlier peneplane, now known as the Grahamstown peneplane, gave the appearance of extensive arable land, but it is in those situations that the thick carapace of infertile quartzite known as silcrete is often best preserved. The bush-choked

---

[1] I. E. Edwards, *The 1820 Settlers in South Africa*, A Study in British Colonial Policy, Imperial Studies No. 9, London, 1934, p. 106.

valleys of the main rivers, like the Kowie, Kap, Fish, were avoided because of their steep valley sides and the airlessness of these valleys in extreme summer heat. Some unfortunate parties found themselves located along the coast where high bush-covered sand dunes and a mantle of grassed drift-sand made arable farming almost impossible.

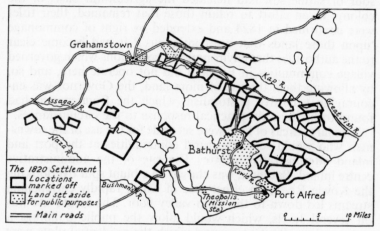

FIG. 26. The 1820 Settlement in Albany.
(After E. A. Walker.)

A second group of locations was centred on the subsequent streams of the Bushmans River. These sub-parallel streams are separated by broad plateau interfluves. Though entrenched, the rivers following longitudinal vales are more open than the transverse consequent stretches. The allocated land was set astride the streams so that each group 'should obtain a portion of garden, arable and grazing ground',[1] like the strip-parish in England. The survival of Salem, which was the only hamlet to have been properly constituted according to plan, has been thought to be due to the unified purpose of the families concerned; but the survival can also be accounted for by the large size of the original settlement covering four open valleys where river terraces would allow ample arable land. The settlement commanded two fords and was a crossroads of significance at this period. All these factors contributed to the survival of Salem in the pioneer phase and its well-being later in the history of Albany district.

[1] Edwards, op. cit., p. 106.

The settlers were composed of 542 men from the land, 326 craftsmen and men in trades, 72 middlemen, 15 professional men and 33 officers and men of the two services.[1] By 1822 three-quarters of the settlers had deserted their locations; those who remained were reduced to conditions of starvation. The defensive aspect of the scheme had obviously failed. Climate and sour or saline soil had defeated the agricultural basis of the colony. In an effort to retain those that remained, their titles were confirmed in 1824 and extended by right of commonage 'upon those lands that are contiguous'.[2] It had become clear to the authorities that environmental conditions which governed village communities in England did not operate here, and so, by allowing them the use of more land, the Governor was encouraging extensive pastoralism which the frontiersmen had found to be the only practical response to the circumstances.

Two large areas of land were set aside for the use of the townsmen who would serve the rural communities at the port and inland administrative centre. The site of the administrative centre inland, Bathurst, was chosen on a blunt spur overlooking the Kowie River, on either side of which rapidly entrenching streams led down to the main valley floor. The actual site was on several levels, which would allow the public buildings a commanding situation around which the residential plots were laid out overlooking the valley head to the west (Fig. 22).[3]

The administrative function of Bathurst was withdrawn within five years (1825) and recentred at Grahamstown. This may be an indication that, although the frontier was still believed to be most vulnerable in the coastal belt, in actual fact the frontier had shifted northwards and the need of a town more directly in touch with the Amatola strongholds of the Gaika peoples was evident. Grahamstown was nearer than either Uitenhage or Bathurst when dealing with the frontier now opening in the interior or with the threat of attack from the militant tribes of the Winterberg–Amatola quarter. Grahamstown had also better communications than Bathurst, both across the Fish River and with the parts of the Colony to the north and west. As military and administrative centre Grahamstown attracted towards itself also commercial, educational and ecclesiastical interests. It became a bishopric, and schools, now famous, were started with the help of the churches. The new town of Bathurst barely survived this eclipse; but

---

[1] Edwards, op. cit., Appendix   A.   [2] Edwards, op. cit., p. 122.
[3] G. E. Cory, *The Rise of South Africa*, London, 1913, Vol. II, p. 62.

twenty years later prosperity accruing from the merino sheep farming encouraged its development into a local regional centre. With Grahamstown and Port Elizabeth so close, Bathurst has never shown vigorous growth and it is now moribund.

The settlers made their way to the land allocated to them by the new coastal road, which crossed the Kowie river by the substantial bar at its mouth. To obviate this tedious journey from Algoa Bay, it was decided to breach the bar and thus give schooners access to the deep water of the dune-buttressed haven behind. A schooner was built and the port, later called Port Alfred, declared open soon after 1820, but, despite dredging, the shifting sands proved too great a handicap and little advantage came from the favourable position of the port, only a little more than 30 miles from Grahamstown.

For a decade the frontier had comparative peace. Discontent among the tribes beyond the Keiskama–Tyumie line grew after the 1830s. Alienated from their ancestral land in the Neutral Territory they had to observe the founding of a military village at Fredericksburg (1825) in the coastal belt, besides the extensive settlement of vagrant Hottentots in the Kat River headwaters from which their important chief Macomo had been evicted in 1829. Crowding of men and stock behind the Keiskama boundary was endured until drought hit the border country in 1834. In search of relief the Xhosa and allied tribes poured across the no-man's-land, and marauding parties reached to the extremities of the border country, even to Port Elizabeth on the south and Somerset East in the north.

While the European farm, because of its large acreage, was able to withstand the consequence of drought, the overcrowded pastures of the tribesmen demanded instant relief. The war that followed the intrusion of the tribesmen brought devastation to the white colonists. When peace was restored the marauding tribes lost their land and the boundary was pushed 80 miles eastwards to the Kei River. Here a new province was created in 1835, between the rivers Keiskama and Kei, and was called Queen Adelaide Province. It was destined to exist for one year only. Thereafter it was more properly named British Kaffraria and brought under the control of Britain. Ten years later the onset of drought again brought violence in its wake. In April 1846 at the end of a torturing summer drought Xhosa poured into the Colony and war broke out again. Movement of troops and cavalry was well nigh impossible because of the lack of drinking water.

In 1848 when the war had dragged to a close new directives were issued to maintain peace.[1] King William's Town, named in the year of Queen Adelaide Province (1835), was once again chosen as the capital of the new dependency of British Kaffraria. King William's Town was the site of an early mission station placed among the Gaika Xhosa, yet near to the territories of other tribes and clans (Fig. 22). The settlement was sited on the left bank of the Buffalo river, where an alluvial terrace (now the Botanic garden) gave some arable land in an area of thin and stony ground. Here too the river valley is open allowing an easy crossing at the ford. Its position 35 miles up the Buffalo River from East London recalls that of the town of Bathurst in relation to the Kowie mouth, where Port Alfred came to be established. The haven (East London) at the Buffalo River mouth was declared part of the Cape Colony to prevent smuggling; and immediately an investigation was begun to improve the anchorage beyond the shallow bar.

Because tribal territory was now to be properly controlled, a series of strong points was established and manned by troops. Certain factors influenced the placing of these forts. Some were placed near the then seat of the tribal chief, e.g. Fort Cox built near another 'Great Place' of the Gaika, Fort Waterloo near the chief Umhala's kraal; others guarded strategic fords or roads down the sides of the entrenched valleys. The majority of the sites chosen were on alluvial terraces near to rivers, whose flow would continue save in the most prolonged drought. The final choice of site was made with an eye to defence. Frequently a full meander curve was favoured as a natural kind of moat, when the rock-cut terraces across the meander spurs would serve as a levelled site for the cavalry barracks and gun emplacements (Fig. 22).

With King William's Town as army headquarters, ten Forts were established in British Kaffraria in 1848 in which 2,000 troops were maintained. In British Kaffraria the forts were strung out in two lines which intersect at Fort Cox, near the 'Great Place' of the paramount chief of the Gaika. One line of Forts commenced at East London, passed inland to Fort Harding (near King William's Town), then to Fort White, commanding the col at Debe Nek, thence to Fort Cox, a ford point and gap site, thence the road continued to Fort Hare, a ford point across the Tyumie and a road junction. From Fort Cox eastwards, a road led to Fort Warden on the Kei River. An

[1] du Toit, op. cit., pp. 20–31.

important strongpoint on this route was Fort Beresford, which lying near the headwaters of the Buffalo River, guarded the area where northward movement outflanks the Amatola escarpment[1] (Fig. 24).

While King William's Town acted as headquarters to the army for British Kaffraria, Grahamstown was the military centre for the Colony, with a subsidiary command at Fort Beaufort to secure the northern part of the territory. Grahamstown and Bathurst were protected by a ring of manned posts established at fords across the Great Fish River and at the mouth of the Kowie. Forts at regular intervals controlled the route from Grahamstown to Fort Beaufort. North of Fort Beaufort, three outposts served to warn the Colony of invasion or infiltration of clans from that quarter.

Among these numerous forts only those of Beaufort, Hare, Elands and Peddie gave rise to civilian settlements. The other forts lie in ruin or came to be perpetuated in other types of public use such as the educational institute at Fort Cox, the University of Fort Hare and the Police Station at Fort Brown on the Fish River.

Besides the erection of pallisaded forts and the manning of military towers, the Governor decided to plant four military villages on the English village pattern in and about the Tyumie valley within protection of Fort Hare. This valley, the most favoured of the Gaika people, was deliberately settled in 1848 at four places: Juanasberg, Woburn, Auckland, and Ely with 247 men, 17 women, and 55 children (Fig. 23). None of these villages has survived, for their presence in the main Xhosa valley drew the first attack on the outbreak of the next war on Christmas Day 1850.[2]

Under the lash of a prolonged drought, the frontier once again became restive and in December 1850, the most arduous war the Border had yet faced broke out. This war is of geographical interest because of the shift of the opposing forces west and north of the Amatola stretch of the escarpment. It is of interest also in that sectional interests and antagonisms between different racial groups showed themselves plainly. First the Boers refused to give aid in a war they termed the settlers' or Governor's war. Only 450 of them came to the aid of the Boer settled district of Cradock.

The Hottentot and Coloured people settled in the Kat River

[1] See E. A. Walker: *Historical Atlas of South Africa*, Oxford, 1922, p. 11.
[2] du Toit, op. cit., p. 53.

area and Albany District, disillusioned by the poor return from holdings, too small for the semi-arid environment, threw in their lot with those tribesmen who had already infiltrated into the plateau-lands around the Kat headquarters. Their defeat brought extinction to two Hottentot villages: Philipton and Theopolis, the latter an old mission settlement in Albany where the Hottentots had also revolted. In the north-eastern regions of the frontier the first onset of the war saw the loss of 5,000 cattle, 20,000 sheep, 300 horses, while 200 of the primitive farmhouses were destroyed by fire.[1]

The settlement following the proclamation of peace in 1853 indicated the extent to which the frontier had shifted away from the coast towards the interior. The coastal belt held by loyal tribes during the recent war survived the upheaval and came through little changed. The tribes living here, the Ndlambe and the Gqunukwebe, once the enemy, now helped to keep open the vital road between the port of East London and the army headquarters at King William's Town.

These war years saw the rise of these towns as entrepôt and distributary centres for the frontier. A borderland in turmoil was to their benefit; each clash between the Colony and Kaffraria saw a corresponding expansion in their size and importance. Later when Bantu power had been crushed and stagnation had settled on the Reserves, these towns experienced an eclipse which continues to obscure their development.

In the coastal belt the relationship between the Dependency of British Kaffraria, the Ceded or Neutral Territory and the Cape Colony proper—separated by the now historic river lines —did not change after the mid-century war, though density of settlement within the buffer zone was considerably increased.

Great change, however, was brought about in the lands along the escarpment foot, and in the plateaux and basins to the north of the mountain line. The rebel and enemy communities of the Hottentots from the Kat River Settlement, the Gaikas from the Amatola Valleys, and the Tamboekies from the Middle Kei and its tributaries, were wholly evicted from their lands or else simply displaced. The rebels amongst the Hottentots had their small plots confiscated and given to Europeans. In time the other plots were also sold to Europeans, and the valley became predominantly one of white settlement. Some of the dispossessed remained on the land as indigent squatters.

After the close of hostilities the Gaika country covering the

[1] Ibid., p. 53.

Tyumie, Keiskama and Buffalo headwater valleys was repeatedly combed by armed patrols seeking pockets of Bantu resistance. Difficult parts were opened by roads for the better movement of troops. Harried in this fashion the territory was abandoned and the Bantu retired back towards the Kei. The tribal lands were then declared a Royal Forest Reserve by the Governor, Sir George Cathcart, to prevent the land-hungry cattle farmer from penetrating beyond the Keiskama–Tyumie River.

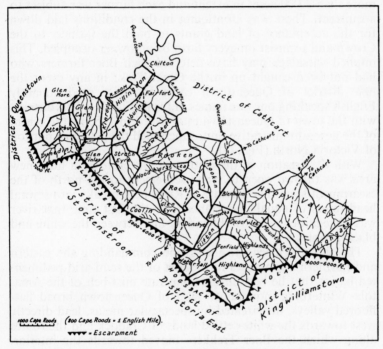

FIG. 27. Grants of land above the Amatola Escarpment.

The Royal Forest was to be guarded by a set of military posts along the escarpment rim where infiltration through the back entrances by returning Gaika tribesmen might be attempted. The boundary of the Reserve ran along the foot of the main escarpment cutting heedlessly across any subsidiary spurs. This has meant in the present pattern of settlement that the face of the escarpment (now planted in government forests) separates the African lands below from the European mountain farmland on the plateaux above the escarpment rim (Fig. 27). To the East and South the boundary was more clearly defined by the two roads leading from King William's Town, which was itself incorporated into the south-eastern corner of the Royal Reserve. Along these roads the forts of the 1848 period gave a succession of strong points.

The warring tribes of Tamboekieland forfeited their territory and had their land given to European men willing to fight and defend the Colony if called upon to do so. No farm was to be more than 3,000 acres in extent and each farmer was subject to a quitrent. There was an attempt in the conditions laid down for the acceptance of land grants to bind the farmers to the Crown and to insist on every farm being owner-occupied. This implied vassalage may have deterred such Boer farmers who had not been caught up in the Great Trek: in any event the new district of Queenstown came to be a predominantly English speaking one (see names of farms Fig. 27). This district, with the town of Queenstown established in 1853 as the centre of the new administrative unit, superseded the detached portion of Victoria North (Fig. 25).

With the creation of the district of Queenstown a huge new area was thrown open to white settlement to the north of the escarpment spur. The Great Kei River here breaks into several headwaters of equal importance. For the first time that river was disregarded as a firm boundary line between the white and black peoples.[1]

The site of Queenstown was one commanding the eastern and northern approaches to the first of the semi-arid pedimented basins that lie beyond the temperate mist-belt of the Amatola–Winterberg mountains. West of Queenstown broad flat-floored valleys, demarcated by spectacular mesas, lead directly west towards the white-settled lands of Cradock and the routes along which the Boer Trekkers moved towards the interior. Queenstown was vigilant of any threat to the Boer life-line; at the same time the new settlers of the district held the 'back door' to the colony in country more easily defensible than the tangle of valleys in which the Highland contingent of the 1820 settlers had been placed (Fig. 23).

To the south of the Royal Reserve, the Governor would allow no occupation of land by white farmers, but he was pleased to consider military villages despite the failure of those already sacked and abandoned in the Tyumie valley. Settlers were also encouraged to take up plots within the precincts of military

[1] Ibid., p. 75.

posts. These provisions gave rise to one new village, that of Keiskama Hoek, within the Royal Reserve. This village, though larger than Bathurst, never developed but has persisted in its function of administrative centre and trading post in a great African location. The town of Alice, where similar plots were granted along with rights to the commonage, is an excellent example of the type of settlement envisaged by the Governor (Fig. 28).

From 1854 loyal tribes and Fingo off-shoots of the Zulu people, seeking sanctuary from Xhosa oppression in Kaffraria, were allowed into the vacant lands of the Crown Forest Reserve and also into unoccupied areas in the Ceded Territory. A government order demanded that the Fingoes should group themselves into units of not less than 20 huts, each householder to pay a quitrent of 10s. a year for the garden plot allocated to him. On the commonage each head of a household was permitted to run ten head of cattle. No provision was made for the future increase of the population and within six years pressure upon the land was already manifest. These homeless Fingo people were added to those already settled in the Ceded Territory; also a Tembu clan, under Kama, were brought from the Queenstown district (where they had fought on the Colonial side), and were placed along the Keiskama River in a portion of land excluded from the Royal Reserve. In this way a string of loyal Bantu were placed in a line from Auckland, at the head of the Tyumie basin, to the coast at Peddie. They were to act as a sponge, absorbing civilization from the white man and transmitting it back to the barbarous tribes (Fig. 24). It is plain from the history of the Frontier that a boundary line between the Colony and the 'Kaffirs', was being continually redrawn, to the disadvantage of the Bantu.

After the war of 1850–3 the Governor tried to freeze the positions arrived at by the opposing forces in a policy of containment or military segregation of the Xhosa within British Kaffraria. Between them the Colonists, the Fingoes and like peoples, presumed more civilized than the rest, would help to defend 'Rome' and maintain peace along the frontier.

Sir George Grey became Governor in 1854. He completely reversed the defensive policy of Sir George Cathcart, his predecessor as Governor. Grey's compelling idea was to lift the indigenous people from barbarism. Thus he would not only introduce them to the benefits of civilization, but also integrate the people into the economy of the Colony and bring them, as

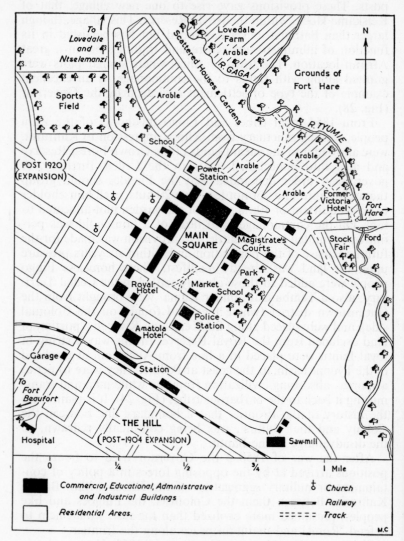

FIG. 28. Plan of Alice, Eastern Cape, 1954.
From *Geography*, July 1954.

full citizens, to contribute to the annual revenue of British Kaffraria.

'We should try to make them part of ourselves, useful servants, consumers of our goods, contributors to our revenue; in short, a source of strength and wealth for this Colony, such as Providence designed them to be.'[1]

It was difficult to bring tribesmen, men who exerted themselves only in war and the chase, to the acceptance of labour through which they could be integrated into a more advanced economy. It was believed an example could be set by education; therefore industrial schools were established at the mission stations of Healdtown, Lovedale, Shiloh, Lesseyton, Salem, St Matthews, and Mount Coke (Fig. 23).

To assure a complete break with the past, Grey intended to bring about other vital changes. The most prominent of these, from a geographer's view, is the recurrence of the theme of the self-supporting agricultural village. This time not only were there to be new villages colonized by military pensioners brought from England, but such nucleated settlements were to be introduced amongst the Bantu also. At King William's Town a pensioner's village was tacked on to the already existing administrative and mission centre; but in fact no military pensioners were recruited from Britain.[2]

In all cases, save perhaps that of Keiskama Hoek, these agricultural villages had failed, as had also those of the Kat River settlement and of the 1820 settlers. The Bantu economy being one of pastoral subsistence was even less able to support the ideal of the agricultural village and, lying outside that of a commercial society, it had no resources whatever to bring about an 'urban' organization.

The Fingoes and before them the Hottentots had been already subjected to planned village organization in the hopes that a more stable agricultural economy would emerge. The first to advocate the village system for all the Africans was the Rev. William Impey. Impey was anxious to fix African settlements on permanent sites with the villagers holding 'personal, indefensible rights in the soil'.[3] By these measures he hoped to break

[1] Speech to Cape Colony Parliament: Enclosure from Governor Sir George Grey to the Secretary of State, 17 March 1855 quoted by du Toit, op. cit., p. 88.
[2] Later the surveyed plots were sold to discharged frontier troops, and, with the money gained, Irish women were brought out to British Kaffraria in 1857 to be the wives of German mercenaries settled there.
[3] du Toit, op. cit., p. 105.

the stranglehold communal tenure has on individual advancement and agricultural prosperity among a tribal people.

Despite doubts the scheme was pushed forward nevertheless. In December 1858, 164 villages had been organized; three years later the number of replanned settlements had risen to 270, of which 28 were beyond the River Kei in Kaffraria proper. Each village contained about 57 wattle and daub huts, but each hut was not a household, for the Nguni people add huts to their living-quarters as Europeans add rooms to their houses. Five huts to a household is not uncommon in a large family. The villages were then considered too small and instructions were sent out that the concentration of settlement should be greater, at least 200 huts to a village, and that their placing should be directed by a plan instead of allowing them to be a mere collection of scattered huts. The Africans in resisting close settlement, were responding to the limitations of their physical and cultural environment. Although in fact a more nucleated and compact village plan was not achieved until the Betterment Schemes of the 1950s, nevertheless, the habit grew among the Bantu to live in loosely agglomerated villages.

This concentration of settlement in Eastern Cape Province has been imposed steadily from above, and with the introduction of boreholes for water the villages have been fixed on a site; but they cannot be considered a spontaneous development as were the *stadt* of the Bechuana, where large villages give the appearance of true agglomeration.

In 1856 tribes on both sides of the Kei, hemmed in by fixed boundaries, debarred from movement by an inflexible frontier, effectively controlled by headmen and police posts in subdivided locations, watched over by vigilant magistrates, pauperized by the epidemic amongst their cattle, resorted to a most fantastic panacea to overcome their plight. If they killed their cattle and destroyed their crops, they believed their ancestors would rise on 18 February 1857 and drive the white men into the sea. The cattle were indeed slaughtered in expectation of the glorious promise to follow, and all grain burned.

The geographical consequence of the 'Cattle Killing Delusion' in the distribution, number and alignment of races, is striking. British Kaffraria and part of Tembuland, except for the Royal Forest Reserve, became a white farming area. The tribes who once inhabited this territory, were decimated either by death or dispersal. To save some of them passes were issued to 24,657 famished people, but it is estimated that at least 30,000 people

24. Koopmans de Wet House in Cape Town, built by Louis Thibault.

25. Cape Town. The Council of Policy recommended flat, tiled roofs to overcome the fire menace of the high pitched roofs of thatch. By 1750 most town houses conformed to the regulations.

26. Oxwagon of the Trekboer. This type is known as the Louis Trichardt wagon.

27. Johannesburg. The first house—similar in style to early farmhouses.

crossed the border to seek help in their dreadful plight. Figures given for 1857 show that within a year the population of British Kaffraria decreased from 104,721 to 37,697. Though probably unreliable the figures indicate the staggering fall in population.[1]

Without power to resist, the remnants of Kreli's Xhosa people in Kaffraria (who were thought to be the organizers of the sorry venture) were rounded up, although nominally inhabiting free Kaffirland, and were driven back eastwards beyond the Bashee river. By this displacement of a people the penetration of European influence into what is now Transkei was first effected.

The close of the Crimean War left Britain with the German Legion on her hands. It was not known what to do with them. Opportunely the need for defence in British Kaffraria gave rise to the idea of ordering them as a regiment, with their officers, to the Eastern Frontier and there maintaining them for three years on land in chosen village sites. Between 1856 and 1857, 2,351 German men, not all from the Legion that had fought for Britain, arrived. However, within three years 1,000 of them had been sent on to put down the Indian Mutiny; a grievous loss to the manpower of the newly occupied lands.

These mercenaries were settled on one-acre plots and had rights to commonage at King William's Town, Breidbach, Berlin, Potsdam, and Cambridge. These settlements were placed at regular intervals along a new road to the east of the Buffalo river (in the territory of the Ndlambe, who had been moved out of British Kaffraria across the Kei into Kreli's lands about the centre of Idutywa). Other German settlements were made north of King William's Town. That at Dohne (Stutterheim) guarded the road between King William's Town and Queenstown (Fig. 23).

The other extensive tracts of country left vacant by the removal of the Ndlambes were filled by colonial settlers, British and Boer. In 1859, 302 farms were granted averaging 1,500 acres each, and granted strictly on the understanding that the land would be owner-occupied under a type of military obligation like those given on quitrent in the Queenstown district.

In 1858 other reports estimated there were in all 1,154 Germans, 2,994 other Europeans and 38,598 Xhosa, Tembu and Fingoes in British Kaffraria. This would give a density of approximately 14 persons to the square mile, half the figure

[1]Ibid., p. 110

A.H.G.S.A.—8

derived at for the densities prevailing before the famine following the cattle killing.[1]

The introduction of European settlers, the economic recovery after 1859, and the stimulus of new colonists, had their effect on King William's Town. The little settlement acquired the demeanour of a regional capital, while East London began to serve the Kaffrarian capital as its port. In 1850 these centres had 626 civilians besides the army and civil service personnel, at King William's Town and 124 at East London. In 1856, when British Kaffraria had been declared a province and a part of the Cape Colony, urban functions crowded into King William's Town. It became the headquarters of troops, a workshop for wagon repair, and an emporium for trade as far afield as the Umzimvubu river in the Transkei. Here were located the Surveyor General, the Chief Civil Engineer, the criminal courts and the medical staff for the frontier hospital. From the date of the dispersal the subjection of the Frontier was complete. British Kaffraria instead of becoming a dependency, or an incorporated native territory like the Transkei, was taken in as a part of the Cape Colony in 1866, albeit an area with many acres occupied by Fingo peasants (Fig. 25).

With the incorporation of British Kraffraria into the Cape Colony the modern framework of the old border had become established and British influence was free to penetrate beyond the River Kei. This was achieved by placing magistrates with resettled tribes. Thus, with the settlement of a portion of the Ndlambe and some Fingoes near Idutywa and Butterworth, British colonial influence had in effect extended to the Bashee River. Furthermore, to the north of British Kaffraria Tamboekie people of the Glen Grey area, restive under direct colonial rule and resentful of its laws, asked to be moved into Kaffraria between the Indwe and Tsolo Rivers. Here too British influence accompanied the shift of the tribe eastwards. By 1860 between the Umzimkulu River and the Bashee River lay the core of tribal territory remaining from the piecemeal reduction of the area by the expanding British colonies to the north and south of it. The Natal Border had now virtually become the Eastern Frontier (Fig. 23).

In 1840 a triangle of land between the Umzimkulu and Umzimvubu Rivers had been claimed by the Boer Republic of Natal, but after the British annexation in 1845 the border of the Colony was withdrawn to the Umzimkulu River. From

[1] Ibid., p. 114.

this river south to the Umtata River, and occupying all the land from the high wall of the Drakensberg Escarpment to the sea, lay the Treaty State of Faku, the paramount chief of the Amapondo people. Beyond this river there had been considerable readjustment of peoples with the banishment of Kreli's Xhosa to land north of the Bashee River. In this sector between the Bashee and the Umtata the recoil from the white man had been eastwards.

The Boer Republics and Basutoland on the high interior plateau were not the concern of the British, since the abrogation of interest under the Conventions of 1854; but much of Kaffraria in 1866 still remained outside British authority. Kaffrarian land was regarded as the only 'free' land remaining east of the Escarpment which, once the tribes were brought into subjection, could be parcelled out. This land might solve two acute problems along the immediate borders of Cape Colony, which, if neglected, might precipitate another expensive war. In Transorangia to the north the Griqua and Hottentot Treaty State centred on the valley of the Orange River, had lost their land to the new Boer republic of the Orange Free State. These people, protégés of Britain through the care of the London Missionary Society, could find new land in Kaffraria, as some Basuto, deflected down the Escarpment by the Free State Boers, had already done in the Matatiele embayment. The second group in need of resettlement were the old Fingo locations of the Ceded Territory beset then by a continuous addition of vagrant tribesmen from as far afield as Kaffraria and Natal; not more than one quarter of the people in these heavily infested locations were the original Fingoes or their descendants. In 1860 reports revealed discontent on both sides of the border; much of it wrongly imputed to the dispossessed Xhosa Galeka chief, Kreli, now banished beyond the Bashee River.

When the Cape Parliament met in April 1861, Sir George Grey referred to arrangements soon to be completed with the chiefs of Kaffraria proper admitting the extension of British influence over much of the country between British Kaffraria and Natal.[1] Grey was a little premature in believing that he could so easily dismiss Natal's interests in the northern portion of the territory; nor could he rouse either the Cape Government or the Colonial Office to the desirability of further expenditure in Kaffraria.

Frontier farmers, land-speculating companies and land-

[1] Ibid., p. 150.

hungry Fingoes pressed for permission to occupy land in Kaffraria. It was widely known that there were vacant areas within
British Kaffraria. Travellers had reported on the unoccupied
lands with amazement; especially remarking on the land along
the foot of the Berg, known as under-berg land, which appeared
never to have been occupied, for no vestige of old hutments or
kraals were to be seen. 'There are no kaffirs in that fine country
under the Berg', John Dobie writes in 1863.[1] These observations
about the neglect of the under-berg land were substantiated in
1860 by Sir Walter Currie, who made a survey of the distribution
of tribes and their numbers in British Kaffraria and found few
lived inland farther than 70 to 80 miles from the coast.

The space between tribal territories can be explained as a
buffer between groups, as reserve land for expansion, or as
reserve forage in time of drought. What explanations may be
sought for this uninhabited belt, named Nomansland by the
colonists of the period? The emptiness along the Berg foot
seems to have occurred also in Natal. The geographical reasons
might give an answer. The great spurs with their doleritic
carapace running out from the Escarpment front divided tribal
land. In country where grazing was still easily acquired the
tribesmen would rather seek the rolling downlands by circumventing the highlands and thus avoid successive barriers to
their migration southwards. More cogent is the fact that these
mesa-like ridges fall into the mist belt in summer and suffer
severe frost in winter. The pastures are therefore less palatable
and are not as continuously nutritious as sweet veld or mixed
veld is at lower altitudes.

In another report on projected settlement in Kaffraria, by
Sir Walter Currie, a sketch map is added to show where Europeans could be settled without displacing tribal groups. In
effect the sketch map must indicate the distribution of vacant
land in Kaffraria in 1860.

The Governments of the Cape and Great Britain, fearful of
further expenditure on 'these mill-stones', put an end to such
schemes; but Sir George Grey, committed to the resettlement
of the Griqua, who had already moved into Southern Basutoland in expectation of land promised them, pressed forward
against official opposition and objections from Natal. The
Lieutenant-Governor of Natal not only claimed that Faku, the
Pondo Chief, had given Natal the land between the Umzimkulu

[1] J. S. Dobie, *South African Journal*, 1862–6, ed. by H. F. Hattersley (Van
Riebeeck Soc. pub., 26), Cape Town, 1945, pp. 104 and 132.

and Umtamvuna Rivers from present-day Harding to the sea, but inland from that point to the base of the Drakensberg.[1] These rights dated back to 1850 and were willingly ceded by the chief on the grounds that his people had ample room for development and deployment of pastures. Ultimately sectional interests were ignored and Natal was authorized to give up the claim to land nearer the Drakensberg in return for the incorporation within her boundaries of the coastal section already outlined. This unsatisfactory solution led to the annexation of this district of Alfred by Natal in 1866. Natal thus ceded almost half the land which ultimately was given to Adam Kok's 2,000 Griqua. This immense country stretched the length of the high Drakensberg for 130 miles, and was 50 miles broad. The Tembu people came to inherit all other land south of the Umtata River and the East Griqualand mountain border, save the coast lands where remnants of the defected independent Xhosa, the Galeka, had taken refuge. These lands were brought under Colonial administration between 1884 and 1886. These Xhosa, occupying the coastal belt, have continued into the present decade to enjoy full tribal life outside the stream of Western economic advance.

The last to lose full sovereignty were the Pondo who came to consolidate their lands between the Umtata and Umtamvuna Rivers, thus covering the great basin of the lower Umzimvubu

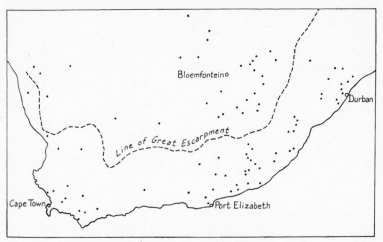

FIG. 29. Mission stations in South Africa, 1850.

[1] du Toit, op. cit., pp. 152 and 153.

River and abutting inland more or less along the line of the present main road on to the territory of East Griqualand. The Umzimvubu River cutting through the fault block at its mouth in a deep channel attracted interest as a possible Port. As early as 1870 the haven of Port St John's was ceded with land around it to Cape Colony for which a solatium was paid to the Pondo. It is instructive in the light of what has been said of the coast lands of Southern Africa that, though these coast lands are amongst the most habitable in the 3,000 miles of shore, yet they have remained tribal areas with the least economic development (Pl. 31).

By 1894 the whole of Kaffraria and Griqualand East had been annexed to Cape Colony. Natal had salvaged the small district of Alfred from the rapacious advance of Cape interest north-eastwards below the Great Escarpment. This may be marked as the highwater of Cape Colony's influence in South Africa. Thereafter her relative importance begins to decline with the rise of the South African Republic on the High Veld interior (Fig. 37).

CHAPTER 4

THE WIDENING ENVIRONMENT

Bʏ the end of the eighteenth century Dutch East India
Company rule over the Cape had collapsed and in 1795
the British arrived. The strategic value of the Cape was
emphasized by the Napoleonic wars and its control was essential to safeguard the route to India and the Far East. British
occupation of the Cape lasted from 1795 to 1803 and, after a
brief period of Dutch rule, became permanent after 1806, British
possession being confirmed by the Congress of Vienna in
1814.

A hundred years of expansion by Dutch pastoralists eastwards from the Cape was checked towards the end of the eighteenth century by the south and east moving Bantu pastoralists.
The previous chapter outlined some of the facets of that expansion; this chapter will deal with the rapid extension from
about 1795 to 1870 of Boer and British rule over the vast plateau
region south of the Limpopo, later to form the Union of South
Africa. This pre-mineral era from about 1795 to 1870 may be
subdivided into two periods from 1795 to 1835, and from 1835 to
1870, the Great Trek marking the dividing line.

Major events during the first period were the final handing
over of the Cape to the British in 1806; the arrival of the 1820
settlers and subsequent economic development in the Eastern
Cape; while to the north the holocaust of the Lifaqane from
1812 onwards and widespread destruction of the Bantu tribes
on the High Veld and in Natal prepared the way for the Great
Trek. Many mission stations were also founded during this
period and missionary influence was of considerable importance both in England and at the Cape.

In the second period from 1835 to 1870 the frontier expanded
rapidly from the Orange and Great Fish rivers to the Limpopo
and the Lebombo; the Boer republics were established across
the Orange and the Vaal; Natal became a British colony, and

99

British rule partially extended over the large Bantu area between the Eastern Cape and Natal.

At the beginning of the nineteenth century the white population of the Cape was still very small,[1] 80 per cent being in Cape Town and the Cape and Stellenbosch districts. A slave-owning class producing wheat and wine had developed in the Western Cape which had become a distinctive region by this time. The frontier districts of Swellendam and Graaf Reinet produced most of the livestock. A guide to the Cape of Good Hope says, 'The near, middle and ulterior Snowy Mountains may be considered as the grand nursery of sheep and horned cattle, particularly of the former'.[2]

By 1806 the original four districts had been increased to six, and by 1815 to seven, i.e. Cape, Stellenbosch, Swellendam, Tulbagh, George, Graaf Reinet and Uitenhage. By 1815 the European population had increased to over 35,000, thus exceeding the slave population of nearly 30,000. By 1832 the Europeans, swelled by the arrival of the British 1820 Settlers, had nearly doubled in number to about 66,000. At the beginning of the nineteenth century De Kaap was still the only town in the Cape, the other settlements such as Stellenbosch, Swellendam and Graaf Reinet being only villages. Uitenhage was founded in 1804, Cradock and Grahamstown in 1812 as military posts marking the ends of a double line of blockhouses designed to clear the Xhosa out of the Zuurveld (Fig. 23). The white population of the Graaf Reinet district doubled between 1804 and 1811, and the number of houses in the village increased from less than 20 to over 70, while little more than ten years later there were 300 houses.

Thompson wrote a long description of Graaf Reinet in the middle 1820s.[3] 'It contains now about 300 houses, almost all of which are neat and commodious brick edifices . . . The streets are wide, laid out at right angles, and planted with rows of lemon and orange trees. Each house has a large allotment of ground behind it, extending in some instaces to several acres, which is richly cultivated, divided by quince, lemon or pomegranate hedges, and laid out in orchards, gardens and vineyards. These are all watered by a canal from the Sunday River . . . The population of Graaf Reinet, of all colours, amounts

[1] 1798 Census—21,746 European colonists, 25,000 slaves.
[2] *A Guide to the Cape of Good Hope* 3rd ed,, London, 1819, p. 39.
[3] G. Thompson, *Travels and Adventures in Southern Africa*, London, 1827, p. 42.

to about 1,800 souls. The town is built in a sort of basin, almost encircled by the deep channel of the Sunday River, and closely environed by an amphitheatre of steep and rugged mountains.'[1] (Fig. 22.)

It was the arrival of some 5,000 British settlers in the Eastern Cape in 1820 that caused a rapid growth of towns and villages here. Failure to make a livelihood on the small farms they were allotted and the constant despoliation by native depredations caused the majority to leave the land and go as artisans and traders to the newly established settlements at Cradock, Grahamstown, Port Elizabeth and elsewhere. With the growth of the coasting trade and the little port of Port Elizabeth, named after the Governor's wife, the overland wagon route via the Karoo declined in importance and with it Graaf Reinet's role as a commercial centre. In 1820, before the arrival of the British settlers, there were only a few houses and huts besides the Fort, but by 1823 the settlement had grown considerably and spread irregularly along the shores of Algoa Bay. It could boast two inns, many substantial houses and stores and a population of about 500. After 1826 the development of the port was marked when restrictions on direct trade with Cape Town were repealed with the relaxation of the Navigation Laws (Pl. 32).

Established as military headquarters for the Eastern Cape in 1812, Grahamstown became the capital of the region in the 1820s, supplanting Bathurst, which Sir Rufane Donkin had intended as 'the seat of magistracy for the English settlers'. By 1826 the population was over 2,500 and in 1838 when James Backhouse visited Grahamstown the population had increased to 4,000. He thus describes it: 'The site of Grahamstown is said to have been that of an old military station, around which the town gradually grew up. The present town consists of a few streets, one of which is spacious and serves as a market place. The streets are regularly laid out; and the houses are neat, and white, or yellow.'[2] It was the seat of local government and military headquarters, and soon became the most important commercial centre in the Eastern Cape with a wide hinterland. The following is a description of Grahamstown before the Great Trek in the 1830s. 'The public market at Graham's Town . . . which is held every day except Sundays exhibits a very lively

[1] Thompson, op. cit., p. 23.
[2] J. Backhouse, *A Narrative of a Visit to the Mauritius and South Africa*, London, 1844, p. 174.

and amusing scene; here is to be found the farmer from the most distant extremities of the Colony, with his wagon laden with curiosities, such as skins of wild animals, ostrich feathers, ivory and the rude but deadly weapons of the Bushmen and Bechuana; here, also, is to be seen the enterprising settler, just returned from a six-months' trading journey to the interior, with a cargo of hides or ivory, together with the rich fur dresses or cloaks of the natives of distant regions visited by him in his peregrinations. By the market register it appears that between October 1831 and September 1832, 1906 wagons entered the market laden with produce.'[1] Ellis who visited Grahamstown in the 1850s must have drawn on Backhouse to some extent. He writes, 'This young African city is pleasantly situated in the midst of an amphitheatre of grassy mountains. The streets are wide, and regularly laid out, the houses neat, generally white or yellow and numbers of them shaded with trees.'[2]

The towns and villages of the Eastern Cape were predominantly English in composition by the 1830s compared to the rural areas, which were largely Dutch until the Great Trek when nearly 10,000 Boers left the Eastern Cape.

A distinctive style of architecture tended to develop with a mixture of English and Dutch styles, and reflecting the insecurity of life on the Frontier. During the Kaffir War of 1834 over 400 farm houses were destroyed. Therefore because of this and other wars farm houses were fortified. A two-storeyed stone house with watch tower, firing slits, a thatch or slate roof, and a Dutch stoep in front, developed as a common type of settler house. The severe lines of the fortified farm house were a contrast to the sedate formal lines of the Cape Dutch house.

The prosperity of the Eastern Cape was based to a considerable extent on the wool industry. During the eighteenth century the Dutch had preferred the rearing of hairy sheep and the production of mutton to the breeding of fine-woolled sheep and export of wool. After the Governor imported Spanish rams and ewes in 1815, and the 1820 Settlers realized the potentiality of the Eastern Cape for sheep grazing, the wool industry, based on merino sheep, expanded rapidly and the semi-arid regions of the Karoo and Eastern Cape were turned to profitable use. Until the 1830s the Karoo was regarded as a negative economic area, only the fringes and river banks being used as winter grazing. But with the advent of merino sheep the Karoo vege-

[1] *The Saturday Magazine*, No. 295, 4 February, 1837.
[2] W. Ellis, *Three Visits to Madagascar*, London, 1858, p. 241.

tation, consisting of small succulent bushes widely spaced on bare stony soil, proved of great value for sheep fodder (Pl. 37).

Thompson says, 'Some of the wool sent home from the eastern districts promises to be of a better quality than any hitherto raised near the Cape, and holds out the cheering prospect of this important produce becoming ere long, one of the staple exports of the interior'.[1] The following table gives the relative values of wine and wool exports from the Cape in 1826, 1842 and 1861. By 1842 wool had become the most im-

Year	Wine £	Wool £
1826	98,000	545
1842	43,000	72,000
1861	34,000	1,460,000

portant export, the value of wine exports having declined to less than half the figure for 1826.

The wine industry of the Western Cape benefited by its connection with Great Britain, and Cape wines were admitted at one-third the duty charged on Portuguese and Spanish wines. By 1830 nearly three million gallons of wine were being produced, three times the amount produced in the late eighteenth century when only Constantia wine was exported to Europe. Over half the total production was exported. As in the eighteenth century the principal wine districts were limited to the area of Mediterranean climate, hocks and muscadels being produced in the Peninsula, particularly the Constantia valley, the more common wines coming from the Piedmont belt stretching north-south along the eastern edge of the Hottentots Holland mountains.

The quality of Cape wine did not improve greatly despite government encouragement and the appointment of an official wine taster. R. Percival, who visited the Cape at the beginning of the nineteenth century, comments: 'The Dutch have never arrived to any perfection in the art of making wine, or the rearing of vine shoots.'[2] In 1831 the duty on Cape wines was raised and in 1860 preference was abolished. This fact plus the strong competition from French and Spanish wines and the lack of labour after the abolition of slavery drastically reduced wine exports, and the prosperity of the wine producers of the Western

[1] Thompson, op. cit., p. 413.
[2] R. Percival, *An account of the Cape of Good Hope*, London, 1804, p. 177.

Cape declined considerably. There was stagnation from 1830 to 1870, after which the local market was stimulated by the mineral discoveries.

The production of wheat in the Western Cape increased greatly from 170,000 to 400,000 muids[1] in the period 1818–53, because of increasing population, improved transport facilities and better farming methods (English ploughs drawn by mules were more effective than the clumsy Dutch ox-drawn ploughs) and better markets. Despite this, yields were low on soils of poor fertility and with indifferent cultivation. As in the eighteenth century, wheat was grown predominantly in the shaley loams north of Cape Town, Malmesbury being the leading producer.

Increasing population and economic activity at the Cape made it necessary in 1826 to increase the number of districts to eleven, i.e. Cape, Simonstown, Stellenbosch, Worcester, Swellendam, George, Beaufort West, Graaf Reinet, Uitenhage, Somerset East and Albany. The Eastern Cape, with its prosperous wool industry and thriving towns, began to rival the Western Cape. Partly because of this, and partly as control of the Eastern Frontier was too difficult from Cape Town, it was decided in 1828 to divide the Cape into two provinces;[2] the Western Province with the districts of Cape, Simonstown, Stellenbosch, Worcester and Swellendam, and the Eastern Province with the remaining six districts. The Eastern Province rapidly developed its own regional and even separatist characteristics as it pressed for political separation from the West.

The Eastern Cape, like Natal, has tended to remain British in attachment, in contrast to the other major regions of South Africa, a regional separation that is largely due to the influence of the 1820 Settlers.

An important feature of the first period from 1795–1835 was the rise of missionary activity and influence in the Cape. First in the field were the Moravians who went back to the old station, first established by George Schmidt in 1737 and abandoned in 1744, which was now renamed Genadendal, the Vale of Grace. The Moravians were successful here and at Mamre also. Burchell describes the plain white church at Genadendal with its steeply pitched roof, the missionaries' houses, knife manu-

---

[1] One muid is equal to about three bushels.
[2] *Report of the Commissioners of Inquiry on the Cape of Good Hope*, Cape Town, 1827, p. 22.

factory, blacksmith's shop, water mill, wine press, tobacco house, poultry house, cow house and store rooms. Water was led off from the Baviaans River to irrigate a number of small gardens. The Hottentot and Coloured population was about 1,400, but fluctuated according to the labour demands of neighbouring farms (Pl. 33).

The London Missionary Society were also pioneers in the mission field. By 1816 there were 20 L.M.S. missionaries in the field and their mission stations spread beyond the colonial border to the Bastaards, renamed Griqua. The problem of creating definite centres for the nomadic Griqua was gradually solved when Anderson persuaded some of them to settle at Klaarwater, renamed Griquatown, and situated at a good spring near the Orange-Vaal confluence.

The number of mission societies in the field increased greatly with the Wesleyans in Kaffirland and Pondoland, the Berlin and Glasgow societies among the Xhosa, and the Rhenish Society and Paris Evangelicals in the Eastern Cape and amongst the Basuto and Bechuana (Fig. 29).

With the growth of industrialization in Great Britain and the rise of the middle class to political power there was increased interest in the colonial territories and missionary activity. During the first half of the nineteenth century the missionary party was strongly represented in the British Government and much heed was paid to reports from men like Dr John Philip about ill treatment of Hottentots and slaves on the frontier. The success of Wilberforce and the anti-slavery party in Great Britain with the passing of Fox's Abolition Bill in 1807 made way for the abolition of slavery by the act of 1833. In consequence of that act nearly 40,000 slaves were freed in the Cape in 1834. The abolition of slavery and the failure to deal with the problem of Hottentot vagrancy added greatly to the perennial problem of lack of farm labour.

Most farmers and many officials were convinced that the mission stations encouraged vagrancy. Field Cornet Maritz wrote to the Klaarwater missionaries complaining that the mission station housed runaway Hottentots and slaves. 'It was according to his opinion, nothing but a receptacle for the idle and worthless.'[1] Settlers complained that labour was withdrawn from the farms; they also disliked the missionary doctrine of brotherly love and freedom of the individual. Officials, too, viewed

---

[1] Burchell, op. cit., p. 377.

missionaries with some suspicion; Somerset considered the location of their stations beyond the colonial frontier to be too vulnerable. Attempts were made by Governor Caledon in 1811–12 to regularize the supply of Hottentot labour by restriction of movement and apprenticeship of children. But by 1828 the missionary clamour against these restrictive labour laws resulted in the passing of the famous Fiftieth Ordinance which abolished the pass system and apprenticeship of children.

Missionary influence was thus strong in official circles both in the Cape and in England. Resentment at missionary interference along the frontier was one of the major factors causing the Great Trek. This was an event of great historical importance for South Africa. Some 8,000 to 10,000 Voortrekkers or nomadic white pastoralists left the Colony from 1836 on and doubled the area of effective white occupation of South Africa in the space of a few years. Towards the end of the eighteenth century the Boers came into contact with the Bantu pastoralists moving south and east. The line of advance of white and black pastoralists had been checked along the Fish River. Cattle raiding and minor skirmishes developed into a series of wars which lasted for a hundred years. The contending parties, both practising an extensive pastoral economy, had constant need of fresh land. This search for new land is epitomized in the Great Trek and later series of treks that took small parties of Boers across half Africa, and in the Bantu migration south from the Great Lakes (Fig. 30).

The reasons for trekking were varied; for many it was merely a continuation of the quest for new land, but for the majority it was more a matter of principle, as they felt that the British were threatening their way of life, undermining the traditional patterns of labour and taking the part of missionaries, Bantu and Hottentots rather than of the settlers. The coming of the 1820 Settlers, a considerable increase in the size of the Dutch population in the Eastern Cape and prevention of further movement to the east, caused a scarcity of land. There was no longer free land for the asking; land became a negotiable asset and values rose as a result when it was decided that in future Crown lands would be sold by auction. In Canada the government controlled the allocation of land and surveyed farms, which being arable were small compared to the large pastoral farms in South Africa. There was no such control over land settlement in South Africa; farms were unsurveyed, and no taxes or land revenue was paid. Thus early in the nineteenth century the great bulk of the potential arable and pastoral areas had been parcelled out among a few white farmers.

Among other reasons were the lack of security along the frontier, drought, and the promise of better grazing across the Orange River. From 1820 on many Boer families had settled between the Orange and Riet Rivers and hunting and trading parties trekking far into the interior had brought back reports of wide, empty grasslands to the north. Another major reason for trekking was Britain's vacillating frontier policy. Governor Sir Benjamin D'Urban attempted to solve the problem of frontier unrest by establishing a strong cordon of colonists in Queen Adelaide Province between the Great Fish and Keiskamma Rivers, but this was reversed by Lord Glenelg, much to the disgust of the Boers. Economic developments in the Eastern Cape also made it possible for the Trek-

FIG. 30. Pre-railway wagon routes to the Interior.

kers to move across the Orange River, as they could be supplied from Port Elizabeth and Port Natal by wandering traders known as *smouses*. Grahamstown, Colesberg, Harrismith, Potchefstroom, Klerksdorp, and Shoshong became forward depots at various times for trade with the interior (Fig. 30).

Trekking, trading and hunting in the far interior were made possible by the ox wagon and the treeless, level surface of the high plateau. Where mountains, as in the Western Cape or the Great Escarpment, proved a barrier a number of easy passes were found to circumvent it. However, in some regions, particularly the highest parts of the plateau, in the Basuto highlands and the steep slopes and deep valleys below the Escarpment in Natal, movement by ox wagon was hampered and wagons often had to be dismantled. Coming down a pass could be a hazardous venture and bushy trees were often lashed behind the wagon to provide extra braking power (Pl. 35). The *Protea grandiflora* often used for this purpose is popularly known as *waboom* (wagon tree) in Afrikaans. On the other hand, if South Africa had been as heavily wooded as parts of North America, travel by wagon would have been far more difficult. Long stretches of navigable rivers and lakes in North America made it possible to penetrate far into the continent by canoe and boat. But in South Africa the lack of navigable waterways made it imperative to open up the region known as Overberg by horse or ox wagon. Many of the trekboers, moving slowly from one *fontein* or spring to another in the Northern and Eastern Cape, knew no other life or home, and thus trekking on to the High Veld was merely a continuation of former practices. The trek wagon was there-fore home, transport and mobile fortress in times of danger, when a cordon of wagons could be linked together to form a fort or *laager* from which Bantu attacks could be driven off effectively by firing between the spokes.

Ox wagons were of two main types. The first was the large buck wagon from 18 to 22 feet long, 5 to 7 feet wide, either with a half tent or no tent at all, holding a great deal of cargo of up to three tons. It was used primarily for transporting heavy goods, particularly in the second half of the nineteenth century (Pls. 36, 40).

The second type was the smaller full-tented wagon, 12 to 17 feet long and three to four feet wide, used by the Trekkers. Ox wagons were unwieldy and strongly constructed to withstand the rigours of travel over rough tracks and in a dry climate. They had no springs, but the many parts comprising the wagon moved freely, so preventing cracking or breaking of the parts. The body was long and narrow with sides built up to a height of about two and a half feet and chests at either end con-taining stores and equipment. The driver sat on the *voorkis* (front chest) and controlled his span of up to 18 or 20 oxen with a long whip and exhorted them continuously by name. Names such as Blauberg and Engeland were in constant use, the latter being the best ox among the Bechuana and the most stubborn among the Boers! Arched wooden supports held up the roof of the wagon. The roof was often composed of three layers, a

28. The Batavian Government, 1803–6, entered into an agreement with Gaika, Chief of the Xhosa. The wooded face of the Amatola escarpment is noticeable.

29. 1820 settlers landing at Algoa Bay. *(Sketch by C. Van der Berg)*

30. 1820 settler family occupying land allocated to them near the Great Fish River.

reed mat underneath and two outer layers of canvas. A *katel* or simple bed, consisting of an oblong wooden framework thonged with leather, was usually carried inside (Pl. 26).

A number of hardwoods were used in the construction of the wagon; stinkwood, yellowwood, pearwood and assegaiwood of which the first named was perhaps the most prized. The wood had to be properly seasoned, otherwise the dry air of the plateau caused it to shrink. A common occurrence was for the spokes and ties of the wheels to shrink, making them fall apart. The wheels were of unequal size, the front being smaller than the back. This was useful on steep slopes when wheels were often transposed, the large back wheels being placed on the down slope, the small front wheels on the up slope. Constant maintenance was necessary, as vital parts such as the main shaft or *dissel-boom* were easily broken. Leather strips or *riems* were used for repair work and were an indispensable part of trekking equipment.

Oxen were essential to draw the lumbering wagons. The Afrikander, a cross between European and Hottentot cattle, was the common transport animal. It became a distinctive type and was first evolved in the eighteenth century with a dark red colour, heavy forequarters and powerful neck muscles. Other types were the smaller speckled or brindled Zulu ox which was humpbacked and faster than the Afrikander, the large Bechuana ox and the smaller Matabele ox, both of which were extremely hardy and able to resist drought. The Bechuana oxen were used individually as riding and transport animals, whereas the Afrikander were used mainly in spans of up to 20 oxen. Oxen had to be treated carefully as they were liable to succumb easily to temperature extremes, overwork or diseases such as nagana, rinderpest, redwater, etc. (Pl. 38).

An ox wagon train was an impressive sight; each span of 14 to 20 oxen and wagon being up to 70 feet long, thus a cavalcade of ten wagons could take up to 300 yards of track. Average rate of travel in an ox wagon varied according to season, type of country, load carried and state of oxen. In the summer two stages of three hours each per day was usual, and the distance travelled was 12 to 15 miles, but in the winter or cool season with three stages a distance of 20 miles could be covered. Trekking through sand in Bechuanaland or below the Escarpment in Natal, slowed down the rate of travel greatly.

Cape and Scotch carts were used by those with less baggage. The Cape cart was a high two-wheeled affair drawn by up to four mules or horses and, as the name implies, was used widely in the Cape.[1] The Scotch cart also had two wheels, but was heavier and longer. It was drawn by four to six oxen and carried just over a ton in weight. Horses provided the quickest mode of travelling and under favourable conditions a distance of a hundred miles could be covered in a day. The Voortrekkers developed the art of firing their heavy guns, *roers*, from horseback and combined with the use of the *laager*, these tactics made it possible for them to defeat large numbers of Bantu, as for example at the battle of Blood River in 1838. Later in the nineteenth century the small, easily manoeuvrable and hardy Basuto pony was used extensively for hunting and on commando. During the Anglo-Boer war the Boers mounted on Basuto ponies were at a considerable advantage compared to the British on their heavy cavalry chargers.

But for the ravages of horse sickness and nagana,[2] horses would have been used extensively for exploration in Southern Africa, as the terrain is well suited to such travel. African horse sickness or *perde siekte* was most extensive in the summer rainfall area, and at low altitudes with a warm damp climate. Areas of high altitude such as the Roggeveld and Basutoland were used for horse breeding. Winter was the usual season for hunting, both because of the summer incidence of horse sickness and nagana, and also because the game collected round waterholes in the dry winter, whereas with the onset of summer rains the wild animals scattered widely. The cause of horse sickness is still not known, but is thought to be due to a virus transmitted by some unidentified insect carrier. High prices were obtained for so-called 'salted horses' which had recovered from *perde siekte* and were supposed to have obtained immunity, although more often than not a salted horse would succumb to horse sickness again.

The widespread occurrence of tsetse fly in Central Africa precluded the use of the ox wagon and here the native carrier was the only means of transport. He could carry a load of 60 to 70 pounds for about fifteen miles a day. Some ten species of tsetse fly are carriers of trypanosomiasis or nagana, *Glossina morsitans* being the most widely known. Other species such as *Glossina palpalis* carry the trypanosomes causing sleeping sickness in man. The fly is found in belts, particularly in the bush along river banks or lake margins. The fly belts vary in extent and were not sharply defined in Southern Africa a century ago.

[1] See Plate 39.   [2] Nagana is another name for trypanosomiasis.

Areas most affected by nagana were the low-lying river valleys of the Limpopo–Zambezi and the Low Veld of Transvaal and Zululand. The High Veld of the Transvaal and the drier parts of Bechuanaland tended to be free from tsetse fly. Control of the tsetse fly is very difficult as many wild animals are carriers of nagana. Various remedies have been tried in the great fly infested areas of Central Africa, such as widespread killing of game, selective bush clearing and grass burning, trapping of insects, vigorous control over movement of man and animals into and out of the fly areas, use of insecticides, etc.

Malaria was another barrier to northward movement and was prevalent in the same type of region where nagana was found. It was thought that malaria was caused by exposure to the miasma borne in marsh and swamp mists. Many died each year and, although quinine was increasingly used after its worth had been proved in the Niger expedition of 1854, it was only at the end of the nineteenth century that the work of Ross and Manson proved the link between mosquitoes and malaria.

Before the Great Trek began much of Southern Africa had been depopulated by the rise to power of the Zulu under Shaka and Dingaan and the widespread devastation and slaughter that resulted from the Lifaqane disturbances.[1] The Tswana were cleared from the High Veld by the Mantatis and Matabele. The former Bantu population fled west to the Kalahari or sought the protection of the broken plateau edge to the north and east. The Orange River valley had been occupied since the late eighteenth century by half-caste Hottentots, later known as Griqua, while on the fringe of the Kalahari were the Batlapin, Bangwaketse, Bakwena and Bamangwato at Shoshong. To the north-west Mzilikazi and his Matabele had established themselves along the Marico River with head-quarters at Mosega. Near the eastern edge of the High Veld, in the Caledon River valley and on the western margin of the high Basutoland plateau were Bantu tribes, mixed clans and missionaries at centres such as Bethanie, Imparani, Meru-metsu, Platberg, Thaba Nchu, Bethulie, Mekuatling, Morija and Thaba Bosigo. The most important Bantu chief was Mo-shesh, centred at Thaba Bosigo, who was gathering round him the broken remnants of Sotho tribes later to become the Basuto nation (Pl. 17).

Backhouse, who travelled extensively in the border areas and

---

[1] Theal puts the loss of human life at nearly two million, although with little authority.

beyond in 1838 and 1839, describes the mission station at Bethulie situated near the junction of Caledon and Orange Rivers. Water from a spring rising between two basaltic ridges was led off to irrigate a strip of cornland. The low circular, thatched Barolong huts were situated at the foot of the basaltic hills. The settlement of some 2,000 people was grouped round the mission buildings, with a brick mission house and school, chapel and wagon shed in clay, situated near the fountain. Farther to the north the number of Basuto and Barolong settlements increased considerably, Backhouse commenting on the fact that from Thaba Bosigo to Platberg the hill slopes abounded with Basuto, 'these people esteeming the plains unhealthy'.[1] The Barolong Wesleyan settlement at Thabanchu was the largest of these Bantu settlements in the western part of the High Veld, and had a population reported to be nearly 10,000 in number.

By 1838–9 many Boers had settled in Transorangia along the Modder River and elsewhere, and the Barolong traded corn with them which they had obtained from the Basuto. By the 1840s there were many mission stations in this region with substantial stone and brick buildings with thatched roofs. The Griqua, some of whom settled between Mohales Hoek and Quthing, copied these and the houses of early settlers and built rectangular thatched cottages reminiscent of the cottages of the Coloured people at the Western Cape.

Fifteen years before the Great Trek occurred parties of hunters and trekboers had crossed the Orange River and settled in the Koesberg area on the slopes of the Koesberg, Elandsberg and Kranskop, in the triangle of country near the junction of the Orange and Caledon rivers and the later town of Zastron. The goal of the Voortrekkers was the great swathe of grasslands restricted to the west by the 15 to 20 inch isohyets, that is the area east of the Harts, Vaal and Orange confluence and the Kalahari, west of the Great Escarpment and bounded to the north by the Bush Veld and Low Veld of the Transvaal. The Trekkers were in seven main parties, and the map opposite shows their leaders and places of origin (Fig. 31). They crossed the drifts of the middle Orange which occur over a distance of about 100 miles from Aliwal North to near Philippolis, and then moved slowly across the grasslands to the north.

One of the first parties was that led by Trigardt and Van Rensburg. Van Rensburg was massacred near the junction of

[1] Backhouse, op. cit., p. 383.

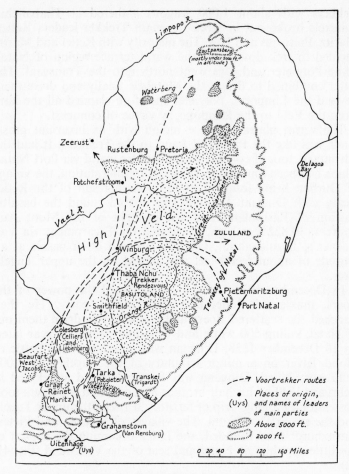

FIG. 31. Voortrekker routes, 1836.

the Olifants and Limpopo Rivers, while Trigardt went right to the Zoutpansberg. He then perished in an attempt to get through the malarial Low Veld to Lourenço Marques. Parties under Celliers and Liebenberg from Colesberg and under Potgieter from Tarka trekked through Griqua territory to the area inhabited by the Bataung north of the Sand River. Potgieter was given land between the Vet and Vaal rivers which formed the first Boer republic of Winburg.

Other parties arrived, and in 1837 nearly half the total Voortrekkers with about 1,000 wagons gathered at Thabanchu. Quarrels broke out between the main Trekker leaders Retief, Maritz, Pretorius and Uys. The majority with Retief and Maritz decided to trek down into the warm terrace region of Natal, while Potgieter and Uys went north into the Transvaal. The latter combined to defeat the Matabele finally and drive them beyond the Limpopo. Potgieter therefore claimed all the land from the Vaal to the Limpopo by virtue of conquest.

The warm plateau terrace region with its luxuriant grasslands was like the Promised Land to the Trekkers. It had the advantage, too, of contact with the outer world via Port Natal, which had been founded in 1824 as a trading station, the village of Durban being founded in 1835. As a result of the Retief treaty with Dingaan the Trekkers curved round the basaltic bastion of Basutoland and within sight of the Mont Aux Sources, 10,822 feet high, descended the Escarpment via Van Reenen's, Bezuidenhout, Oliviershoek and other passes at an altitude of about 5,500 feet and settled on the upper Tugela river.

In December 1837 Dingaan, who feared the power of the Boers, massacred Retief and some of his party. He then attacked the scattered Boers and attempted to drive them out of Natal, killing 500 white and Coloured people. A year later, on 16 December 1838, Dingaan was defeated at the battle of Blood River on a minor tributary of the Tugela and 3,000 Zulu were killed. Dingaan was finally defeated and killed in February 1840 by his half brother Mpande, and the Boers took possession of a long strip of territory between the upper Tugela and the sea at Port Natal. The villages of Weenen and Pietermaritzburg[1] were founded, the latter becoming the capital of the little republic of Natal and seat of the Volksraad (Pls. 41, 42).

In 1840 the site of Pietermaritzburg was surveyed and laid out in the form of a parallelogram approximately one and a half by one mile in extent, with about 400 *erven* or plots, and water laid on from the Little Bushman River. By 1841 some 80 houses had been built and a church erected in thanksgiving for the defeat of Dingaan.[2] By mid 1844 over 130 houses, the majority of brick or stone, had been built. The *Raadzaal* or Court House,

[1] Named after the Voortrekker leaders Pieter Retief and Gerrit Maritz.
[2] 16 December is a significant date for Afrikaners, and on this day, formerly called Dingaan's Day and now the Day of the Covenant, services of commemoration are held and the fires of Afrikaner nationalism rekindled.

gaol and powder magazine were built. In 1844 British troops arrived and the town expanded west to Fort Napier. By the 1850s Pietermaritzburg was an attractive small town with whitewashed cottages on a gently sloping ridge at a height of over 2,000 feet and about 50 miles from Durban. The houses and streets were lined with hedges of quince, pomegranate and syringa, willow and oak trees.

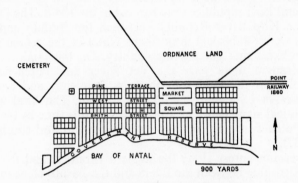

FIG. 32. Early plan of Durban (1855).

Port Natal on Durban Bay was of great importance to the Boers who gained possession of a good harbour. The settlement was founded in 1824 and named after Governor Sir Benjamin D'Urban in 1835. The village of Congella was established on the shores of the lagoon, which is sheltered by a headland 200 feet high and offers quiet water. The entrance to the lagoon was closed by a sandbar until dredging was begun and groynes built to throw the drifting sand seaward. Once access was established the site had great potentialities. The mud flats made quay excavation easy while the deltaic area was later easily reclaimed for industrial undertakings. The first raised beach gave flat land available for the commercial area and the succeeding terraces, like that of the Berea, behind the town offered fine residential sites (Pl. 44).

A sandy *vlei* lay between the Point and the straggling village of Durban with oxen grazing in the main streets, and market gardens on the outskirts. The early inhabitants complained of the sand, and it was only in the 1870s that the principal streets were macadamized. As elsewhere the first buildings were only wattle and daub structures (Fig. 32).

The British, however, were alarmed at the prospect of Boer

control of coastal Natal. In 1842 troops were sent overland from the Cape to reoccupy the port. An additional reason for British action was an attack by the Natal Trekkers on Ncapaai, chief of the Baca, and the capture of cattle and child apprentices. Natal was annexed in August 1845 as a district of the Cape. The majority, disgusted at another manifestation of what they considered British perfidy, left Natal and established themselves on the high plateau.

Several Boer republics were formed in the 1840s. The Utrecht and the Klip River Republics between the Buffalo and Klip Rivers were established in northern Natal in the region where the Trekkers first entered the country. On the High Veld, in Transorangia there were the Vet River and Potchefstroom Republics in the lands obtained by Potgieter, and also the republics of Lydenburg and Zoutpansberg. The Vaal was of no political significance as a boundary at this time as the Winburg-Potchefstroom Republic stretched north and south of it (Fig. 37).

Increasing unrest along the Eastern Frontier, and the prospect of trouble between the Boers and the Basuto clans rallying to Moshesh in the Caledon River valley, led the somewhat impetuous Sir Harry Smith to proclaim the Orange River Sovereignty in 1848. The land between the Orange and Vaal came under British control and the Vaal became a political frontier for the first time. In December 1847, as a result of the War of the Axe, the land between the Keiskamma and the Kei was formed into the separate colony of British Kaffraria with its capital at King William's Town. In the space of a few years British authority was extended over an area almost the size of the Cape.

The effect of the Great Trek was thus to cause the net of British authority to be cast in increasingly wider circles over South Africa, despite the desire to avoid further colonial commitments. The area between the Orange and Vaal known as Transorangia was divided into two main districts, the Caledon River District in the south, and the Bloemfontein District to the north. The Caledon River District was comparatively well populated with Boers in contrast to the very thinly populated northern district. Even in 1854, of 200 farms marked out between Winburg and Harrismith, only three were occupied.

Major Warden as Resident decided to establish his headquarters at Bloemfontein which soon outgrew the importance of Harrismith and Smithfield, the administrative headquarters

of the two districts and both bearing Sir Harry Smith's name!
Bloemfontein[1] became the capital of the Orange River Sovereignty, and after 1854, of the republic of the Orange Free State.
In 1852 by the Sand River Convention the republics north of
the Vaal gained their freedom. In 1854 the British withdrew
from the Orange River Sovereignty leaving the Boer republic
more or less to its own devices until the end of the nineteenth
century, when the Boer War embroiled all the European states
of South Africa. The northern and southern boundaries of the
Orange Free State were the Vaal and Orange Rivers and therefore easily defined, but to the east there were the valuable
Caledon River lands, whose fertile soil and average annual rainfall of thirty inches enabled good crops of wheat to be produced without irrigation, a region contested by Boers and
Basuto.

Moshesh had established himself in the broken defensible
mesa and butte country between the Caledon River and
the Malutis, the western wall of the high basaltic plateau forming the Orange River watershed. His headquarters were at
Thaba Bosigo, a flat-topped mesa with steep slopes leading to
a vertical-walled rampart of cave sandstone. This palisaded
rampart was only breached in three or four places by doleritic
dykes, so that the large flat area on top, which could shelter
large numbers of cattle and people, could be defended easily.
Thaba Bosigo formed an impregnable fortress and was never
captured, although assailed by Bantu, Boer and British.

After the Lifaqane, the defeat of Mzilikazi and Dingaan, and
the return of some security to the High Veld, the Basuto clans
came down from the protection of their natural fortress and
reoccupied the Caledon River Lands. The familiar story of the
Eastern Frontier was repeated with cattle stealing, commandos,
burning of huts, destruction of farm houses and a number of
minor wars. The only difference was that the contestants were
more easily matched, the Basuto also having horses and guns
and being helped by their table mountain fortresses. The final
outcome was uncertain, but in 1865 after nearly thirty years of
intermittent warfare the Basuto were finally defeated, and, but
for the intervention of Britain their territory would have been
annexed by the Orange Free State. President Brand's object in
breaking up the Basuto nation and seizing their land was forestalled by the British decision in 1868 to protect Moshesh.
Initially Basutoland was incorporated in the Cape, but after

[1] Pl. 43.

the Gun War it was finally placed under the authority of the Imperial Government, and became a British protectorate surrounded by the Cape, Natal and the Boer republics in 1886.

The other two protectorates of Bechuanaland and Swaziland are on the north-western and north-eastern borders of South Africa and were established as British protectorates some twenty to thirty years later than Basutoland.

Bechuanaland has an area of about 222,000 square miles, more than ten times the size of Basutoland with an area of 11,716 square miles, and Swaziland with 6,705 square miles. Bechuanaland consists largely of the waterless Kalahari, the majority of the population being situated on the eastern fringe near the Transvaal border. Less than forty per cent is native reserves, over half being Crown land, compared to Basutoland where all the territory is owned by the Basuto and no land can be alienated to Europeans. The population at the census of May 1946 was nearly 300,000, the vast majority being Tswana divided into a number of tribes, the biggest being the Bamangwato. This compares with a population of nearly 642,000 in Basutoland (April 1956 census) and an estimated population in 1959 of about 264,000 in Swaziland.

There was constant trouble during the latter half of the nineteenth century between the Boers and the Tswana who had earlier been threatened by the Matabele. Contact was made with the Tswana early in the nineteenth century by the missionaries, notably Moffat and Livingstone. Captain W. C. Harris, who travelled through Bechuanaland in 1836 comments very favourably on the work Moffat was doing at Kuruman.[1] The Boers attempted to annex their lands by a familiar process of infiltration and set up two small republics of Stellaland and Goshen.

The British were concerned over Boer and German expansion to the interior which might threaten the Missionaries' Road to the north. Cecil Rhodes was particularly anxious that this route should remain under British control, as it gave access to Central Africa. An expedition was sent under Sir Charles Warren to southern Bechuanaland to pacify the area. The three most important chiefs of northern Bechuanaland, Khama being the best known, appealed to the British for protection in 1885. This was granted and, after a preliminary period under Cape Colonial rule, British Bechuanaland was placed under the British Government through the High Commissioner in South Africa.

[1] *Expedition into Southern Africa*, Bombay, 1838, p. 49.

Swaziland is by far the smallest of the three High Commission territories. It is bounded on the north, west and south by the Transvaal and to the east by Mozambique and Natal. The country extends across the terraces of the Great Escarpment, thus comprising north-south strips of high, middle and low veld similar in character to the Transvaal and Natal at equivalent altitudes. Swaziland is far better watered than Bechuanaland and much of Basutoland, and the Komati, Usutu, Umbuluzi and Ingwavuma rivers provide much water for irrigation projects in the Middle and Low Velds. Subtropical crops of cotton, tobacco, citrus, sugar and rice are produced here, while on the High Veld there are great softwood forests which will supply pulp for export, and the asbestos mines at Havelock, whose exports are worth over £2m. yearly. Swaziland has a varied and prosperous economy compared to the more poverty-stricken Bechuanaland, which relies on exports of cattle, and Basutoland, whose exports are predominantly wool and mohair.

White concession hunters towards the end of the nineteenth century obtained so many grants of land that most of Swazi territory was alienated. Gradually, however, land has been bought back and now the Swazi own about half the country, the rest being owned by European farmers. Swaziland was administered by the Transvaal from 1895 to 1907, when it was placed under the High Commissioner (Fig. 33).

The Protectorates with the native reserves in the Republic of South Africa form part of the great belt of African-owned land half circling the High Veld (Fig. 34). They are a reminder of a more successful struggle by a minority of the Bantu against the Boers, and of rescue by the British, to form three small quasi-independent states embedded in the body politic of republican South Africa. The South African government has made repeated attempts to incorporate the protectorates into the Union, now the Republic of South Africa, but without success, as the British Government has resisted these demands in the knowledge that the African inhabitants of the Protectorates are bitterly opposed to Afrikaner rule.

In the 1850s the Orange Free State was inhabited by about 12,000 Trekkers who were widely scattered and practised extensive pastoralism. The republic occupied an irregular oblong area of nearly 50,000 square miles, so that the density of white population was about one person to four square miles. Compared to the Transvaal, political and economic development was rendered easier by its smaller size, less broken terrain and

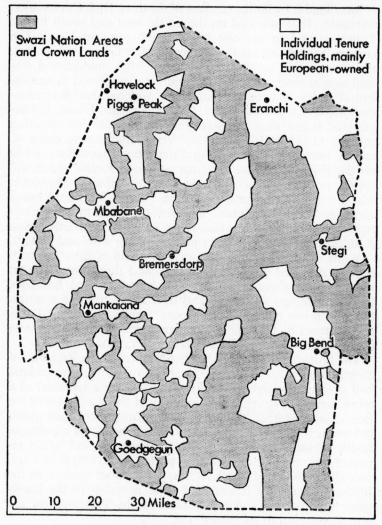

FIG. 33. Alienated land in Swaziland.

From Green & Fair, *Development in Africa*, by permission of the Witwatersrand University Press.

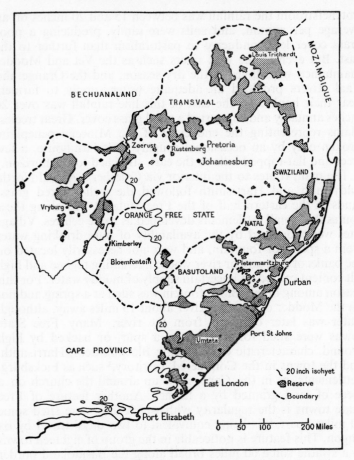

FIG. 34. African reserves in South Africa.

the great stretch of High Veld. Closer proximity to the Cape also meant more contact with outside influences than in the Transvaal, which tended to attract a higher proportion of adventurers and lawless elements than the Free State. The bulk of the Free State was grassland and ideally suited to pastoralism, but not to cultivation, although wheat was grown in the Caledon River area and later in the century the area east of Winburg began to grow maize. This now forms part of the maize triangle which produces much of South Africa's maize.

To the west of the line from Philippolis–Bloemfontein–

Potchefstroom the rainfall was between 15 and 20 inches on an average per annum, and soils were sandy, producing a poor grass cover less conducive to pastoralism than further to the east. But even in the west rivers such as the Vet and Modder maintained waterholes in the dry season, and the Orange and Vaal Rivers provided an adequate water supply to farmers near their banks. To the east of this line rainfall was over 20 inches annually and supported a good grass cover. Great treeless plains representing the end cycle of the Miocene peneplain, broken only by an occasional roughly built farmhouse, a few trees and flat-topped hills to the east, stretched to the horizon.

The main routes to the interior via Colesberg, Aliwal North, Ladysmith and Harrismith followed the well-watered grasslands in the eastern half of the Free State. It was along these routes that small settlements developed as route centres. Village sites were governed by the availability of pure drinking water from a spring or fountain, and were not necessarily located on the banks of a stream or river whose fluctuating régime and high silt content caused an uncertain supply of muddy water. For this reason among others Bloemfontein was sited at a spring and not on the Modder or Muddy River about 15 miles away, although water was later obtained from the river. Many Free State towns were sited for defence on a spur, or backed by high ground, characteristic of this being Bloemfontein, Harrismith, and the towns in the Conquered Territory,[1] such as Ficksburg. Settlements, as in the Cape, grew up around the church on a piece of land granted by a farmer. Another feature of Free State towns is the regularity with which they were sited some 30 miles apart, this being equivalent to two days' travel by ox wagon. This feature is noticeable in the group of eighteen towns in a swathe some 60 miles broad along the Basutoland border from Smithfield and Zastron in the south to Reitz and Harrismith in the north. Both roads and towns tend to form a hexagonal pattern, as may be seen from the map of roads and towns in the eastern Free State (Fig. 35).

For the first thirty years the settlements, except for Bloemfontein, were only villages or hamlets. In the 1850s there was only Bloemfontein and the nuclei of four small towns, but by the 1870s there were thirteen so-called towns. After Bloemfontein the most important were Harrismith, Kroonstad, Bethlehem, Bethulie and Fauresmith. They had the spacious

[1] Conquered territory is the name given by the Basuto to land wrested from them by the Boers.

layout and regular street pattern characteristic of towns in the Cape, geared to the needs of ox-wagon transport and self-sufficiency based on locally grown fruit and vegetables, produced on large *erven* or town allotments. Theal comments, 'The villages are small, but some of them are neatly built and ornamented with trees'.[1]

Bloemfontein developed on the site o a spring at the base of two flat-topped hills, later called Naval and Signal Hills. Its fountain or spring was called after Jan Bloem and the present site selected by Major Warden in 1846. Set on the wide flat plains of the Free State and over a hundred miles from the crossing places over the Orange River at Norvals Pont and Aliwal North, Bloemfontein grew into a pleasant little town, a green oasis in the dusty expanse of the High Veld. In 1851 it was only a hamlet with a few houses scattered about, some being situated on the open furrow with large gardens irrigated from the spring, a few stores, the usual Dutch Reformed Church and a fort.[2] It became the capital of the Free State after Winburg and in 1852 was large enough to have a Village Management Board (Pl. 43).

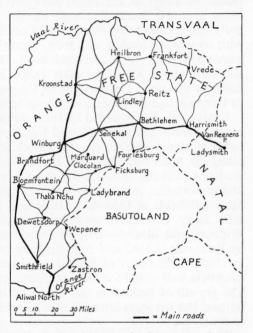

FIG. 35. Road pattern in the eastern Orange Free State.

Muller described the Bloemfontein of 1856 as only a small village occupying a large area. The government office, a simple building, fronted on to the market place, while streets and paths were overgrown with grass and ruined barracks were a re-

[1] *Compendium of the History and Geography of South Africa*, London, 1878, p. 133.
[2] W. W. Collins, *Free Statia*, Bloemfontein, 1907, pp. 20–21.

minder of the English occupation.[1] Later comments on the town varied, but most travellers were favourably impressed by its spacious layout and attractive appearance, somewhat reminiscent of Potchefstroom and Pretoria. The majority of public buildings in the 1870s were still one storey in height, being grouped round the large market square, which had a daily market except on Sunday, and on Saturday was crowded with ox wagons loaded with fruit, vegetables, skins, etc. There were about forty stores and three hotels. The population, which was only about 500 in the early 1850s, had increased to over 3,000 by this time. The majority of the population were English or German, and the English ran the commercial life of the town.

Fauresmith was founded in 1848, 40 miles west of the main route to the interior. Kroonstad followed in 1856 and, owing to its strategic position on the Valsch River almost half-way along the main route between Bloemfontein and Pretoria, has tended to outstrip most of the other Free State towns in size and importance, particularly since the growth of the new Free State goldfields at Odendaals Rust and Welkom less than 40 miles away. Bethlehem, on the main route from Harrismith to Winburg and Bloemfontein, was established in 1860, followed by Rouxville in 1863 and Brandfort, named after the President, in 1865. Collins says of Brandfort's location: 'The locality is doubtless well suited for the establishment of a thriving town'.[2] The growth of Bethlehem was slow and in 1872 it had only 12 houses, but ten years later the number of houses had increased to nearly 80.

The successful conclusion of the Basuto wars by 1866 and accession to the Free State of the Conquered Territory to the west of the Caledon River, meant the laying out of many hundreds of farms, each of 3,000 acres, and the establishment of towns, Ladybrand, Wepener, Ficksburg and Fouriesburg, on 12,000 acre sites. The first three towns, some 40 miles apart and near the Basutoland border, have made rapid progress and have become important commercial centres handling a considerable proportion of the trade with Basutoland.

Harrismith, founded in 1849, has become one of the main urban centres of the eastern Free State. It is less than 20 miles from the Natal border and commands the passes into Natal, and via Van Reenen's pass is on the main route from the Free State to Pietermaritzburg and Durban. It is situated on the

[1] H. P. N. Muller, *Oude Tyden in den Oranje-Vrystaat*, Leiden, 1907, p. 71.
[2] Op. cit., p. 149.

31. The mouth of the Umzimvubu River, Port St. John's, Transkei. Block faulting has given a deep water trough but even so a sandbar blocks the mouth.

32. Port Elizabeth in 1866. The town grew up on the first raised-beach, spread up the facet of the second and suburbs deployed on the upper raised-beach. Shallow water covering the sandy bay made lighters when under-loading cargoes imperative, until 1940 when deep water quays were constructed.

33. The Mission Station at Genadendal, was founded by George Schmidt, a Moravian missionary in 1737. *(After a drawing by G. F. Angas, 1849)*

34. Sheep and goats in the present day Ciskei. Eroded slopes are apparent.

Wilge river and is backed by the 7,500-foot-high Platberg which supplies water to the town. Sanderson, who visited the town in 1851, only two years after its foundation, describes it as follows: 'At the time I visited it, Harrismith consisted of some 25–30 houses, laid out on a regular plan, with water led through the main street. The situation is bare and inhospitable in the extreme . . . Still the situation on a main road between Natal and the interior is good, and it is likely to progress.'[1] It has progressed and is now one of the largest market and route centres of the eastern Free State with a population of nearly 13,000 (1951).

The agriculture of the Free State in the mid-nineteenth century was backward and dominated by pastoralism. As in the Transvaal, farms were large and little or no attempt was made to improve the natural pasture or breeds of livestock.[2] In the late 1840s sheep farming based on merinos spread from the Cape districts of Colesberg and Cradock across the Orange River. By 1852 the Orange River Sovereignty exported 23,000 bales of wool worth £230,000, and by 1891 the number of sheep in the Free State had risen to nearly six million. Wheat was an important cereal in the Free State soon after the Voortrekkers arrived. The Barolong acted as middlemen for the sale of Basuto wheat to the Boers. It was not grown on a large scale, however, until the mining era created larger markets. During the period 1880 to 1891 the production of wheat in the Free State was more than doubled, most of it coming from the Conquered Territory where more fertile soils and adequate rainfall encouraged the growing of winter wheat.

Maize only became an important Free State product at the beginning of this century. In 1880 only 100,000 bags were produced, compared to over seven million bags in 1923. The north-eastern Free State is the heart of the maize triangle. Maize should thrive here on flat land with loamy soils and with a well-distributed annual rainfall of over 25 inches, and a summer rainfall reliability of over 70 per cent, yet yields are low, and only a third to a half of those achieved in the Argentine and United States of America. This may be due to rainfall variability, soil poverty and backward farming methods.[3]

---

[1] *Memoranda of a Trading Trip into the Orange River Free State, and the country of the Transvaal Boers*, 1851–2, pp. 235–6.

[2] Note that agriculture in the Boer republics is treated in more detail in the section on the Transvaal.

[3] J. H. Wellington, *Southern Africa*, Cambridge, 1955, Vol. II, p. 12.

After the conclusion of the Basuto Wars in 1866 the Orange Free State prospered and developed slowly in the few years before the discovery of diamonds on and near the Vaal. It was a modest prosperity based on extensive pastoralism. Farms were large and far apart, and the small white population widely scattered. The white population of about 15,000 in 1854 had increased to about 80,000 in 1890. Bloemfontein was the only town of any size, the rest being mere villages. Nevertheless, a semblance of political unity had been achieved earlier than in the Transvaal, and the Free State was able to derive considerable economic benefit from the diamond discoveries in the fifteen-year period before gold was discovered on the Witwatersrand in 1886.

In the 1850s the Transvaal consisted of four separate republics—Potchefstroom (at first part of the republic of Winburg and later the nucleus of the South African republic), Utrecht, Zoutpansberg and Lydenburg. Independence was granted with the Sand River Convention of 1852 and this great area of 110,450 square miles stretching in a semicircle from the Vaal northwards for nearly 400 miles to the Limpopo achieved recognition as a separate political unit. Nevertheless, it was only in 1864 that partial unity was achieved when the four separate republics were formed into a single republic under the presidency of Pretorius. Unity was far more difficult to achieve than in the Free State, as the Transvaal had a far greater area and more broken country than the Free State. Great size, ruggedness of terrain, lack of communications, and until the 1880s, lack of exploitable mineral resources delayed unification. It was only through the crucible of the mineral discoveries and the Anglo-Boer war that Transvaal Afrikaner nationalism was forged.

Geographers in the nineteenth century recognized three major natural divisions in the Transvaal, the Hoogeveld, Bankenveld and Boschveld.[1] The Hoogeveld corresponding to the High Veld has an area of about 35,000 square miles, almost equal in size to the Orange Free State, and situated at an altitude of 5,000 to 7,000 feet had a cool healthy climate. 'The general elevation of the Transvaal is a most important feature. It is this which fits it to be the abode and work place of the European settlers.' This sentiment is contained in Silver's *Handbook to the Transvaal*.[2] Bryce writes with less enthusiasm about the Transvaal, 'It is a country whose aspect has little to attract the

[1] A. H. Keane, *The Boer States*, London, 1900, p. 30.
[2] S. W. Silver & Co's *Handbook to the Transvaal*, London, 1877, p. 11.

settler.'[1] This is, however, countered by Theal who is most enthusiastic, 'The South African Republic is a land of magnificent promises', and 'It contains within itself such an abundance and variety of agricultural resources that it is commonly termed the garden of South Africa'.[2] Most visitors saw the southern Transvaal, and were pleased by its cool temperatures in summer and its winter warmth in places like Pretoria, but rarely penetrated to the hot, damp and unhealthy Low Veld and Limpopo Valley to the north.

North of the ridge of the Witwatersrand the Karoo cover of the High Veld breaks down and pre-Cape rocks are exposed, causing an irregular surface relief. The second region of the Bankenveld begins here. It covers nearly half the Transvaal and was subdivided into two smaller regions. First was the Low Veld between the plateau edge and the Lebombo Mountains with an area of 15,000 to 20,000 square miles, a low, hot, undulating region between 2,000 and 3,000 feet in altitude, much of it now occupied by native reserves and the Kruger National Park. Secondly, the lower part of the interior plateau intersected by hills trending east-west and north-east to south-west. Much of what geographers such as Wellington and King now call the Bush Veld must have been incorporated in this region. According to the nineteenth-century geographer the third region of the Bush Veld was further north and included the Limpopo valley. This region of the Bush Veld was hot, moist and unhealthy and afforded winter grazing.

The earliest settlements were in two main groups: first, along the Vaal River and the Magaliesberg Mountains (Potchefstroom was founded in 1839, Rustenburg in 1851, and Pretoria in 1855); secondly, south of the Zoutpansberg at Ohrigstad, founded in 1845, and Schoemansdal in 1858. The bulk of the population lived on the High Veld and the southern border of the Bankenveld with the two main centres at Potchefstroom and Pretoria.

The total white population was very small at first, probably less than 25,000 in 1854, although estimates as to its size vary considerably.[3] The Boer republics of the Orange Free State

[1] J. Bryce, *Impressions of South Africa*, London, 1899, p. 40.
[2] G. M. Theal, *Compendium of the History and Geography of South Africa*, London, 1878, Part II, pp. 154 and 155.
[3] E. A. Walker, (1947 ed.) p. 352, footnotes 3 and 4, gives the white population of the Free State as 12,000 and that of the Transvaal as 15,000 in 1854. J. Maud, *City Government*, Oxford, 1938, p. 13, however, estimates the Transvaal's white population as 25,000 in 1854.

and Transvaal consisted of isolated communities with a very thinly scattered population and density of one white person to about four or five square miles. Farms and families and villages were separated by great distances. Keane writes, 'The eye sweeps over vast grassy plains or gentle rising ground, and lights on nothing but a few clumps of low shadeless trees marking the sites of the Boer farmsteads which are dotted at long intervals over the steppe, affording here and there a little relief to the monotonous landscape'.[1]

Each burger was entitled to two farms, each of 3,700 morgen, on the High Veld and on the Low Veld. This was made possible by the abundance of land and the necessity for transhumance between these two regions. The usual practice was for the farmer to move to the lowlands with his stock in winter, when disease was least likely and ticks inactive, and retreat back to the high plateau in summer, when the onset of the rains brought a new flush of grass to the mixed and sour veld. The large farm of 6,000 acres or more was a necessity in the Karoo, where water was at a premium and many acres were needed to feed one animal. This idea of the large farm became a regular pattern and was adopted widely on the High Veld regardless of the suitability of soil and climate. The attainment of political rights was bound up with possession of large land holdings, and was another factor in the continuance of these large farms.

The standard of agriculture was low and the average Boer farmer was not interested in the production of meat or milk, in scientific breeding and the growing of winter fodder, root crops, etc. His main concern was the breeding of trek oxen and the sale of cattle to natives for *lobola* (bride price). Veld burning was necessary to keep down the grass, and farms were understocked. When the grass on one part of the farm was eaten up the animals were moved to another part, using a form of nomadic grazing.[2] The wealth of the Voortrekker lay in land and livestock. There was little ready capital and little necessity for an exchange economy. Land was plentiful and very cheap. The head of the household selected land and registered with the landdrost the area claimed. Only in 1864 were farms surveyed and beacons put up. Prior to this there was no fencing and no provision for water, while animals were herded by day and kraaled at night.

The Transvaal Indigency Commission Report says, 'The system of farming of the Boer is still that of the Voortrekker. It

[1] Op. cit., p. 53. [2] Not unlike that of the Bantu pastoralists.

cannot really be called farming at all. It is unsystematic, primitive and wasteful. It consists mainly in tending a few cattle and a flock of sheep and goats. The principles of scientific stock breeding are not understood and their importance is not appreciated. Cattle are simply treated as a convenient form of property and are left mainly to themselves. Agriculture is limited to scratching a piece of ground in which to grow the mealies which form the staple food of the inhabitants of the farm, and of which a few bags may be sold to a neighbouring storekeeper. The whole existence of the backward Boer farmer is arranged on a hand-to-mouth basis.'[1]

The most intensively cultivated region was between Rustenburg and Zeerust, although the percentage of cultivated land was very small. A variety of crops were grown, maize, fruit and tobacco. In the early 1850s Sanderson reporting on Magaliesberg said that, 'This district has the reputation of producing fine fruit in great quantity'.[2] Crop production was greatly subordinated to pastoralism and hunting. During the 1850s ivory was the most important article of trade, and was obtained from the Zoutpansberg and Lake Ngami areas and sold to traders. Ivory did not deteriorate and was easily transported, and hunting required only a small outlay of capital.

Elephant hunting later spread to the High Veld of Southern Rhodesia and Matabeleland. Elephants were the most valuable animals and until 1870 the area adjoining the Shashi and Tati Rivers was a popular hunting ground. In the Zoutpansberg African hunters operating on foot were employed by whites, as horses could not be used because of the ravages of nagana and *perde siekte*. Wholesale slaughter of elephants by white and black hunters—between 1872 and 1874 Matabele and white hunters shot about 2,000 elephants—soon caused the supply of ivory to dwindle.

The northern Transvaal was only used for hunting and winter grazing. In summer the grass was too rank and the climate too unhealthy for man or stock. Many died from malaria which was prevalent from October or November to nearly June. Ohrigstad, altitude 3,824 feet, which was founded in 1845, was abandoned in 1850 because of malaria.

The northern part of the Transvaal attracted the more restless and adventurous type of person and was even more of a frontier

[1] Report of the Transvaal Indigency Commission, 1906–8, Pretoria, 1908, p. 61.
[2] Sanderson, op. cit., p. 246.

and pioneer region than the southern Transvaal. Hunting was an attraction, and also the possibility of obtaining free land through the fomenting of native wars. This area was not properly occupied and settled until well into the twentieth century. A hot unhealthy climate, lack of water and the presence of large numbers of Africans prevented the area from being settled by whites. An Occupation Law was passed in 1886 to encourage white farmers to settle in the north and provide a garrison against the Africans. Any applicant could get a farm in the Zoutpansberg provided he lived on it. Farms were from one to three thousand acres, but the majority of settlers failed because of lack of experience, effects of pests and diseases, and the great distances from markets.

By 1880 over 10,000 farms in the Transvaal belonging to private individuals had been registered at the Land Office. The white population had nearly doubled, an estimate in 1876 put it at 40,000 with 36,000 Boers and 4,000 English. There was increasing realization that the Transvaal possessed large mineral resources. 'The Transvaal possesses remarkable wealth in minerals which will contribute greatly to the future prosperity of the country.'[1] The first recorded discovery of gold was made by Carl Mauch near the Olifants River in 1868, and in 1870 discoveries were made in the Murchison Range. The crushing of auriferous quartz was started near Pietersburg in 1872 and in the same year alluvial gold was found in the Lydenburg District at Pilgrim's Rest (Fig. 60). In 1875 alluvial gold was found in De Kaap Valley[2] (Pl. 47).

As in the Orange Free State most of the towns in the Transvaal were more like villages in size, and as elsewhere, the growth of the settlement was closely related to the building of church and parsonage and the establishment of trading stores. No agricultural villages developed as in Europe and the Far East, farms were too large and the rural white population widely scattered. Many of the small Transvaal settlements acted as service, market and route centres for a wide hinterland and thus were more like towns than villages in function.

Potchefstroom, Pretoria, Rustenburg and Lydenburg were the chief towns until the period of mineral discoveries. Potchefstroom was for long the biggest town and was known first as Mooi River Dorp. It was founded by Potgieter in 1838

[1] *Precis of Information Concerning the Transvaal Territory*, London, 1881, p. 59.
[2] For more details of early mineral discoveries in the Transvaal, see Chapter 6.

on the Mooi River some 15 miles north of the Vaal. It was the capital of the Transvaal until 1860, when Pretoria in a more central position was chosen as the capital. After 1870 it bene-fitted by its position midway between the diamond and gold fields of the western Transvaal. In the 1870s it had a population of over 2,000 and covered an area of nearly 1,000 acres and like many South African dorps had a three-mile-long, straggling main street. Water was led off from the Mooi River to irrigate the town gardens. The wide streets, grid patterned and lined with willows, eucalyptus and other trees, gave the town an attractive appearance. 'Potchefstroom has a thriving trade, and an excellent daily market . . . It has its commercial bank, two newspapers . . . printed in Dutch and English, twenty general stores, about twelve water mills . . . three Dutch churches, two English churches . . . a municipality, the station office for the pas-senger wagons between the Diamond Fields and the Gold Fields, two public hotels, several private boarding houses and a brewery.'[1]

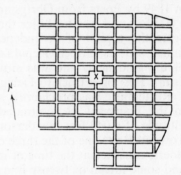

FIG. 36. Plan of Pretoria.

Pretoria was founded in 1855 on the Aapies River, and named after Andries Pretorius. It became the cap-ital of the republic after 1860 and was more favourably and centrally situated in relation to the core of the nascent state. It was near the fertile Magaliesberg district and midway between Zeerust, Rustenburg and Lydenburg and near the junction of contrasting land forms, Bankeveld, Bushveld and High Veld. It lay about 100 miles north-east of Potchefstroom in a basin below the Witwatersrand at an altitude of 4,593 feet. The lower altitude gives it a warmer climate than Johannesburg, particularly in winter.[2] Water was led off from the Aapies to irrigate gardens, and willow poles, planted as fences, soon took root and flourished as trees. These have been replaced by other trees now, particu-larly jacarandas which bloom in October and November and beautify the streets which are broad and well laid out (Fig. 36).

[1] *Handbook to the Transvaal*, p. 30.
[2] Johannesburg—mean annual maximum 70·7° F.; Pretoria—mean annual maxi-mum 77·8° F. Johannesburg—mean June maximum 60·3° F.; Pretoria—mean June maximum 68·3° F.

The large central square was used for the outspanning of wagons. Round it were grouped the main buildings and a large Dutch Reformed Church. The population was smaller than that of Potchefstroom. Although Pretoria was on the route between the diamond and gold fields it was off the main route to the interior which led through Potchefstroom and Rustenburg and then on to the north through Bechuanaland. Reclus writes, 'Originally laid out on an ambitious scale with boulevards and streets crossing each other at right angles, Pretoria long remained in a state of transition between town and country, presenting somewhat the aspect of a large garden relieved here and there with a few groups of low buildings' (Pl. 21).[1]

Lydenburg, meaning the Town of Suffering, was established in 1849 by Boers from Ohrigstad, It lies at an altitude of nearly 5,000 feet and was healthier than Ohrigstad. It was for eleven years the capital of an independent republic which in 1858 joined with the Utrecht Republic. It developed as the chief town of the gold fields and was situated about 30 miles from Pilgrim's Rest on a track to Delagoa Bay which was used fitfully.

Rustenburg was proclaimed a town in 1851, the third oldest in the Transvaal. It is situated near the Magaliesberg at an altitude of 4,049 feet. Sanderson describes it, 'Rustenburg (the Town of Rest) one of the three or four villages of the Transvaal Boers, consisted at the time of my visit of a church built of clay and some fifteen or twenty houses, half of them only in course of erection. The water is led out from the river, a small but beautifully clear stream.'[2] The stream was a small branch of a tributary of the River Crocodile. The warm climate and water enabled tobacco, citrus, vegetables and other crops to be grown.

The poor state of communications in the Transvaal delayed economic and political development. 'The road system throughout the Transvaal is in a most rudimentary condition.'[3] Roads were only tracks worn by traffic and often followed hunter's tracks, native trails and elephant paths. There were no bridges over the rivers and floods in summer might often delay the traveller for days. The main route from the south passed through Potchefstroom and Heidelburg to Pretoria. The route from Durban came through Pietermaritzburg and Harrismith to Potchefstroom, and then two branches led via Rustenburg

---

[1] Elisée Reclus, *The Universal Geography*, London, Vol. XIII, p. 212.
[2] Op. cit., p. 247.
[3] *Precis of Information Concerning the Transvaal Territory*, London, 1881, p. 19.

or Zeerust and Shoshong to the far interior. A second route from Natal went from Utrecht and Wakkerstroom to Pretoria. Another route to the interior went from Port Elizabeth to Graaf Reinet, and after Colesberg or Kimberley (1870) thence to Kuruman and Shoshong (Fig. 30).

There was no route to Central Africa via the northern Transvaal because of the hot unhealthy climate. The bulk of the roads in the Transvaal were thus limited to the southern third. The main route to the interior went west from Potchefstroom and then turned north through Bechuanaland, where a long north-south semi-arid strip on the fringes of the Kalahari had sufficient grass and water and was tsetse free. Ox wagons and horses could use this route, the famous Hunters' or Missionaries' Road. Shoshong, the main town of the Bamangwato people, was a route centre of major importance, as two main routes from Durban and Port Elizabeth to Central Africa converged here. It had a large population of nearly 30,000 until the mid 1870s, when lack of water caused a decline in numbers and importance. In 1889 Khama moved the capital to Palapye under British protection. Shoshong consisted of hundreds of Tswana homesteads and a considerable white trading community with nine stores.[1]

Meanwhile the coastal colonies were progressing slowly. The total population of the Cape had increased from an estimated 130,000 with 66,000 Europeans in 1832 to nearly 500,000, including 180,000 whites in 1865. Economic progress was considerable, particularly with the growth in wool exports from the Eastern Province which compensated for the decay of the export trade in wines and is shown in the table below. An un-

Year	Wine	Wool	Hides and Skins	Mohair, Ostrich Feathers
1826	£98,000	£545	£30,000	£3,000
1861	£34,000	£1,460,000	£97,000	£24,000

favourable balance of trade until 1825 was made up by defence expenditure at the Cape and receipts from passing ships. The main exports until the 1830s were wine, grain, hides and skins, aloes, horses, ostrich feathers and butter to the value of about £250,000 yearly. After 1840 wool dominated exports until the

[1] For a description of the town at this time, see *Zambesi and Matabeleland in the 70s*, ed. by E. C. Tabler, London, 1960, p. 22.

period of the mineral discoveries. Economic progress in the latter half of the 1850s was slowed down because of a long period of drought. Droughts have always been a recurrent feature of the South African scene causing great crop and animal losses at times.

During the first half of the nineteenth century Cape Town grew comparatively slowly. In 1860 Cape Town harbour works were begun, the breakwater and inner harbour being opened in 1870. The town expanded south round the flanks of Devil's Peak and on the road to False Bay in a line of villages—Papendorp, Rondebosch and Wijnberg. From here there was a sandy stretch with few houses until the coast of False Bay was reached. Here were the small fishing villages and resorts of Kalk Bay and Fish Hoek and the naval station of Simon's Bay. There was little expansion westwards till after 1850, as the coastal terrace was terminated by Lion's Head, while to the east growth was restricted by the shifting sands of the Cape Flats. The village of Maitland was built along the hard road over the Flats after 1845.

Wijnberg was the resort of invalid officials of the East India Company and was an attractive, tree-embowered village on the slopes of the Wine Hill and backed by the mass of Table Mountain. 'In the charming valley which connects the two bays, and which is flanked on the west by the superb rocky walls of Table Mountain, lies the picturesque little village of Wijnberg, a delightful group of residences nestling in the shade of oaks and pine groves.'[1] Further expansion of Cape Town had to await the railways and the period of mineral exploitation. In 1863 a railway was built to Stellenbosch and Wellington (Pl. 25).

In the Eastern Cape King William's Town, or 'King' as it is locally known, was founded in 1825 as a mission station and rapidly became of considerable importance. W. Ellis, who saw it in the 1850s, described it as, '. . . a place of some importance, and the chief military post on the frontier, pleasantly situated on the banks of the Buffalo River. Most of the houses appeared to be recent erections . . .'[2] Until 1864 Kaffraria was administered separately from the Cape, and King William's Town was the Capital[3] (Fig. 22).

King William's Town is about 40 miles from East London, one of South Africa's main ports. Fort Glamorgan was built in 1847 and in 1848 the town was founded on the west bank of the Buffalo River. The port was used in the Kaffir Wars for a

[1] Reclus, op. cit., p. 128.   [2] Op. cit., p. 237.   [3] See pp. 84 and 94.

brief period, as it was the nearest accessible harbour for military operations on the Eastern Frontier. For long the bar at the mouth of the river restricted its use to ships drawing less than nine feet of water.

The growth of communications in the Cape was slow until 1879, but by the 1850s it had the beginnings of a road network about thirty years before the railways. In 1824 the Fransch Hoek Pass was opened over the mountains to Worcester. In 1830 an important link was improved with Sir Lowry's Pass, named after Governor Sir Lowry Cole, replacing the dangerous eighteenth-century Hottentot Hollands Kloof. In 1840 the Queen's road was built from Grahamstown to Fort Beaufort to assist in the wars along the Eastern Frontier. In 1845 the Montagu Pass was built from George to the Langekloof. The completion of Mitchell's Pass to the Bokkeveld and Karroo opened up the merino sheep areas. In 1853 Bain's Kloof from Paarl to Worcester formed a useful alternative to the Fransch Hoek Pass.

The voyage from Europe to the Cape took two to three months during the eighteenth century, but by the mid-nineteenth century this was reduced to one month. In 1826 151 ships with a tonnage of 47,000 called at Cape Town, but by 1862, 1,140 ships with a tonnage of 386,100 called at Cape and Natal ports, reflecting the rapid growth of the pastoral industry.

In August 1845 Natal was annexed as a district of the Cape, but in 1856 it was separated from the Cape and given its own Legislative Council. In 1840 the white population of Natal was only about 6,000, nearly all of whom were Boers. But the withdrawal of the majority of the Trekkers on to the High Veld when Natal became a British colony, and the arrival of over 4,000 British immigrants in the period from 1848 to 1851 caused a change in the composition of the white population from Boer to British which has persisted. In 1856 the white population was still only 8,500, but by 1861 this had increased to 12,500, and by 1876 to 17,500. The Bantu population was estimated at 100,000 in 1848, but this had increased greatly by the end of the century to well over half a million through a large natural increase and the annexation of Zululand in 1897.

The economy of Natal was for long in a precarious state, and based on ivory brought from the interior, or the fluctuating fortunes of tropical crops such as coffee, tea, pepper, arrowroot, cotton and tobacco, grown along the coast. Cotton and coffee which seemed to hold out prospects of success failed partly because of pests and labour troubles. Coffee exports were worth about £3,500 in 1873, while cotton exports varied from £2,000 to £6,000. The standard of farming was low and income from many farms on the plateau terrace region was based on rentals from Africans leasing small plots of land on the farm. There was little incentive to improve farming methods, partly because of the lack of local markets and high costs of transport.

After the partial destruction of the Zulu the original Bantu population began flooding back, causing considerable congestion and problems of administration which were partially overcome by the creation of reserves. In 1851 eight reserves were set up, largely under the influence of Shepstone who tried to reconstruct the tribal system. The African population of Natal proved unwilling to work on the European farms, and so after 1860 Indian indentured labourers were imported to work in the coastal region.

Sugar cane was first grown successfully in 1849, but it was the arrival of Indian labour that made the sugar industry become the mainstay of Natal's economy towards the end of the nineteenth century. From 1870 to 1891 the number of Indians in Natal increased from 6,000 to over 40,000. By 1913 the import of Indian indentured labour to Natal had stopped, but over a period of about fifty years nearly 150,000 labourers were brought from India to work in Natal. The majority elected to stay after the expiration of their contracts. The Indian population of South Africa has grown to nearly half a million, concentrated mainly in Natal. Great changes in occupation have occurred since the nineteenth century. The bulk of the workers on the sugar estates are now Africans and a significant proportion of Indians are today engaged in manufacturing and commerce. About 80 per cent of the Indian population are Hindus and 14 per cent are Muslims. There are great religious, social and economic differences within the Indian population, and between them, the Europeans and Africans.

Three-quarters of the sugar is grown in the coastal belt north of Durban, the area to the south of the city being far more undulating, as the monoclinal axis of Natal comes close to the coast, with a greater altitude and therefore higher incidence of frost.[1] Rainfall from about 40 inches to nearly 60 inches yearly makes Natal marginal for the cultivation of sugar cane. Here

[1] Frost-resistant varieties of cane have allowed an extended cultivation on the 3,000-ft. terrace and well within the frost area.

the frost hazard is only slight. The soils are mostly recent sands and some are productive. Yields vary greatly according to variety of cane and the amount of rainfall.

Production was small initially, although there is a reference to 20 bags of Natal sugar being sold on the Bloemfontein market in 1861.[1] The problems were the high cost of machinery for the sugar mills, the instability of the market, fluctuating prices and costly transport. This was partially solved by the opening up of high-veld markets after the discovery of diamonds and gold. It was only after the first world war that an export trade in sugar developed. Production in 1910 was only 82,000 tons, whereas in the 1959–60 season it was over a million tons. The table below shows the value of some of the main exports from Natal by sea in 1868 and 1874. The largest increases were in pastoral products, hides, skins and wool from the

CROP	1868	1874
	£ sterling	
Arrowroot	5,501	2,226
Hides	9,501	82,473
Skins	16,117	70,688
Ivory	8,077	8,580
Ostrich Feathers	8,839	3,138
Coffee	2,425	3,348
Cotton	2,263	1,165
Sugar	90,387	159,079
Wool	91,630	338,936
Total	234,740	669,633

interior plateau and plateau slope regions. The value of sugar nearly doubled during this period, while other tropical crops, except for coffee, showed a marked decline. Total imports and exports for Natal for the period from 1854 to 1857 were £¾ m., while for the period from 1880 to 1883 they had increased many times to about £5 m.

The agricultural economy of the plateau slopes in Natal was based on pastoralism. Those Trekkers who had stayed behind in Natal were settled on large farms in the Upper Tugela and Umvoti valleys. These farms consisted of open, unfenced pastures, farm boundaries being marked by stone cairns. Large herds of cattle and sheep were moved from hill summer pastures to valley winter pastures on the farm. The experience of the first English settlers in respect of land grants was rather

[1] Collins, op. cit., p. 217.

similar to that of the 1820 Settlers in the Eastern Province. 'But the land made over to the settlers was cut up into regular parallelograms without any consideration for its character and fitness, and besides this the allotments were very much too small for profitable occupation in the circumstances of the colony.'[1] Later farms increased in size, but, compared to the Boers, the English farms were close together and there was more cultivation.[2] The position of the homestead, at first a primitive wattle and daub affair, was marked by Australian bluegums (*Eucalyptus globulus*) which grew very quickly. The principal crops were maize and Kaffir corn, but the chief activity was pastoralism, and butter and wool were the main products.

Natal's economy, like that of the interior republics, suffered from the poor state of communications, made more difficult in Natal by the highly accidented relief. 'The one influence which has been operative beyond all else in retarding the industrial advances of Natal has obviously been the cost and uncertainty of transport.'[3] The cost of ox-wagon traffic for the 54 miles from the port to the capital was £5 a ton, for a distance of 230 miles from Durban to Newcastle £20 a ton, and for the 437-mile journey from Durban to the diamond diggings on the Vaal River £42 a ton. The average rate of 1s. 9d. a ton for a mile worked out at about twenty times the cost of railway transport in England at the time. This emphasized the great need for railways, but apart from a short line from the Point to Durban built in 1863, there were no other lines before the period of mineral discoveries. The main road from Durban to Pietermaritzburg and Van Reenen's Pass made use of the Umgeni Ridge and other watersheds in order to avoid the steep and difficult descents and ascents of the deep river gorges. The coastal road could not avoid this and every three or four miles had to ford a river.

By the 1870s Pietermaritzburg, backed by the scarp of Town Hill over 1,000 feet high and overlooked by Fort Napier on the western edge of the ridge on which the town was situated, still kept the same layout as when laid out by the Voortrekkers over 30 years before. However, the original two-acre allotments were subdivided in the centre of the town, the open watercourses were gradually being enclosed and the original one-

---

[1] H. Brooks and R. J. Mann, *Natal*, London, 1876, p. 239.
[2] Although of 7,500,000 acres alienated by 1866 only 38,000 acres were cultivated.
[3] Brooks and Mann, op. cit., p. 317.

storeyed Dutch houses replaced by more pretentious two- and three-storeyed buildings.

In the 1870s Durban sprawled along the sandy flat between the Umgeni River mouth and the Inner Bay. The wharves and landing stages at the Port were connected by a two-mile-long railway to the town, which was divided into long parallel streets and quadrangular blocks like most South African towns. The street names—West Street, Smith Street and Grey Street— reflected Durban's English influence compared to the Afrikaans named Burger, Kirk and Loop Street in Pietermaritzburg. Durban's white population, composed largely of the commercial class as compared to Pietermaritzburg's officials, numbered nearly 4,000, slightly larger than that of Pietermaritzburg. As in Pietermaritzburg, the simple wattle and daub houses were replaced by more permanent structures roofed with corrugated iron; the larger houses spreading up the steep slopes of the Berea took advantage of altitude and a sea breeze location to escape some of Durban's summer humidity. From the luxuriant subtropical gardens of the Berea there were wide views of Port Natal with its piers, docks and warehouses at the entrance to the lagoon bounded by the wooded Bluff, and the village of Congella where the Boers had first settled.

The 1849–50 settlers founded villages at Verulam, Pinetown, Richmond and Ladysmith. The principal town in northern Natal was Newcastle, situated near the coalfields. Brooks and Mann say, 'Coal occurs in Natal amongst the carboniferous sandstones in various places and in considerable abundance', and, 'It is for the most part poor in bituminous ingredients but rich in fixed carbon, and is of useful quality'.[1] Coal seams in Natal occur in four basins in the Vryheid, Utrecht, Newcastle and Dundee districts over an area of some 4,000 square miles. The 'useful quality' of Natal coal is illustrated by the fact that the Natal fields now supply about 20 per cent of South Africa's coal production. Describing Newcastle in 1884, E. P. Mathers says, 'Instead of that [a small collection of hovels, lining a thoroughfare of mud] I found a well built, well laid out town, with streets admirably kept . . .'.[2]

Until 1870 South Africa consisted of four separate political units; the coastal colonies of the Cape and Natal with the most advanced economy based on wine, wool, and sugar; and the

[1] Brooks and Mann, op. cit., pp. 29 and 30.
[2] 'Gold Fields of South Africa', Reprinted from *Natal Mercury*, Durban, 1884, p. 164.

interior republics of the Orange Free State and the Transvaal practising extensive pastoralism. The country was thinly populated by whites, agriculture was backward and communications poorly developed. The long series of wars between the Bantu and the British and Boers had ended along the Eastern Frontier and in the Free State, and a period of uneasy peace set in. A vast region had been brought under a very loose political control by the British and Boers, a factor of vital importance for the successful exploitation of the very valuable deposits of diamonds, gold and other minerals.

35. Storm's River gorge bridged in 1956. Gorges such as these hampered coastwise movement below the escarpment.

36. Buck wagons, Scotch carts and Trekker wagon at Kimberley Market in 1888. Buck wagons could carry up to three tons when pulled by 18 oxen.

37. Merino sheep.

38. Afrikander ox.

CHAPTER 5

BORDERLANDS INTO BOUNDARIES

THE concept of a fixed boundary line was alien to the way of life of both the Boer cattlemen and the African tribesmen, though of course not unknown to the white farmers. A boundary defined by written record or established by surveyed cairns was considered by both groups as a needless barrier to occupation of land which, where empty, could be occupied freely, and where disputed, could be seized by force.

The regulation of land ownership by a fixed boundary line was introduced by the Dutch and British, who, coming from old established and heavily populated countries, could not conceive of space so great that boundaries could be belts of no-man's-land, where the grazing rights of one man or tribe slowly gave place to that of another individual or group. The frontier burger on his 6,000- to 10,000-acre farm seldom grazed the periphery of his land where it impinged upon that of his neighbours. The stock of each farmer was generally penned at night to prevent depredation by rieving. But some white farmers so little considered the fault of trespass that their cattle were left to graze untended for months at a time. A certain Mr Hart on the Eastern Frontier 'was in the habit of turning out his cattle to graze for three months at a time, night and day, totally left to themselves, being counted once in that period'.[1]

Although the social life of the Bantu was inextricably linked with his cattle, yet Sandile, chief of the Gaika Xhosa of the Eastern Frontier, told a Governor of the Cape that land and men counted more to him than cattle. But the territorial boundaries might be so ill-defined that if two chiefs claimed the same sector of grazing, then both tribes would graze the debatable ground in amity, while the men of each tribe remained subject to their respective chiefs.

The Dutch East India Company, in their possession of the

[1] Eric A. Walker, *A History of South Africa*, London, 1947, p. 221.

Cape Colony, had attempted to contain their free colonists and limit their dispersal by naming lines beyond which land should not be taken up. The British were even more punctilious about boundary lines, and throughout the history of the British administration one reads of boundary commissions delimiting land between black and white, besides the repeated attempts to regularize individual grants of farms by a proper system of survey and the issue of title deeds on the basis of recognized quitrent.

It was partly the limitation to free occupation of land after the annexation of Natal as a district of the Cape Colony in October 1844 that caused the Trekkers to leave Natal and return to the High Veld. Earlier the dissatisfaction at the terms of land occupancy demanded by the British on the Eastern Frontier was one of the reasons for the Great Trek of the frontier burgers.

The British officials, likewise the high personnel of the Dutch East India Company and those of the Batavian Republic, were drawn from the governing classes of Europe. These men were not only very much aware of the exact limits of their own country estates (it was the age when men were 'self-conscious' of their country estates), but they were familiar with the long-drawn-out land disputes following wars in Europe. The Congress of Vienna was fresh in the minds of the British officials, many of whom were veterans of the Peninsular War under Wellington. Besides the British administrators, there were the missionaries, who also introduced the concept of the defined boundary and the sense of 'state' organization, to peoples who had not been concerned previously with these matters.

The presence of missionaries beyond the Orange River from 1803 (20 by 1816), must be counted as a vital factor in the political and historical geography of the interior. The Boer Republicans were right in believing that the missionaries of the London Missionary Society (L.M.S.) frustrated their free expansion and helped to deny them their hard-won heritage of free and spacious land. They were blind to the fact that these missionaries were spokesmen of the inarticulate African, who had as much claim to land as they had.

Missionary influence by bringing European ideas to bear on the peoples of the Griqua States, on Bechuanaland and on Basutoland, materially contributed to the fixing of the boundaries of those territories. As early as 1820, or shortly thereafter, men of the L.M.S. had given status, based on written grants,

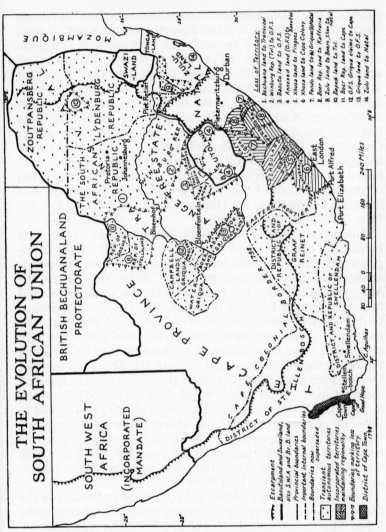

Fig. 37. Evolution of the Union of South Africa.

to three Griqua States centred on Griquatown, Campbelltown and Philippolis[1] (Fig. 37).

Later the boundary dispute between the captains of Griquatown and Campbelltown on the one hand and Philippolis on the other was arbitrated by the missionary agents of the dis-

[1] Walker, op. cit., p. 185.

putants. The missionaries laid down a line separating the Griqua States, which, starting at Ramah on the Orange River, crossed the Modder River near its confluence with the Riet at a grave called David's Graaf, to end at Platberg, a flat-topped mountain standing above the diluvian terraces of the Vaal. This, the first recorded land delimitation (1838) on the interior plateau, came to play a vital part in the rival claims set out after diamonds were discovered. With some small modification the line was stabilized (1877) as the western boundary of the Orange Free State, thus depriving the Republic of the vital triangle of land, between the Vaal and the Orange, which contained the diamond fields. In compensation for the deprivation of that part north of the Vetberg line[1] where ownership was especially in question, the Orange Free State accepted £90,000 from the British Government.

Among examples of missionary forethought in having land boundaries laid down and recorded, is that of the Paris Evangelical Station at Bethulie on the Orange River, situated downstream from the confluence with the Caledon river. There the Mission Station existed as early as 1835, in a rectangle of land facing the Orange River on the south side. This reserve, defined by the Warden Arbitration Award of 1849, might have preserved its identity to modern times had not the chief quarrelled with his French missionary and sold his land in 1860 to President Pretorius, then joint President of both the Transvaal and the Orange Free State. The peoples of Beersheba mission lying on the right bank of the Caledon sold their land also, thus losing the opportunity of preserving their legal identity established in 1849. By contrast, the Wesleyan Mission Reserve surrounding the Barolong headquarters at Thaba Nchu established since the 1830s, and delimited again by Warden in 1849, remains to this day as the largest and almost the only reserve in African possession within the Orange Free State (Fig. 34).

Sir George Grey laid down the pattern of settlement in the Ciskei, following his policy of mixing white settlers among the tribes. This policy he had brought with him from New Zealand, where it had worked well in bringing Western culture to the Maoris. Likewise the foundations of the Protectorates in South Africa, built upon the Treaty system introduced from India, illustrate the spread of British imperial ideas.

---

[1] The Vetberg line was a boundary which Adam Kok, Captain to the Philippolis Griquas had laid down between his lands and those of Cornelis Kok of Campbelltown in 1855.

Britain, exhausted by the Napoleonic wars and exercised at home by a depressed economy, was fearful of commitment in a country as turbulent and as little productive as Southern Africa appeared to be before her mineral wealth was known. Governors on the spot and missionaries aware of the necessity for imperial troops to prevent clashes between settlers and tribesmen, advised and sometimes clamoured for British annexation of territory beyond the Cape Colony and Natal. In many instances, to quell a restless frontier or prevent the too ruthless displacement of weak and disorganized tribes by the land-obsessed burgers, the Governor or High Commissioner annexed territory in the name of the Queen, only to have his action repudiated and himself censured by the Colonial Office.[1] Instead the Treaty System was preferred, and in the first half of the nineteenth century the Cape Colony came to be surrounded by a number of Treaty States under the supervision and protection of Great Britain.

The Trek leaders, and later the Volksraden of the various Republics, would not have concerned themselves with the proclamation of boundaries nor the recording of treaties entered into with chiefs, had they not been forced to do so for fear of their occupation of the land being challenged by the Colonial Office. Piet Retief, the greatest of the Trek leaders, hailed from the Winterberg of the Eastern Frontier, and there he had observed the British practice of treaty-making with unsophisticated chiefs. Thus in 1837, on his passage across the High Veld, Retief made treaties in the present-day Basutoland area with Chiefs Moshesh, Siconyela and Moroko; at his request the Zulu chief, Dingaan, set his mark to a paper whereby Retief acquired legal right to Natal, as far south as the Umzimkulu River. Dingaan thought so little of the agreement (to him a meaningless document) that the paper was left on the murdered Retief; it was later retrieved, and used by the Boers in their attempt to establish their legal right to Natal.

After the annexation of Natal by the British, the Trekkers on retiring northwards in 1846, again attempted to establish unquestionable right to land by inducing a minor, and therefore a powerless son of the Swazi king, to cede land to them. This dubious agreement was actually used to prove independence against one of the Trek leaders, Potgieter, when he claimed authority over this territory in the name of the rival Boer republic based on Potchefstroom.

[1] du Toit, op. cit., p. 14.

In the scramble for legal right of occupation, 'blanket' claims to large stretches of land were often made though hardly ever substantiated. Among such wild assertions of ownership is that of Jan Mocke, leader of the pre-Trek Boers in Transorangia, who rode down to the Orange River (Allemain's Drift) in 1842 to proclaim a republic. There he was met by Judge Menzies of the Cape Colony, who in the name of Great Britain set the Royal hand on all land south of latitude 25° S. and east of longitude 22° E. (save for such land already in recognized possession). Downing Street disclaimed all knowledge of this ambitious annexation.

The Portuguese on the other hand, held that as first comers from among the European powers to Southern Africa, their influence was paramount in Africa north of 26° of latitude. Thus, unhappily for the Afrikaners, Potgieter's claim in the name of the South African Republic to the territory between the Orange, the Zambezi and Lake Ngami, found no recognition, and the Republic was too weak to enforce this wide annexation.

Since none of these claims could be implemented they remain as historical curiosities. Less ambitious and with more substance to it was the claim of Adam Kok's Philippolis Griqua, who in answer to the threatened Mocke Republic, laid right of ownership to the land between the Orange River and the Modder. In the treaties that followed between the Griqua State and Great Britain, that of November 1843 affirmed that Adam Kok III of Transorangia, i.e. the Philippolis Griqua, had control of the land between the more southerly Riet River and the Orange, with the exclusion of two areas—one at Touwfontein, and the other downstream from the confluence of the Riet with the Modder River. Had the Modder-Riet area received definition by this Treaty of Sovereignty in 1843, and had this land been recorded as inalienable, as was that round the Griqua capital at Philippolis, then it is possible that these parts might have been absorbed eventually into the Cape Colony. For at that time there were a considerable number of Afrikaners, who even as late as their republican independence achieved in 1854, considered themselves subjects of the Cape Colony.

The inalienable lands, laid down for the Griqua in 1843, were later illegally dispersed and sold to the Free State burghers with the connivance or indifference of British officials, intent on relinquishing their responsibilities in areas now excluded from British influence. By this eviction of the Griqua the Cape

Colony lost land which might have come within its borders in the final declaration of fixed boundaries. These Griqua were given land in Nomansland of the under-Berg adjacent to and at the expense of Natal and Pondoland (Fig. 37).

The southern boundary fixed for the Griqua's inalienable land ran from Ramah along the Orange River eastwards to the mission lands of Bethulie. This river line came to be the border between the Orange Free State and the Cape Province. West of Ramah, the other Griqua domain (Waterboer), delimited in 1838 from that of Philippolis by the Platberg line, continued to function under the aegis of missionaries and the protection of British interests. Hence, in the final adjustment between Boer and British in 1871, this remaining Griqua territory was annexed by the British, but was later included within the Cape Colony. Thus the Cape inherited the diamond fields along with the city of Kimberley (Fig. 38).

In the hope of recognition by the Sovereignty Treaties of 1843–5, the Basuto under Chief Moshesh likewise made known at that time their right to the territory between the Caledon and Vaal Rivers. This land is counted as the most rewarding and fertile in the Union. The Basuto argued that in the period of despoliation (the Lifaqane) by the Matabele and Mantati hordes (1820–34) they had temporarily vacated these lands. The British having no direct interest in these then little-known parts, which in any case were patchily settled even by the Trekkers, allowed the Basuto plea of ownership to pass unnoticed. Indeed in any event, from 1830 onwards there was a steady movement of Basuto across the Caledon River into lands now freed from the menace of the tyrant hordes. By the time the white farmers began to appear in noticeable numbers, the spearhead of occupation was already 40 miles west of the Caledon River.

Instead of giving fair hearing to Basuto claims in the general land adjustments decided upon in the Treaties of 1843, the Napier Line was announced. By this proclamation it was decided which land was free to be occupied at will by white farmers, and which land was held to be inalienable, i.e. reserved on behalf of the Africans. By the Napier Award much of the land west of the Caledon was excluded from Basuto use, yet they were given all the land between the Caledon and the Orange, in the south-western parts of which, near the confluence of the two rivers, Boers were already settled. This unfair delimitation sowed the seed of future discontent and war. Yet later still, after further white encroachment had taken place, Moshesh reverted in a new appeal for justice to this badly drawn Napier Line, when he realized Basuto losses were to be even more drastic and crippling than those he had suffered by the first award (Fig. 37).

In a new continent, pioneered by a people alien to its shores and indifferent to the point of callousness of the African way of life, boundaries were chosen for their ready recognition. Thus in the eastward advance of the Cape frontier, except for occasional lapses, a series of rivers marked the shift of the Cape Colony boundary. Starting with the lower Gamtoos in 1770, resting longest on the unsatisfactory Great Fish River, using the Keiskama as a stepping-stone, the frontier came to rest on the Great Kei river in 1866. Beyond and north-eastwards, the territory came to be called the Transkei. Into this territory the Cape Colony's frontier would have pushed further east yet, had not the resilience of the close-knit tribal front deflected the white emigrants northwards. At all events beyond the Great Kei various tribal divisions were recognized as being delimited by certain rivers for a certain period, then readjusted along other river lines, as was expedient in the interests of the British. Until the year 1857 these tribal units were sketched on a large scale: thus the Pondo were recognized as holding land from the Drakensberg to the sea, between the rivers Umtata and Umzimkulu. From this last river to the Tugela-Buffalo river line lay the Boer colony of Natal (1838–46) and north again of the Tugela lay the bulk of Zululand abutting on the coastal plain. Beyond the Mkuse River lay the kingdom of the Shangaans.[1]

Marginal to the interior plateau the rivers, as boundaries, had the advantage of rising along the front of the Great Escarpment, which was everywhere a well-marked feature, even if, on near acquaintance, the front was fretted by a labyrinth of valleys. West of the Stormberg front, routes across the Escarpment were easily achieved and the Escarpment as a natural wall or frontier was already set aside, when Governor van Plettenberg set up his Beacon in 1778, near the present site of Colesberg.

Once the frontiersman was working northwards in his search for land, the frontier fixed by a despairing Government was forced to move after him. In the early history of the Diaspora in the Western Cape, the desert and semi-desert to the north of the Mediterranean lands and in the rain-shadow of the Cape

[1] Walker, op. cit., p. 240.

fold ranges, dictated the limits of effective settlement. In a haphazard way the lowest reach of the Olifants River, the Namaqualand Coast, and the more striking stretches of the western-
most escarpment in the Nieuwveld, served as ready reckoners
to officials reviewing the size and extent of their Colony. Dispersal from Graaf Reinet, north-eastwards across the Escarpment had none of the additional difficulties of water scarcity
encountered in the Western Cape. The first recorded crossing
of the Orange River is that of Jacobus Coetzee in 1760; by 1815
the missionary and trading stream was flowing strongly; soon
to be augmented by pastoral farmers—the forerunners of the
great stream of migrants of 1837 to 1840, who carried white
settlement to the Limpopo.

The Orange River, after its emergence from the high core of
the Drakensberg at the point where it is joined by the Caledon,
continues the trend of that river; then in an angular bend swings
away north-westwards, taking with it travellers making in that
direction. At the great southerly bend of the Caledon-Orange,
where the important fords lie, diverge the two most important
routeways of the central plateau. The one has its destination in
Central Africa, the other, after circumventing the Basutoland
bastion, makes its way to the few suitable harbours along the
east coast. These roads known as the Great North Road, and
the Road to the Sea, were instrumental in defining the limits of
the Union that was to come.

The Orange River, set transverse to the line of settler movement from the Cape, became a natural halting place and a
recognizable limit to authority. The boundary of the Colony
was first declared to lie along its banks in 1835—along that
stretch of the river where the main fords cross. The boundary
was recorded as stretching between the recorded point of Ramah
and upstream from that mark to a north-trending tributary,
known as the Stormberg Spruit (Aliwal North). This stream
meets the Orange at the point where the river emerges from its
mountain foreland of residual buttes and mesas. East of the
Stormberg stream the land was largely unoccupied by Trekkers,
since the land there lay to the right of the main trekker movement. These mountain valleys of the Stormberg became filled
by Bantu, slowly spilling southwards, since their natural expansion on to the Free State plains had been deflected by the
Boer occupation there. The presence of so many Africans near
the stormy Eastern Frontier made the Governor uneasy. In his
capacity as High Commissioner, he annexed in 1846 the large

triangle of land between the Stormberg Escarpment and the Orange River as far east as the Kraai tributary. East of the Kraai River, the high altitude of the Drakensberg crest (8,000 to 11,000 feet), deep entrenchment of the rivers and the complete isolation, daunted all men except the persecuted Bushmen, until the late nineteenth century when the Basutos took up the land.

At the same date as the Kraai annexation (1846), the Governor, taking the opportunity of regulating the whole Orange River frontier (left undefined downstream of Ramah), proclaimed the Cape boundary to be along the whole length of the river to its mouth. By this action the Cape came into undisputed ownership of the coastal diamond field, which lies to the south of the Orange River mouth on the raised beaches of Namaqualand.

After 200 years of endeavour the Cape Colony had finally absorbed the Karoo in all its vegetational aspects, sclerophyllous macchia, xerophytic succulents, and deciduous thorn scrub and bush. Beyond the great bend of the Orange-Caledon lay better lands, and these, from the Drakensberg to the River Vaal, the Governor declared by the same proclamation of 1846 to be the sovereignty of Transorangia. These great leaps of British influence towards the north measure the rapid sequence of events after the initiation of the Great Trek in 1836.

The Boers were at this date of 1846 uninterested in the Great North Road which lay to their west and still mainly frequented by the elephant hunters, missionaries and traders. Along the trekker route the rendezvous was at first the Barolong headquarters at Thaba Nchu, established there by Wesleyan missionaries in 1833. Later, the route to the north-east was marked by the equidistant stations of Bloemfontein, Winburg and Harrismith. This last settlement stood on the crest of the Escarpment at the first practicable descent to the coast after outflanking the 800 miles impassable Drakensberg 'wall'.

Along the route the rivers were near to their headwaters and kept a show of water for most of the year; yet they were not so large as to defeat a crossing at times of high water. Also the route lay to the west of the broken country of residual heights, which marks the approach to the 6,000-foot sandstone plateau of central Basutoland (Pl. 9).

The fringe of this mesa country was occupied by a number of remnant people surviving the wars of despoliation (Lifaqane) of the years 1820–34. The fiercest of these were survivors of the

Mantati horde, who under Sikonyela, drove the accepted leader of the Basuto, Chief Moshesh, from Buta Bute, in the district of Leribe, farther into the interior, to the very edge of the really inhospitable and then uninhabitable Maluti Mountains.

With his rear secure from attack, Moshesh, functioning from an undisturbed and impregnable stronghold (Thaba Bosigo), could exercise his leadership over the outlying tribes, without himself becoming involved in depredations of one tribe on another, or of the burger commandos on neighbouring people.

While the Barolong chief at Thaba Nchu was forced by the circumstance of his position on the road to the sea to throw in his lot with the Boers and to call them allies in the breaking of the Matabele scourge in 1837, Moshesh could bargain from a position of strength. Twice Thaba Bosigo was beset by white forces without falling, while Thaba Nchu, though remaining a reserve, did not save the Barolong from incorporation into the body of the Orange Free State.

The peripheral tribes were used by the Europeans to weaken the power of Moshesh. This was cleverly done by recognizing the independence of each. By the Warden Line of 1849 in pursuance of the High Commissioner's plan to settle disputes bordering the Cape frontier, the British Resident at Bloemfontein delimited two mission reserves at Hebron and Beersheba, and three virtual principalities, those under Sikonyela, Taaibosch and Moroko (Fig. 37). These puppet territories stretched from Mont Aux Sources in the Drakensberg (10,822 feet) in a belt to the Modder River boundary of Moroko's Thaba Nchu mission lands. Save for a small part of the lands of Sikonyela, no 'principality' land lay to the left of the Caledon River, but Moshesh continued to hold territory on the Free State side of the river. They illustrate very well an example of a buffer zone or shatter belt of small ephemeral or constantly changing territorial units, which appear to arise along the frontier between two powerful and opposing spheres of influence (Fig. 37).

In the Napier decision of 1843, Moshesh had resented the diminution in the Winburg sector of his best cornland; but was surprised to find his less established claim to the land between the Caledon and the Orange confluence granted to him.

In this Smithfield sector, Warden, the British agent in settling its boundary, made another adjustment in favour of the Boer farmers. Drawing a line from the south-west corner of the Thaba Nchu mission lands, he projected the line through a conspicuous peak, Vecht Kop, to the confluence of the Kornet

Spruit and the Orange, thus allowing for the expansion of the Cape Colony to that point five years later (1853). Warden, before he became British Resident at Bloemfontein, had been the agent to the Governor in Aliwal North, the northernmost magistracy in the Cape Colony at that time. Hence he was more familiar with the Smithfield frontier than he was with the Winburg frontier to the north. In the Smithfield area farmers had been long established, some of them dating their residence from the years before the Trek. By pushing the boundary far into the interior of Basutoland, Warden could assure the burgers a steady advance, as new land was needed, without the Basuto vassals having grounds to recourse to legal appeal. At the same time Warden placated the missionaries at Beersheba and Hebron by drawing rectilinear lines to enclose their areas of jurisdiction.[1] The Warden Line cut off over one hundred Basuto villages, thereby depriving these numerous people of right to the land or any hope of further expansion, as the natural increase of population took place.

From the first the Basuto refused to accept the new ruling. Warden's troops sent to overawe Moshesh were defeated in October 1850, and by 1855 Moshesh had beaten Sikonyela and Taaibosch of the 'principalities' and the Baputi of Quthing to the south back into submission.

This unrest coincided with the war on the Xhosa frontier. There was fear that the greatly extended 'black' frontier stretching now from Mont Aux Sources to the sea, would rise as a man against the white encroachment. The High Commissioner, more informed than any man of the danger of an organized and concerted attack on the thin white line, investigated the reasons for the general unrest in the Orange River Sovereignty. This commission condemned the unfairness of the Warden Line; the Governor, conscious that only imperial troops could prevent the trespass of the insatiable burger farmer on to tribal land, or cordon off the tribesmen from raiding European stock, appealed to Downing Street for troops to man the area.

The British Government, exercised by the events in Eastern Europe, leading finally to the Crimean war, felt only irritation at the continuous trouble in a country which was an economic drain rather than an asset to the Empire. It was therefore decided to withdraw control rather than enforce it. So in February 1854, the abandonment of the Orange River Sovereignty was completed, accompanied by the abrogation of all Treaties,

[1] See E. A. Walker's *Historical Atlas of South Africa*, 1922, pp. 16–17.

which was understood by the burgers as freedom 'to act in the matter of boundaries as in the days before the Napier arbitration of 1843', when as President Pretorius put it: 'There being no law there could be no transgression.'[1]

The British Government, like the Dutch East India Company before them, could only regret that settlers and colonists had been allowed to escape inland from such military and naval stations as the protection of the African stretch of the route to the Indies demanded.

With interest centred on the wars along the coastal frontier, the weight of numbers of the Basuto between the years 1850 and 1853 allowed them to hold the initiative against the numerically inferior Boers. Sir George Grey saw how Moshesh, playing the role of spider from his Thaba Nchu stronghold, twitched whatever thread of the web he wished to agitate. Grey therefore persuaded the Boers and the Basuto to re-enforce the abrogated Warden Line; but his intervention was too late to prevent the outbreak of the war of 1857.

Peace brought the First Treaty of Aliwal North which confirmed the Warden Line, with some modification, however, in favour of the Basuto in the area between the confluence of the Orange and the Caledon, where before Warden had been too ruthless in his expropriation of tribal land.

So seriously did Grey view the power of Moshesh, placed advantageously in the centre of a weakly held frontier, that he actively planned to isolate him from closer contact with the Xhosa in the Kaffrarias. Indeed, had it not been for the high wall of the Drakensberg, Grey would not have achieved an effective barrier to Basuto influence, when planting the displaced Transorangian Griqua of Philippolis in the Nomansland of the Transkei. To the west of the Griqua he settled loyal Tembu and Fingoes, who as hereditary enemies of the Xhosa, separated the Basuto from their allies. Grey envisaged the armed and mounted Griqua of East Griqualand 'as a wall of iron' separating these tribes, that were now dangerous to peace because they were seeking desperately to forestall complete eviction from their lands.

During the greater part of the late fifties and sixties, the Europeans in South Africa struggled in an acute economic depression, made the more intolerable by the harsh droughts of 1865–7. The subsistence economy of the Africans escaped the

[1] Walker, op. cit., p. 260.

consequences of commercial depression, but it was especially sensitive to the crippling effects of drought.

To find relief for his people, Moshesh again laid claim to, and made hostile demonstrations for the return of, Sikonyela's lands between the Drakensberg and the Vaal, i.e. the well-watered plains of the north-eastern Free State.

British arbitration between the Boers and the Basuto could do no better than to re-emphasize and consolidate the Warden award by undertaking a careful survey and separation of 'white' land from 'black' by beacons. The sight of white farmers waiting to take tribal territory, once the beacon points had been set up, gave the Basuto the courage of despair and they determined to test the issue in war. Moshesh gambled on a 'blitzkrieg'. He would direct the fighting from an almost impregnable headquarters, on shortened lines of communication served by a store of sure-footed mountain ponies free from the dreaded horse sickness, and against an enemy numerically five times smaller in numbers than the warriors and mounted men he commanded.

So important a role had Basutoland come to play in the geopolitics of South Africa, that all settlers, Boer and British, were determined to break the Basuto Confederacy.[1] When war came in 1867 most of the uncommitted tribes joined one side or the other. The High Commissioner for Southern Africa, as always, was sensitive to the danger of defeated landless Basuto pouring into the Cape upon the restive people of Kaffraria. To avert this possibility and on the plea from Moshesh asking for imperial protection, the Governor annexed Basutoland and sent up a police force in March 1868 to restore calm and security.[2]

The second Treaty of Aliwal North (1869) brought the long struggle to a close, but not before the notorious Warden Line had been shrunk yet further to the benefit of the Free State. By the new treaty the boundary came to lie along the Caledon River and its headwaters from Mont Aux Sources on the crest of the Drakensberg, downstream as far as Wepener. At this point a line parallel to the old Warden Line, but some ten miles east of it, even further reduced what remained to the Basuto of their vital grain lands along the lower Caledon. In effect, Basutoland was reduced to a kernel of a high treeless lava plateau, deeply entrenched, where snow at high altitudes could occur in any month of the year. The excision of all grain-

Walker, op. cit., p. 326.   [2] Walker, op. cit., p. 329.

lands and their addition to the already alienated territory of the Free State, allowed the Basuto family man little choice but to export himself to work on farms or in the mines in order to keep his family alive within this barren mountain state (Fig. 37).

The political role of the Basuto State (given a measure of self-government in 1959) set within reach of the area of greatest industrial development in the Republic, remains an explosive issue between South Africa and Great Britain. Of the three British Protectorates, Basutoland has most cause to fear for the future should the Government of the Republic impose an economic siege on her; for by the settlement of February 1869, Basutoland was left a trunk without supporting limbs.

The Quthing border down the Kraai stream to its confluence with the Orange, defined in the annexation by the Cape in 1854, remained unchanged in the last Aliwal North Settlement. No consideration of the Free State aspirations was allowed in this quarter, and the lands belonging to the Chief Morosi of the Baputi (not claimed in the general annexations of the Free State in 1866) were left to the Protectorate.

By these decisions the Cape Colony and Basutoland came to have a common border, and thereby the outlet the Free Staters had gained through African territory, and which it was suspected they held so as to reach the Umzimvubu River and Port St John's harbour, was sealed off.

Once the Boers were established on the plateau, their search for a sea route as an outlet from their land-locked states may be counted as an important factor in the emergence of boundary patterns and their emplacement.

The early Trekkers did not follow the Great North Road passing through the mission and tribal capitals of Griquatown, Kuruman, and Kolobeng. Relatively empty lands straddling the Vaal River and recently dominated by the Matabele, whom the Boers evicted in 1837, drew the Trekkers into this area and thence east and north-east along the high divides, following the open grasslands wherever possible.

North of the Witwatersrand, the disease-infested Low Veld and Bush Veld were crossed expeditiously to reach plateau residuals, like those of the Waterberg, Zoutpansberg and north-eastern stretches of the Escarpment. Beyond the Zoutpansberg (at their highest 6,699 feet) lay the deep trough of the Limpopo. Threat of disease to man and beast and the experience of intolerable temperatures of 100° F. sustained for weeks in summer, made the achievement of a route to reach the sea at Delagoa Bay impossible in the age of wagon transport.

In the early history of the Zoutpansberg these environmental difficulties and the hostility of the tribes drove many Trekkers back to the easier lands of the southern Transvaal. By May 1870 the Zoutpansberg was all but deserted. Those farmers that chose to remain began to pay African chiefs for the privilege of holding land. By 1874 Potgieters Rust, like the early settlement at Andries Ohrigstad, had had to be abandoned because of fever and isolation.

Nevertheless, the excellent elephant country in the Low Veld, and a hand in slave dealing, organized by the Portuguese through their coastal stations, kept sufficient men in the area to substantiate the claim of the Limpopo as the northern boundary of the South African Republic after the amalgamation of the three Boer Republics in 1857. There were none to dispute the claim on behalf of the tribes that inhabited the Limpopo lands. Missionary enterprise arrived after Boer occupation, and in the case of the Hermansburg Missionary Society, were invited in by the South African Republic in 1857 to counteract the liberal, and, as the Boers thought, detrimental policy of the London Missionary Society. In any event the boundary of the Limpopo was not linked to a land dispute, as in the case of the Vaal provincial boundary, and the Limpopo passed unchallenged into history as an international frontier line.

Eastwards as late as 1857 neither the Zoutpansberg Republic nor the Lydenburg Republic had a defined boundary. The high land was fitfully held by farmers seeking the heights and avoiding the anopheles- and tsetse-infested valleys. The plateau spurs end along the line of the old escarpment, here fretted and destroyed by complete dissection. Eastwards is the broken residual-dotted country of the unhealthy Low Veld, which in turn is separated from the sandy maritime plain of the Mozambique, by the Lebombo Mountains running from the Limpopo south to the Pongola River. The straightness of the Lebombo Mountains invited the placing of a boundary along the crest when the time came to settle the division between Mozambique and the Transvaal.

By the nature of the desultory settlement of the Europeans along the high erosion surfaces and away from the broken Low Veld, the Swazi retiring to the dissected country were never wholly brought into subjection, though they ceded to the burgers most of their land. Indirectly their survival may be

39. The Cape cart, a conveyance used throughout South Africa until the introduction of the motor car.

40. Empty transport waggon crossing the Sandy River drift.
(From A. B. Balfour 'Twelve Hundred Miles in a Waggon' 1895)

41. King Dingaan's Great Place, Unkunginglove, Zululand. Here Piet Retief was murdered, 16 December 1837, which day has since become the Day of the Covenant.

42. The Voortrekker monument, Pretoria, opened 1949 to commemorate the Battle of Blood River where the Zulu power was broken.

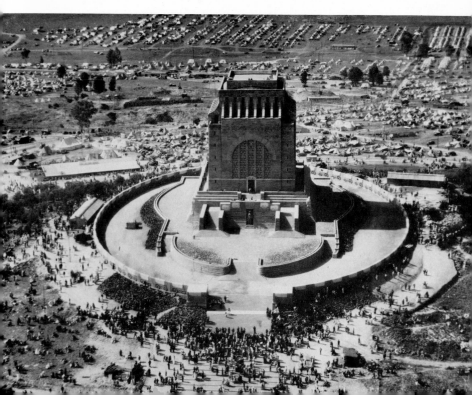

accounted for by the disposal of hostile peoples about them. The militant Shangaan kingdom lay in the plains of Mozambique due east, while Zulu power was strong to the south of the Swazi. To the north of Swaziland the extremely broken face of the Transvaal Escarpment, and the malaria-infested Low Veld, held off white penetration from that quarter. To the west at Laing's Nek, lies the natural entry into Natal from the Transvaal High Veld. This meant, in effect, that the Swazi people occupied a kind of eddy in the flow of movement round them, sometimes impinged upon by aggressive Zulu and Shangaan currents, although these seldom reached the core of their country, while white penetration from the west was linked to the plateau spurs. To the south, between the Swazi and the Zulu, lay the strip of tribal no-man's-land—here especially broad because of the war between the two peoples. After Port Natal had been closed to the Trekkers, Republicans sought access to the coast along this no-man's-land bordering the Pongola River.

At this time, 1856, the Swazi gave ready access to land not really theirs. Ten years later further acquisition and extension of this strip of land between the Swazi and the Zulu was made by the Republicans, but still the strip did not reach to the coast. To end the impasse, President Burgers suggested that the Swazi subject themselves to Transvaal rule. In this way the Republic would obtain direct access to Delagoa Bay without fear of British interference. The Swazi would not comply. Baffled, the Transvaal returned to consider the Pongola cul-de-sac and decided in April 1868 to announce the annexation of a corridor enclosing the Maputa River for a half-mile on either side of its channel to the sea.

The storm this annexation precipitated compelled the Transvaal to withdraw, but in the negotiations with Portugal that followed, a clearer definition of boundaries in Gazaland was reached. These, by implication and indeed by geographical design, rested along the straight crest of the Lebombo. The Victoria Convention of October 1881, following the first Boer War against the British, confirmed much of the Lebombo boundary; but final agreements were made between the Transvaal and Portuguese East Africa as late as 1895 (Fig. 37).

In 1875 the Transvaal again turned its attention to the upper part of the Pongola strip. It was hoped to consolidate the base of the Pongola bridge-head and to gain more land for those Trekkers drifting from the Zoutpansberg and eastern Lydenburg.

The Transvaal's Executive proclaimed full jurisdiction over the Blood River Territory (still inhabited by the Zulu); distributed all the land among their followers and levied onerous land taxes on the 15,000 Zulu resident there.

After a show of force by the Zulu, arbitration was called for, and despite the Zulu cession of the territory to the Boers in 1861 and the ratification of that agreement in 1868 (now repudiated by the Zulu, when they realized they were to be evicted) the Commission found in favour of the Zulu and the land was returned to them, along with the 75 Boer homestead units. But this award of June 1878 carried with it clauses designed to ensure the dissolution of Zulu power. In consequence of these thoughtless actions, the Zulu War broke out. At the close in 1879, a protectorate for Zululand was hinted at but never realized. This lack of foresight was an unfortunate omission, for once again, in 1884, the Afrikaners made an attempt to establish a republic within Zululand. The new king, Dinizulu, ceded land round Vryburg for services rendered him. At first the demands for payment in land by the Boers who had helped him amounted to nearly four-fifths of Zululand but were wisely scaled down later. When cession of St Lucia Bay to a German, in league with the new independent republic of Vryburg was made, Great Britain, through the agency of Natal, invoked the treaty of 1843 and decisively annexed the Bay. Thus ended the last attempt of the Afrikaners to reach a sea outlet. But many acres proper to Zululand passed in this way into white hands, and although Zululand continues to have a distinctive character, the territory is much disrupted by enclaves of white land. In 1887 Natal at last brought the remains of Zululand under her direct control and put an end to further alienation of territory by white encroachment.

By unwise action, excessive expropriation of native land and intrigue with Germany, the Afrikaners lost the republic of Utrecht, the Blood River Territory and their hold on Zululand. Later, because of these actions, Britain in the settlement of Pretoria, which followed the first Boer War of 1881, seriously debated whether all land east of 30° E. should not be removed from republican control. The argument was strengthened by the fact that most of the tribes lived in broken country east of the line, none of whom had rights under Transvaal law. Also, at this time British miners in the Barberton area of the Transvaal to the east of 30° E. had set themselves up as independent of the Republic and had formed yet another little state. The

miners, like the diamond miners before them, had complained
of lack of protection and inadequate control by the Transvaal
Government, which they maintained justified their rebellion.
Longitude 30° E. was probably chosen as a possible line for
an eastern frontier to the Transvaal, because it lay nearest to
the knot of the then international boundaries between Natal,
the Free State and the Transvaal which meet near Laing's Nek,
and is guarded by the town of Volksrust.

The 30° E. line never became more than a suggestion, for the
British feared renewed hostilities with the Transvaal if they had
attempted to implement the plan. Instead, the Pretoria Convention of 1881 fixed the boundary of Swaziland. The peculiar
circular shape enclosing the Protectorate marks the extent to
which land had already been alienated by the Swazi habit of
freely ceding land to the burgers, or any other European group
(Fig. 33).

Significantly, the 30° E. longitude cuts across the difficult
country of the eastern Transvaal, but unfortunately divides in
half the lands of the Bapedi in the Lulu Mountains of Secocoeniland. By the 1881 Pretoria Convention, these people, like the
other tribal units within the Transvaal, were given certain
inalienable rights to land. It was hoped that some security
from encroachment would bring the wars of the defiant Seco-
coeni of the Lulu Mountains and the Batlou of the Waterberg
plateau to an end. Europeans and tribesmen battled here for
residual heights and uplands which stand free from disease
amidst the hot malevolent lowlands. Bush cover and rough
terrain in the lowlands also restricted movement by horse and
wagon and made such environments impossible for the Boers.
In neither the Waterberg area nor the Lulu Mountains were the
tribes in large enough units, nor near enough to the main stream
of European commercial interest for them to have achieved
anything more than 'reserves', when the final boundary fixing
came about. These areas, though local borderlands big enough
in the case of Secocoeniland to merit the name of the Basutoland
of the Transvaal, did not give rise to international or provincial
boundaries as happened in the areas now designated British
Protectorates (Fig. 37).

In the case of the British Protectorates, the lands disputed
were the healthy open grasslands along which the major routeways of the subcontinent passed. The Kalahari border is the
most interesting of those borderlands which came to mark
interstate frontiers. In this area, more than in any other frontier

district, the failure of the Colonial Office to grasp the problem of South Africa is manifest.[1] It has been fairly stated that Downing Street allowed the tribesmen to be crushed in the interests of the white man, only then to intervene to prevent the white man from enjoying his victory to the full. From the point of view of the British Government their policy was designed to spare the British taxpayer, encourage recognition of local responsibility, and save the African from gross exploitation and deprivation.

This last concern led to the creation of residual tribal lands as inalienable reserves, whether as integral parts of the South African states, or as direct protectorates of the Crown. Bechuanaland has the distinction of part being vested in the Cape Colony, and part being directed by the Colonial Office.

The study of the frontier along the margins of the Kalahari is especially interesting because of two special features, the occurrence here of diamonds and the situation also of the Great Trunk Road to Central Africa (Fig. 38).

The 'pipe' diamond diggings of Kimberley concern the frontier between the Orange Free State and the Cape Colony, and the history of the boundary dispute hinges on the early treaties between the Governor of the Cape and the Griqua people, and on boundaries drawn up by missionaries to separate the Griqua States.

North of the Vaal-Orange, the boundary dispute became focused first on the alluvial diggings and farther north upon the Great North Road. Both areas lay in the possession of the Bechuana people, from whom the Transvaalers attempted to wrest them. The record of attempts to deprive the Bechuana of his land is so sordid as to make this history read like the conquest of Mexico.

The Great North Road is an enduring feature in the historical geography of Southern Africa. Near Mafeking the bottleneck of this route between desert and malarial lowlands begins. The road coming up from the Cape crossed the Orange River near or at the present Hopetown. Proceeding north, the Vaal River is met at Klip Drift (Barkly West), thence the road took to the broad interfluve, between the lower Harts and the Vaal River to a point where the upper Harts strikes towards its source in the dolomitic plateau of the western Transvaal. The

---

[1] J. A. L. Agar-Hamilton, *The Road to the North; South Africa, 1852–1886*, London, 1937, and C. W. de Kiewiet, *British Colonial Policy and the South African Republics, 1848–1872*, Imperial Studies No. 3, 1929.

road crosses the river by a ford, on the farther bank of which the Bechuana *stadt* of Taungs was established. The road continued along the watershed and on reaching the Molopo source area, picked up one headspring after another. Each spring, according to its capacity, supported a tribal unit closely set about the water point. These *stadts* contained several thousand inhabitants. In the case of the Batlapin capital of Lithakoo, 15,000 were believed present in the thirties of the last century.

The villages were organized in a manorial pattern with their arrangement of arable land placed near the settlement and therefore nearest to ground water. Beyond lay the common pasture and beyond again the waste land or hunting territory, used in good years for cattle pasture if surface water persisted for any length of time.

This route was viable at all seasons, save in the most intolerable of droughts. It lay between the Orange and the Molopo in the belt transitional between sweet veld and Karroid scrub or bush veld. Ten inches of rainfall occur at Hopetown to feed the semi-arid Karoo. Farther north at 26° S., in the headwaters of the Molopo, 20 inches of rainfall support low thorn and tropical bush veld. Thus in good seasons grass and water were assured along any section of the road (Fig. 38).

An alternative route north to Central Africa lay along the western margin of the Kaap Plateau. This was the Missionary Road which, crossing the Orange at Prieska, led north through Griquatown to Kuruman, using the line of 'vauclusian' springs in the dolomite. Thence the road strikes north-east, picking up the water holes near the junction between the Kalahari sand and bedrock. In drought these springs fail and the route becomes impossible. Life at such times concentrates on the great perennial springs, many of which, like those in the Kuruman hills, give more than 500,000 gallons a day (Fig. 38).

The Missionary Road and the settlements upon it lay for the most part beyond persistent depredations of the Matabele and Mantati hordes. But the Matabele from their chief place Mosega on a headwater spring of the dolomitic Marico, impinged upon the Mafeking stretch of the Great North Road, just at the point where the Missionary Road joins it.

The Matabele chief expected, in the nine years he remained at Mosega, that his permission be asked for a safe passage through to the north. It is said he slew the Liebenberg party of Voortrekkers for failing to observe this courtesy. After the defeat of the Matabele by the Voortrekkers and their Barolong

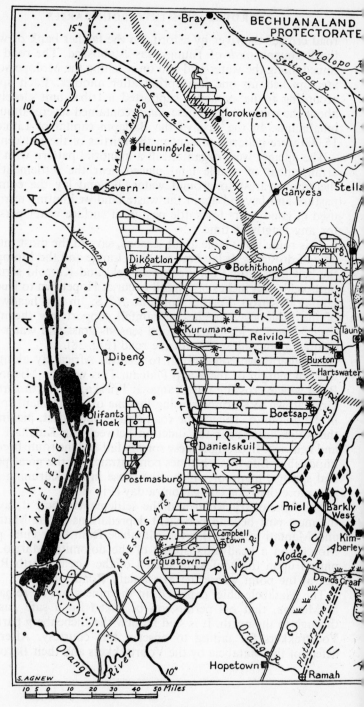

FIG. 38. The Kalahari Frontier.

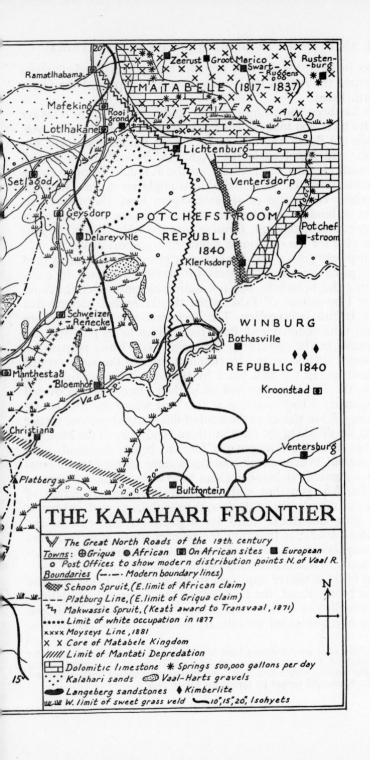

THE KALAHARI FRONTIER

🅥 *The Great North Roads of the 19th. century*

Towns: ⊕ Griqua ⊚ African ▣ On African sites ▣ European

○ *Post Offices to show modern distribution points N. of Vaal R.*

Boundaries (—·— *Modern boundary lines*)

〰️〰️ *Schoon Spruit,(E.limit of African claim)*

- - - *Platburg Line,(E.limit of Griqua claim)*

ʓʓ *Makwassie Spruit,(Keat's award to Transvaal, 1871)*

····· *Limit of white occupation in 1877*

xxxx *Moyseys Line, 1881*

X X *Core of Matabele Kingdom*

////// *Limit of Mantati Depredation*

▤ *Dolomitic limestone* ✳ *Springs 500,000 gallons per day*

⛰️ *Kalahari sands* ⬭ *Vaal-Harts gravels*

🌑 *Langeberg sandstones* ◆ *Kimberlite*

〰️〰️ *W. limit of sweet grass veld* ﹏ *10", 15", 20", Isohyets*

N

allies in 1837, the Trekker republic centred on Potchefstroom assumed the role of the Matabele as toll-keepers of the Great North Road.[1]

It has been shown how on the establishment of the Trekker States their first interest was fixed on finding a route to the sea. When the Boers were driven back from the Zoutpansberg Republic and Natal on to the High Veld by sickness or British annexation, then the pressure on the Kalahari frontier began to make itself felt. Paradoxical as it might seem, the Transvaal Republic by reason of its extravagant land allocations was short of land to distribute among the burgers. With no other economic development, farming was the only livelihood possible save for the occasional hunter or transport driver.

Displacement of the Bechuana tribes, who previously had been given land by the Boers for services rendered in overcoming the Matabele, was not noticeable until after the Sand River Convention of 1854, when the Transvaal became free from British intervention. The Bechuana rose in war and on defeat were saddled with huge indemnities to be paid in head of stock. In the case of the Batlapin, when being pressed for payment, they answered by claiming right to the land wrested from them, in the first place by the Matabele, and following them, the Trekkers who had taken their place. They recovered a boundary which, starting at the Vaal where the Makwassie stream joins it, passed to the head of this watercourse and thence along the divide to the most northern headwater of the Molopo.

This claim the Batlapin put forward before diamonds were discovered. When the alluvial fields came to light, the Transvaal reiterated its blanket claim to ownership as far west as the Langebergen, but with no success. Since occupation of land was nine-tenths of the law, the republicans were chagrined that their outermost farms lay a good distance east of the diamond lands; at that time the pioneer fringe stretched from the neighbourhood of Rooigrond near Mafeking, to 20 miles downstream from Christiana on the Vaal.

To effect a nearer approach to the diamond fields and the Great North Road, the President of the Transvaal proclaimed the new district of Bloemhof downstream along the Vaal, and in the north enlarged the military authority of the Zeerust dis-

---

[1] In 1864, after the missionary John Mackenzie had settled at Shoshong in far Bechuanaland, he received a message from the Transvaal Government saying authority must be sought first from it, for him to settle among the Bamangwato people. Mackenzie replied by raising the Union Jack.

trict to the west so as to straddle the Road. This measure was more practical than the usual blanket claims.

Insecurity of his claim to the diamond fields proper, and fear of the English element flocking to the diggings, next induced the President to issue a monopoly of the diamond area to a triumvirate of friends. This brought prompt reaction. First, the miners declared themselves independent of any neighbouring State, then the Batlapin declared themselves outside the authority of the Transvaal, and last, the Griqua, though few were resident, drew attention to Treaties which in 1842, reaffirmed in 1864, gave them possession of this land between the Harts and the Vaal. Having no power to enforce their claim the Griqua appealed for protection from Britain. The urgency of claims redoubled in 1870 when 'dry' diamonds were found south of the Vaal in a rocky hill near Kimberley (Pls. 49, 51).

Not to be outdone, the Baralong, resident at Taungs and Mamusa (the old Koranna stronghold, renamed Schweizer-Reneke) before their eviction by the Matabele at the beginning of the century, brought evidence to show claim to their ancestral lands, as far east as the Schoon Stream, to which they had returned on helping to defeat the Matabele in 1837. Arbitration was sought to quell the conflict, but the Orange Free State refused to subject the land south of the Vaal to a British decision. On the strength of their present jurisdiction over the Piniel Reserve, the Free State Government began to administer the disputed lands claimed also by the Campbelltown Griqua.

Despite a reluctant Cape Parliament, the Governor forced through an act of annexation of this and all land remaining to the Griqua States—and named the area Griqualand West, in contrast to the Griqualand East established in 1854 on the borders of Natal.

To the north of the Vaal, the diamond area and farms thus fell to the British also. In settling the western border of the Transvaal Republic, Keate took cognisance of the early Batlapin claim and asserted the line of the Makwassie stream northwards along the divide to Ramatlhabama. This excluded a considerable belt to the west of the line, which was already considered as in possession of Afrikaner farmers. The Keate award of 1871 caused deep bitterness among the Boers and was repudiated by them in 1874.

British officials viewed the anarchy prevailing in the Transvaal with misgiving. Trouble between farmers and the tribes was recurrent in all the borderlands. Unwisely, Britain annexed

the whole of the Transvaal on 12 April 1877. This did little to
alleviate the distress on the various borders, where tribes, driven
desperate by loss of land, turned to make a last stand. Wars
between the years 1878 and 1880 flared up in the Lulu Mountains of Secocoeniland, in Griqualand West, in Basutoland and
in the Transkei.

To crown the general turmoil and frustration of the borderlands, the Transvaal Boers rebelled in 1880 and succeeded in
repulsing the British at Laing's Nek, the gateway to the Transvaal High Veld. Peace called for a new consideration of Transvaal independence and its frontiers. These were embodied in
the Pretoria Convention of 1881, which laid down the Bechuana
frontier also. Here, where might has proved right, the Transvaal boundary was set west of the limit of white occupation as
known in 1877.

The new line started at the dispossessed Bechuana *stadt* of
Rooigrond, thence the line led along the watershed, south to
the republican settlement of Delareyville, so on to the Harts
river and along it to Mamusa. Here the boundary crossed the
river to proceed south to meet, at right angles, the old Griqua
Campbelltown boundary which started from the Vaal near the
famous Platberg boundary point. This line was called the
Moysey Line, but it too found no favour among the landless
Afrikaners. The new frontier so drawn, traversed the last 'good'
lands of the tribes.[1] It passed through or narrowly skirted three
stadts which were once important native strongholds, but were
now already European settlements. (That of Mamusa had been
raised to the ground and the Korannas scattered at gun point.)
The shift of the line westwards brought Phokwani (Hartswater),
Manthe, Taungs and Khunwana (Geysdorp) into the frontier
position. Mafeking had long suffered the role of a besieged
frontier town in constant fear of attack.

The announcement of the new frontier brought panic to the
tribes and they turned to fratricide in seeking elbow-room for
their constrained herds. The wars were supported by white
volunteers, Boer and Briton, who expected payment for their
help in land and cattle within the tribal areas. Eventually, the
Afrikaners persuaded the demoralized Batlapin and Barolong
to cede all their land to them to the very desert verge, but excluding the chief perennial springs of the Kuruman hills. These
became the republics of Stellaland and Goshen (Fig. 38).

The Afrikaners were indifferent at that time to the land on the

[1] See Fig. 38 for the western limit of grass veld.

desert side of these new republics, for by these new possessions they had established right of entry into the 'dry' Harts Basin, which was the best of the grazing land of Stellaland, and also access to Mafeking which had a better water supply than the brigand den of Rooigrond. In the Harts River basin a new administrative post at Vryburg was established.

From their new station at Vryburg, and after the eviction of the Barolong from Mafeking, the republicans could take toll on the Great North Road, and could thieve Bechuana cattle with impunity. If need be, the Transvaal, already implicated in the plot, could be asked for protection and in this way the little republic would amalgamate with the mother state as the Crown Colony of British Kaffraria had done with the Cape Colony.

The missionaries, so active in the history of the Road, now once again entered the scene. Barbaric actions by white men against the luckless Bechuana brought the powerful humanitarian group in Britain into protest. The British Government, impelled by public opinion to intervene, called the London Convention of 1884 to make a final settlement in the land disputes. The tribes regained no ground already lost, but Stellaland and Goshen, those ephemeral states, disappeared leaving Geysdorp and Vryburg as witnesses to posterity.

Britain, in the name of the Cape Colony, then made a blanket claim to all land south of the Molopo, and up the lower Mossop river to longitude 20° E. Because Britain was at the height of her power, the line was honoured and did not suffer the fate of Pretorius's pretentious assertions in 1868.

The frontier of the Transvaal had been so laid down that the roadway from Taung, through Vryburg, thence to Mafeking gap and north to the next nodal point at Kanye, lay outside the jurisdiction of the Transvaal. This did not preclude the republicans from having their own road through Schweizer-Reneke (Mamusa) and Geysdorp (Kunwhana) and so north to Rooigrond and Central Africa.

In the Mafeking sector settlements like the Matabele's Mosega, Bechuana's Ramatlhabama, Afrikaner's Rooigrond, were set right on the frontier; thereby each was devitalized as organizing centre for further republican expansion. Lichtenburg and Zeerust, placed some distance back from the frontier, inherited these functions and grew in consequence (Fig. 38).

The railway to the diamond fields and its extension to the Tati gold field of Central Africa, were built outside the republican frontiers, following in the tracks of the Road. Those Bechuana towns reached by the railway, such as Mafeking, soon became Europeanized and out-distanced others like Taungs which lay to the side of the rail route.

The Road to Central Africa had been invested first by the Matabele who had themselves retired north along it, and then by the Transvaalers who hoped to ride it in their covered wagons in search of yet more land. The Trekkers who moved into Angola, and those who reached East Africa, were undoubtedly the precursors of a great movement strangled by the British intervention in Bechuanaland and the declaration of a Protectorate over the northern part of it.

The Great North Road, linked in its history to the Kalahari frontier, will not remain the main route to the north. Geographical determination first established it, and historical accident perpetuated it in a railroad, which from the Cape to the border of Rhodesia passes through one of the least productive areas in Africa (see page 190). The true road to the north is the route first followed by the Voortrekkers north-eastwards to the Zoutpansberg. After crossing the Orange River somewhere at its great bend, the natural trend of movement is axial to the oval of grassland that covers the High Veld between the Karoo-Kalahari margin on the one hand, and the Drakensberg highlands on the other. Pretoria, as the capital of the Union of South Africa, commanding both the heartland in Halford Mackinder's sense,[1] and facing the most active frontier in Vaughan Cornish's sense,[2] is a truer exponent of geographical reality than Potchefstroom, which so briefly led the fortunes of the nascent Transvaal.

On the Kalahari front, the incorporation of all land south of the Molopo into the Cape Colony welded the last link in a proper geographical borderland. Except for the brief break at the Mafeking gap a zone of dearth and difficulty separates South Africa from the healthy highlands of Central Africa to the north of the Orange–Molopo–Limpopo river frontier. The exclusion of the lower Limpopo from the frontier gives a tantalizingly unbalanced look to a map showing the eastern coastline of the Union. This is the more striking when Delagoa Bay is remembered as the antechamber to the Witwatersrand economic nexus.

[1] Sir Halford Mackinder, *Democratic Ideals and Reality*, 1909; and *Geog. Journal*, vol. xxiii, pp. 421–37, 1904.
[2] Op. cit., *Great Capitals*, London, 1923.

CHAPTER 6

MINERAL DISCOVERIES

THE historical geography of South Africa was treated on a broad scale in Chapter 1 which outlined the long proto-historical and historical period before the Dutch settled at the Cape. This was followed by one hundred and fifty years of expansion by Dutch pastoralists who collided with Bantu pastoralists along the line of the Eastern Frontier of the Cape. During the first half of the nineteenth century the British occupied the Cape and the Voortrekkers moved rapidly on to the high plateau of the interior. The next period of mineral discoveries from 1870 to 1910 was short, but momentous, with swift economic growth in all parts of South Africa. The industrial revolution caused by diamonds and gold, and not by coal, iron-ore or textiles, reached South Africa towards the end of the nineteenth century and changed the economy of the country almost overnight from a basis of extensive pastoralism to that of a modern capitalist state. Economic, social and political changes of serious magnitude mark this mineral period as one of great stress. Repercussions from these radical changes such as the Boer War and its aftermath, and the rise of Afrikaner political power, the social and economic enmeshing of the Bantu in the white industrial and mining economy, and strained race relations resulting from these factors, affect the South African state more and more deeply.

Minerals have been of great significance in Africa south of the Sahara for a very long period. It was partly the gold of the region that became known later as the Gold Coast in West Africa and Monomotapa in south-east Africa that drew the Arabs and the Portuguese along the coasts and into the interior of Africa. The Negroes of West Africa and the Bantu of East and South Africa knew how to work iron, copper, gold and tin. The craftsmanship of the Benin bronzes and Nok figurines and recent finds of bronze figures and ornaments in southern

169

Nigeria reaches a high order that was not achieved in South Africa. Because there were no states in South Africa with a high degree of culture comparable to those of the medieval states of the Sudan belt, the economic history of South Africa dates from the late nineteenth century mineral discoveries of diamonds and gold. They are ideal media for rapid economic development. Abundance of cheap land, exports on a large scale of primary commodities such as wheat, wool, fish, lumber and, later, meat and dairy products, the availability of markets and the growth of modern transport, help to explain the swift economic growth of North America and Australasia. But in South Africa it was diamonds and gold that brought the economic frontier which slowed down the ever moving pastoral frontier. The age of unlimited pastoral expansion was over and a new mineral-agricultural era suddenly dawned after 1870 (Fig. 4).

Initially the attitude of the Boers to prospecting for minerals was hostile and the law prohibited the search for mineral deposits. It was feared that the influx of foreign influence would destroy the isolation and security of the Republics. Their attitude was changed in the fifties when in retaliation the British forbade the export of gunpowder and arms to Transorangia. President Burgers, who was anxious to develop the Transvaal economically, encouraged prospecting, offered a reward for the successful discovery of gold and passed the first Transvaal Gold Law.

The distribution of South Africa's minerals emphasizes the importance of the high plateau and the interior states. Except for diamonds and copper in Namaqualand and coal in Natal the valuable mineral fields are located north of the Orange River and on the plateau. Namaqualand's copper was discovered by Governor Simon van der Stel in 1685, but as the deposits were too remote and the region too arid they were not touched for nearly two hundred years. In 1852 the firm of Phillips and King started mining operations at Springbokfontein. A large number of prospectors came into Namaqualand and mining companies were floated in the main towns and villages of the Cape. By 1855 the wave of speculation had subsided and mining operations were only carried on with any success by two companies at Springbokfontein and Spektakel. Later, however, a dozen firms worked the copper despite difficulties of transport and lack of water (Pl. 46).

The first mineral discovery of major importance in South

Africa was that of diamonds near the Vaal River in 1867. Diamonds are found particularly in volcanic Kimberlite pipes and fissures and in alluvial terraces. The pipes are of late Cretaceous age extending in a belt from Premier Mine in the Transvaal to the Kimberley region. The pipes have vertical sides and are filled with blue ground of a tough soapy texture which weathers at the surface to friable yellow ground. In the Kimberley area Karoo shales cover the pipes. The Vaal River has cut into the pre-Karoo rocks and for a hundred miles to the north-east of Pniel mission station and Klip-Drift (Barkly West) where the first alluvial diamonds were found, it flows through a series of rocky gorges.

Several sub-cycles of erosion are present along the banks of the Vaal forming alluvial terraces containing diamonds. The older terraces have been found at heights varying from 100 to over 300 feet above the river, while a second series of younger terraces vary in height from 15 to 40 feet above the river. Their origin is uncertain, but may be due to alternations of wet and dry periods of climate. The diamonds within these gravels are obtained from the igneous plugs of eclogite and ultrabasic intrusions linked with the ejection of the Basutoland lavas on the break-up of Africa following on the Stormberg desert phase in the Jurassic period. The bulk of the diamonds have been carried to the mouth of the Orange River where they are now mined in marine terraces in the rich Namaqualand fields, and farther to the north along the South West African coast.

The first diamond was obtained in the Hopetown district and soon diamonds were found over a wide zone on the north bank of the Vaal, and a large population of diggers spread out along both banks of the Vaal, from Delport's Hope at the junction of the Vaal and Hart rivers to beyond Hebron on the Vaal. In 1870 a large number of diamonds were found in a depression on the site of the later Du Toit's Pan mine, and in 1871 on a *kopje* which later became the Kimberley mine. The dry diggings proved far richer than the river diggings which many deserted, while thousands came from all over South Africa and oversea. In 1872 the population of the dry diggings was estimated at 50,000 whites and Africans. The early miners had little idea of the extent and value of the diamondiferous ground, previous experience having been obtained at the alluvial diggings. The two poorer mines of Dutoitspan and Bultfontein were found first and worked somewhat haphazardly. Enough experience had been gained by July 1871, when the Kimberley mine was discovered, to enable a more rational exploitation to be carried out from the beginning. The four mines, Dutoitspan, Bultfontein, De Beers and Kimberley, are located in a circle three miles in diameter. The farms on which the diamonds were found were sold at prices ranging from £2,000 to £6,000, good for the period, but pitiful in comparison to the £450 m. of diamonds recovered from them in the period 1867–1955.

The effects of the diamond discoveries were immediate; almost overnight Kimberley became the second largest town in South Africa. Large amounts of capital were brought in, prices of agricultural produce soared, trade improved greatly and a large internal market developed. The poverty of South Africa's communications was emphasized by the fact that Kimberley was 350 miles from the nearest ports of Port Elizabeth and East London, and over 500 miles from Cape Town, the journey taking three to four weeks by ox wagon. In 1870 the Inland Transport Company ran coaches once a week from Wellington to the Vaal, the journey taking eight to nine days. Railways were thus an urgent necessity. Harbour and dock facilities at Cape Town were greatly improved to cope with the increased traffic and in 1870 the Docks were opened. Despite the opening of the Suez Canal in 1869 the amount of shipping calling at the Cape ports did not diminish greatly. In 1873 the Castle Steamship Line was founded and in 1900 it was amalgamated with the Union Line. Better ocean links with Europe were obtained with regular sailings and the voyage to Britain was reduced to twenty-five days.

Imports for the decade after 1870 trebled, while exports from Cape and Natal ports rose from £3 million in 1870 to £9 million in 1882. The revenue of the Cape increased from little more than half a million pounds in 1870 to nearly two and a half million pounds in 1881. The value of diamonds exported was nearly £4 million by 1892. Indirect effects on agriculture were marked, both locally in the attraction of a large internal market, and externally with greatly increased exports of pastoral products, wool hides, mohair and ostrich feathers. According to De Kock[1] agriculture became better organized with improved methods, although the impression gained by travellers through the interior in the 1870s is still that of backward methods and extensive use of land. Soil poverty, drought, numerous plant and animal diseases, conservatism and the use of inefficient native labour made

[1] M. H. De Kock, *The Economic Development of South Africa*, London, 1936, ch. 4.

43. View of Bloemfontein, 1854.   (*From a painting by H. S. Wright*)

44. West Street, Durban, 1888.

45. De Wet's Commando crossing a ford of the Orange River during the guerilla phase of the Boer War.

46. Springbokfontein, Namaqualand copper mining town. The archean complex is here revealed stripped of Karoo mesozoics.

better farming difficult. In addition mineral rights on farms near the Rand caused very high land values and discouraged the development of agriculture. Improved agricultural methods were adopted, however, in the more settled regions of South Africa.

Because of the boom immigrants streamed into South Africa. The total white population of South Africa in 1870 was only about 250,000, whereas by 1891 the population increased to over 600,000 and by 1904 to over a million. Railways extended their mileage from 69 miles in 1870 to over 2,000 miles in 1890. New demands were created for labour and the migration of adult African males to the new mining areas developed on an ever-increasing scale. The Bantu had sought work on the settlers' farms along the Eastern Frontier at the beginning of the nineteenth century. The discovery and exploitation of diamonds and then gold turned the labour trickle into a flood, so that today well over 500,000 Africans are engaged as migrant workers in the South African mines. But in the early 1870s there were only 10,000 Africans working on the Kimberley diamond fields, and wages were paid partly in cash, partly in guns. This latter fact caused considerable trouble leading to the Langalibalele affair in Natal in 1871 and the Basuto Gun War with the Cape in 1882. South Africa was also faced for the first time with complex problems of labour relations in a mixed mining-urban economy, problems that were to prove increasingly difficult to solve.

The town of Kimberley mushroomed and a sprawl of tents and corrugated iron shanties soon covered the dry dusty plains near the Colesberg Kopje (Fig. 49). Cecil John Rhodes as a boy writing to his mother describes Kimberley, 'Fancy an immense plain with right in the centre a great mass of white tents and iron stones . . .'. The Colesberg Kopje was about 30 feet high and measured approximately 180 by 220 yards. Herbert Rhodes, whom young Cecil had accompanied to the diggings in 1871, had three claims. There were about 600 claims in all and many thousands of people working on the kopje, which soon became a gaping hole hundreds of feet deep (Pl. 52).

Trollope was scathing about the appearance of the town. 'I cannot say that Kimberley is in other respects an alluring town; —perhaps as little so as any other town that I have ever visited.' He goes on, 'The roadway is all dust and holes . . . an uglier place I do not know how to imagine'.[1] Yet Rhodes loved the

[1] *South Africa*, London, 1878, Vol. II, pp. 190 and 194–5.

town and had a small, ugly, corrugated-iron-roofed house next to the Club. Kimberley went through difficult teething troubles, water was scarce, dust-storms were frequent, there were no trees for miles, and fuel and food were expensive. Kimberley is situated at an altitude of about 4,000 feet, so that frost is frequent and June and July have mean minimum temperatures of 36° F. The region is semi-arid with an average annual rainfall of about 18 inches, 80 per cent occurring in summer, and with a dry winter. Fuel supplies were a problem; wood was costly and coal almost unobtainable until the coming of the railways and the development of the Free State and Transvaal coalfields. The town developed fairly compactly round the Kimberley mine in a typical gridiron pattern. The census of 1877 gives the total urban population on the diggings as over 18,000 of whom nearly half were whites. By 1891 there were nearly 30,000 people in Kimberley (Pl. 36).

The Kimberley mine is an irregular ellipse in shape, the diameter of the pipe at the surface covering 38 acres, the depth of the open working finally reaching over 1,300 feet. To facilitate easier working the mine was originally divided into sixteen north-south compartments separated by fifteen-foot-wide roadways. There were eventually sixteen hundred separate claim holders, and claims were worked on each side of the roadway soon achieving a pseudoscopic effect of tall buildings projecting into the ground. As the depth of the claim being worked increased the roadways became more and more unsafe. Parts crumbled away, gaps formed and men and animals fell in. Carts were constantly trundling back and forth along the roadways removing the excavated material, while ledges bracketing the pits were crowded with miners digging and filling receptacles. It was an animated and congested scene somewhat akin to an inverted ant-heap.

By 1873 the roadways were not safe, and the mine became surrounded by a host of timber erections containing windlasses almost like opera boxes, surveying the massed chorus of miners delving below, and supporting a cobweb of ropes and buckets. To the clang of wheels and whirring of ropes the diamondiferous ground was carried off to decompose for a period of three to six months on the depositing floors, finally to be washed and sorted for diamonds. After 1875 steam engines replaced the windlass and rope system. Great problems of loose rock and flooding had to be solved, and in 1874 a Kimberley Mines Board was set up. By 1878 a quarter of the claims were covered by rubble and the Board had a deficit of a quarter of a million pounds. Open pit mining could not be carried on below a depth of 400 feet. Shafts were sunk, at first inclined and later vertical, at the side of the pipe and connected to it by means of tunnels.

Problems of rising costs and marketing were even more severe and amalgamation of claims soon occurred. By 1880 to 1881 most of the private holdings in the four mines had been converted to companies. The greatest amalgamation took place in the De Beers mine, and this was achieved by the De Beers Mining Company. In five years yields improved by over 40 per cent and costs of production were reduced by nearly 40 per cent. In order to overcome the problem of theft and limit the prevalence of illicit diamond buying the compound system for housing African labour was introduced. African workers were kept under strict supervision in a guarded compound for the period they worked on the mines.

The process of consolidation was forced on by Rhodes who outmanoeuvred Barney Barnato and his Central Company, so that by 1890 De Beers Consolidated controlled 90 per cent of the production of diamonds in the Kimberley area. Diamonds are far more subject to price fluctuations and market whims than gold; amalgamation was thus essential for the orderly development of the industry. De Beers have gone from strength to strength and by 1960 were able to conclude agreements with mining concerns in Tanganyika, Sierra Leone and the U.S.S.R., whereby De Beers continued to operate as the world's main selling organization for diamonds (Fig. 39, Pl. 50).

The result of amalgamation was to reduce the numbers employed on the mines, and in 1892 the average number of white employees was less than 1,800, and of Africans about 7,400. Two-thirds of the white workers had come from Great Britain and many of them went to the Rand after becoming redundant on the diamond mines. The numbers on the river diggings increased, however, and in the 1890s there were about 4,000 in all, including about 1,000 whites. The value of production from the river diggings was, however, only worth about two per cent of that of the mine diamonds. In 1890 the Premier mine at Wesselton was discovered a mile to the east of Dutoitspan, and was bought by De Beers. In the Orange Free State the only mine of importance was the Jagersfontein mine. The De Beers, Koffiefontein and Kimberley mines are no longer worked, and the principal mines in South Africa are now the Premier mine in the Transvaal and Dutoitspan, Bultfontein and Wesselton

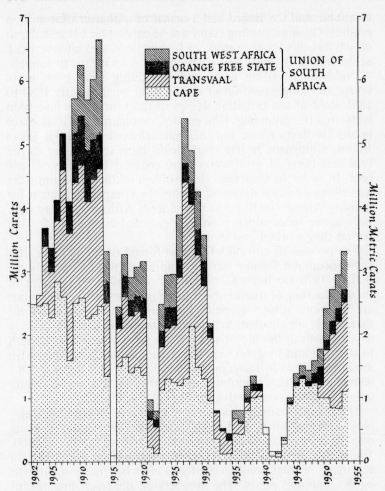

FIG. 39. The diamond production of the Union of South Africa and South-West Africa, 1902–53.

(Note the unshaded columns show the output of the Union other than that shown by individual provinces. Production 1902–21 in carats, 1922–53, in metric carats.)

From Cole: *South Africa*, by permission of Methuen & Co. Ltd.

in the Kimberley area. The Orange Free State benefited considerably by its proximity to the diamond fields at Kimberley and by the discovery of small diamond mines in the Free state at Koffiefontein and Jagersfontein. There was an air of prosperity and the affairs of the little state were well managed by President Brand. There were high prices for agricultural commodities and for twenty years before the coming of the railways there were rich rewards for the transport rider carrying goods to and from the mines.

The average annual value of diamond exports for the five-year period from 1888 to 1892 was about £4 million. By 1955 the total value of diamonds produced in South Africa since 1867 was about £450 million. Diamond mining was undoubtedly the initial stimulus which wrenched South Africa out of her agricultural slough and hustled her into the modern world. The lack of an economic catalyst such as diamonds was serious in the Transvaal before 1886, and the Republic faced bankruptcy. President Burgers's endeavours to raise a loan for railway development were fruitless, and the position seemed so desperate to Kruger that he asked the Cape Colony twice in 1886 for a customs union, the second time only a few months before the spectacular discoveries of gold on the Rand (Pl. 54).

The pace of economic development was quickened by diamonds, but greatly accelerated by the opening of the Rand goldfield in 1886. Gold was first discovered in 1866–7 in the Tati district on the borders of Mzilikaze's and later Lobengula's territory of Matabeleland which was later to become Southern Rhodesia. Little was then known of the Witwatersrand gold fields.[1] The first recorded discovery of gold in the Transvaal was made by Carl Mauch near the Olifants River in 1868. The search for gold had been going on for a long period fired by earlier reports of ancient gold workings in Mashonaland. Eventually payable quantities of alluvial gold were found in the Lydenburg district in 1872 and the De Kaap Valley north of Barberton in 1875. There was a considerable influx of prospectors and diggers and the town of Barberton developed with some 5,000 inhabitants. This south-eastern part of the Transvaal was thought to be a rich gold-bearing region, but apart from the Sheba mine in the Komati Poort area the placer workings

[1] Although, according to C. W. De Kiewiet, *A History of South Africa*, Oxford, 1941, pp. 115 and 116, the Boers appear to have known of the existence of gold on the Witwatersrand in the 1850s. Cf. J. H. Wellington, *Southern Africa*, Cambridge, 1955, Vol. II, p. 121.

were shallow and soon exhausted. As a result of extensive prospecting over a period of twenty years it was only a matter of time before the vast Rand deposits were discovered. There is some controversy as to the actual discoverers of gold on the Rand. A memorial at Langlaagte to George Harrison commemorates his reputed discovery of the Main Reef at this spot. The Struben brothers and Walker are also claimants to the honour of being the first to discover the gold-bearing reef.

In July 1886 the first sample of conglomerate ore was brought to Kimberley and tested. Its richness prompted J. B. Robinson to travel straight up to the Rand, and he bought the farm Langlaagte for £7,000. Rhodes, Barnato, Beit and other Kimberley diamond magnates followed, and in a few years the vast extent of the Witwatersrand gold field was realized. It is unlike any other gold-bearing region of the world. Gold is associated with the pre-Cambrian Witwatersrand system consisting of a succession of quartzites and shales. The outcrops on the Rand form the northern part of a great syncline extending for 50 miles from east to west, dipping steeply at first then flattening out with depth. The gold occurs in reefs of quartz conglomerate, the rounded quartz pebbles set in a quartzite matrix known as banket, and containing the tiny grains of gold not visible to the naked eye. Nearly all the reefs contain some gold, but most of it has come from the Main Reef, the Main Reef Leader and the South Reef. The Main Reef Leader, from a few inches to ten feet thick, is the main source of ore on the Rand (Fig. 40).

There are conflicting theories as to the formation of the Rand deposits, suggesting either a deltaic or glacial origin or that they were derived from deep-seated emanations. The amount of gold in the reefs varies considerably, the payability of a reef depending on costs of recovery rather than on richness of ore. The Rand gold-bearing deposits are the most extensive and yet the poorest in the world with a very low pennyweight content of gold, now less than 4 dwt. to the ton of ore milled. The major problem has been one of payability, and the continued exploitation of the Rand gold deposits has only been possible owing to a number of favourable factors. Undoubtedly the experience gained in mining techniques, both on the mining and organizational side, and the large amounts of capital amassed at Kimberley, proved of the greatest benefit in the initial stages. A complex financial organization and the Group system of mining were set up and the exploitation of the gold

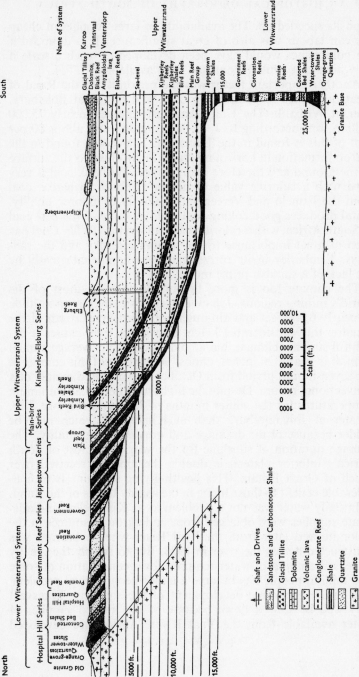

FIG. 40. Geological Section of the Witwatersrand Goldfield from Wellington, *South Africa*, I, by permission of the author, the Government Printer, Pretoria and the Cambridge University Press

deposits speeded up. The availability of large supplies of cheap African labour was also of great significance. It is doubtful if the gold mines would have been developed on such a scale if only high-cost white labour had been available (Pl. 55).

Another important factor was the proximity to the Rand of great quantities of good cheap coal, first mined at Boksburg, later at Witbank. The Union has vast reserves, nearly 75,000 million tons according to J. H. Wellington,[1] and about 80 per cent of this is found in the Transvaal. The coal is found in the Karoo formation in horizontal seams fairly close to the surface of the ground and therefore easily mined. Witbank coal is very hard with a calorific value of nearly 13 lb./lb., whereas coal from the Ermelo and Vereeniging fields is of poorer quality. Natal produces good coking coal and has some of the best coal in South Africa, with a calorific value of over 13 lb./lb. Coal has been of great importance to the mining industry and the railways. Kimberley in its early stages was hampered greatly by the lack of a suitable prime mover.

The climate too is more favourable than in most of the world's mining regions. Johannesburg is situated at an altitude of nearly 6,000 feet and although only 26 degrees south of the equator this considerable height above sea level causes a delightful summer climate, but a cold winter. The average annual rainfall is nearly 30 inches, almost 90 per cent of this coming in the seven-month period from October to April, and mainly of a convectional nature. Despite the higher altitude mean minimum temperatures for the winter months of June and July are 5° F. greater at Johannesburg than at Kimberley, which may be colder because of air drainage and greater continentality. The average duration of sunshine for the year over most of South Africa's interior plateau is double the amount received over much of Great Britain. This health-giving sunshine is of considerable benefit to those living in the shanty towns of the Rand.

Initially water was not a problem as at Kimberley, and adequate supplies were obtained from underground sources in the dolomite and later from the Vaal River when a barrage was constructed across the river in 1923. But to supply the greatly increased amount of water required for a conurbation of some two million people has become a major geographical problem. The future economic development of the southern Transvaal may well be slowed down because of the limited supplies of water available from the Vaal River. Agriculture developed

[1] Op. cit., Vol. II, p. 146.

47. De Kaap Pioneer Battery at Moodie's mine near Barberton, Transvaal, 1888.

48. Alluvial diamond digging in Vaal river gravels. Prospector watching gravel being washed.

49. Kimberley, diamond working, 1871. A time when each prospector staked a claim.

50. Horse-driven power for hauling diamond rich 'blue-ground' to washing racks and sorting sheds of the Kimberley Mine, 1872.

51. Kimberley Mine, 1873. A tangle of haulage lines carrying gravel to the washing stations, leads from the ever deepening claims to the mine edge.

52. Kimberley Mine. The Big Hole after it was abandoned.

53. The siege of Kimberley, South African War, 1899–1902. Cecil Rhodes beside a fortified colonial type house.

54. Paul Kruger, President of the South African Republic, 1883–1900, epitomised the Afrikaner way of life and outlook. He had taken part in the Great Trek as a boy.

rapidly owing to favourable physical factors, a fairly reliable rainfall of over 25 inches yearly and high veld prairie soils, particularly the fertile doleritic black clays, and the attractions of a large market.

Prior to the discovery of gold the Transvaal was in a parlous financial state. British annexation in 1877 led to the first war of independence in 1881, when the Boers were successful in regaining their freedom. During the early 1880s the revenue declined and trade stagnated. The discovery of gold changed the situation completely, and the revenue rose from less than £250,000 in 1885–6 to £1½ million in 1889–90. In twelve years from 1883 the revenue increased by twenty-five times. By 1898 the value of gold production had risen to £16 million. Men and capital poured in, and soon the foreigners, or Uitlanders as they were called by the Boers, outnumbered the latter.

In September 1886 the Witwatersrand Goldfields were proclaimed a Public Diggings and at the end of 1886 land was being sold in the new town of Johannesburg. As in the case of Kimberley, a goldrush camp of tents, iron shacks and wagons developed on the site of the Witwatersrand. Theodore Ruenert writing in 1893 says, 'Johannesburg cannot at present be called a beautiful town, though it is undoubtedly destined to become one of the finest cities in South Africa and probably the largest'.[1] Growth was far more rapid than in the case of Kimberley, and by 1892 Johannesburg, including mines and suburbs, had a population of nearly 80,000. Substantial houses were being built, streets macadamized and gas and electricity installed. In October 1896 the Sanitary Board Census estimated the population of Johannesburg at about 102,000 including 50,907 whites (Pl. 56).

The Sanitary Board established in 1887 was empowered to make regulations on a variety of subjects relating to the health and welfare of the inhabitants of Johannesburg, such as sanitary-pail collection, overcrowding of houses and control over those who were misguided enough to drive taxis at more than seven miles per hour! It was able to insist on a certain standard of building which helped to make Johannesburg appear less dirty and unkempt than Kimberley in the early days. Nevertheless, for the first fifteen years Johannesburg was constantly short of capital for development, and the concession system meant that the Sanitary Board and the Stadsraad (Government) were un-

[1] *Diamonds and Gold in South Africa*, London, 1893, p. 88.

able to provide adequate services.[1] The central part was laid out as a stand-township with a great many narrow streets and crossings and tiny plots of land.[2] Corner sites were valuable, particularly to publicans. Johannesburg tended to develop as a mosaic of townships unrelated to each other.

The factors which hindered the growth of Johannesburg in the 1890s were that deep levels in the gold mines were only proved in 1894 and the political tension engendered by events leading up to the Boer War. After the war the burgomaster tradition of government was abolished and municipal government introduced. In 1902 the Council was given jurisdiction over a greatly enlarged area of 79 square miles, and also planning powers to control the setting up of new townships. But it was only in 1931 that wider town planning powers were obtained. The vast problem of housing a large varied racial population was not tackled with any success until the 1950s; little or no provision was made for housing Africans who formed half or more of the population. Increasingly the African population of the Union of South Africa is becoming urbanized, the urban percentage of Africans having doubled in the last thirty years. An unofficial estimate of the African population of Johannesburg in 1959 placed it at 555,000; there was an increase of nearly 170,000 for the period from 1936 to 1946. Many of the slums have been eliminated, but the inhabitants have been rehoused at a considerable distance from the centre of the city. The new suburbs such as Meadowlands, Zondi, Dube and Mofolo stretch for miles across the High Veld.

Today Johannesburg is the centre of a string of towns stretching for nearly 50 miles along the Reef from Krugersdorp in the west to Springs in the east and including Roodepoort, Germiston, Benoni, Boksburg and Brakpan. On the northern edge of the High Veld Johannesburg has become the most important industrial and commercial centre in Southern Africa, far outstripping its nearest rival Cape Town. And this despite the distance of 400 miles from its nearest port. It has also developed as the focus of the Union's communications network. Johannesburg's skyscrapers rise from a framework

---

[1] The Sanitary Board was not responsible for local services such as water, gas or electricity, which were granted as concessions.

[2] The stand was a plot of ground on which the digger or prospector could pitch a tent or erect a temporary home. The erf-township characteristic of most of the interior had wide 'farm lands' for the use of visiting farmers, and wide streets, a great contrast to the narrow streets and lack of open spaces in the mining towns.

of white mine dumps that glisten in the sun, not unlike Cornwall's china clay dumps. The metropolis of today had its origins in the tented and hutted encampment that was formed hastily on the windswept ridge of the Witwatersrand in 1886 (Pl. 58).

The effect of the Rand gold discoveries on the Transvaal was profound and far more significant for the future of South Africa than the exploitation of the diamond mines at Kimberley. The vast deposits of low-grade ore plunging deeply into the earth could not be worked by individual miners or small companies, in contrast to subsequent exploitation of gold deposits in Southern Rhodesia. Mining was first carried out by digging open trenches along the line of the reefs and sinking small shafts to follow the dip. This was soon changed in favour of vertical shafts south of the outcrop so as to intercept the different reefs by means of cross tunnels from the main shaft. Elaborate and costly processes were required for extraction of the gold from the quartz conglomerate. The ore had to be reduced to powder by the use of Californian stamp mills, some 2,000 of which created a thunderous roar. After this, mechanical and chemical operations were needed to separate the precious metal from the gangue or worthless ore. Initially the mines used the simple plate amalgamation process, but the recovery rate was little more than 60 per cent, which by 1891 was not profitable. A crisis ensued until the cyanide process was introduced, which with other processes enabled a 90 per cent gold recovery rate to be obtained. The cyanide process was widely used after 1892. During the 1890s the geological structure of the Witwatersrand deposits was carefully studied and mapped, and by 1894 their great extent had been indicated by the deep levels to which they reached (Fig. 40).

The centre of mining soon shifted from the Central Rand, and from 1898 to 1911 the main centre was on the West Rand, while from 1924 to 1938 the Far East Rand was predominant. Since 1948 the Far West Rand and the Orange Free State Goldfields have come into prominence. Before the Boer War the amount of gold obtained from each ton of ore milled was nearly half an ounce, but fifty years later it had dropped to less than a quarter of an ounce. Despite this great decrease in the value of gold won from the ore, mining has continued to be profitable as the result of a constant and successful endeavour to keep down production costs. The mean yield on the vast capital invested during the period 1887–1932 has been estimated

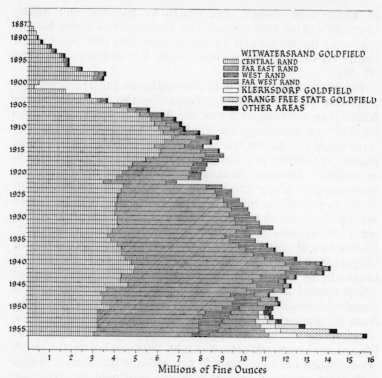

FIG. 41. The gold production of the Union of South Africa and of the leading goldfields, 1887–1956.

(Compiled from data given in the annual reports of the Transvaal Chamber of Mines and the Transvaal and Orange Free State Chamber of Mines.)

From Cole: *South Africa*, by permission of Methuen & Co. Ltd.

at only about four per cent.[1] The nature of the gold deposits, their vast extent and fairly low uniform grade of ore has made it possible to calculate to a considerable degree of accuracy their payability. These factors have necessitated large-scale financial organization and production (Fig. 41).

In 1893, out of 183 gold mining companies, so called, 104 produced no gold. The great need for stability and efficiency meant that control of the industry passed gradually into the hands of powerful companies or groups. The Transvaal Government also determined to make the mining industry pay

[1] S. H. Frankel, *Capital Investment in Africa*, London, 1938, p. 91.

as heavily as possible through taxes and concessions. There are now six groups controlling 53 mines, 43 in the Transvaal and 10 in the Orange Free State, employing nearly 50,000 European workers and 335,000 Africans, and producing gold to the value of over £200 million yearly. The Group organization has been of great importance in the efficient working of the gold mining industry. It supervises all important scientific and technical matters such as the purchase of supplies and machinery, the collection and distribution of labour, health and welfare and the marketing of gold. But apart from these matters each mine forms an independent and separate unit. The Groups are associated together in the Chamber of Mines.

The effect of the Rand on South Africa's population has been profound. According to De Kock the European population of the Cape rose from 181,000 in 1865 to 377,000 in 1891, and that of the Transvaal from 30,000 in 1872 to 119,000 in 1890. In the Orange Free State the white population increased from 35,000 in 1865 to 78,000 in 1890, and in Natal from 18,000 in 1867 to 47,000 in 1891.[1] Approximately half the white population of the Transvaal were Boers in 1891, and of the remainder nearly half were from the Cape, nearly 12,000 were from the Free State, 9,000 were British and 5,000 were non-British aliens.[2] The proportion of South Africa's white population living in the Transvaal has steadily increased, and by 1951 it was nearly half, with well over a million whites compared to less than a million for the Cape.

Perhaps the most obvious social effects of gold mining are to be seen in the tremendous growth of African migrant labour, the rapid break-up of the tribal system, and the emergence of a poor white class. The latter problem arose partly because of the type of society which has evolved in South Africa. Unskilled native workers received only about a tenth to a twentieth of the wage of a white skilled worker. The unskilled or semi-skilled white man was, therefore, unable to exist on an unskilled wage, and yet unable at that stage to acquire the necessary skill to earn the higher wage. This problem has, to a certain extent, been solved by the absorption of the Republic's poor whites into secondary industry.

Cheap African migrant labour was available in large quantities, an extremely important factor in the early and rapid

[1] M. H. De Kock, *The Economic History of South Africa*, Cape Town, 1924, pp. 138, 139, 141, 142.
[2] J. P. R. Maud, *City Government*, Oxford, 1938, footnote pp. 17–18.

development of the Rand gold mines. Nearly 100,000 Africans were employed on the gold mines before the Boer War. One of the pressing problems of the post-war period was the lack of native labour. This was partially solved by the import of some 50,000 Chinese coolies who were all repatriated by 1910. By then, however, the number of African miners had risen to well over 100,000 and gradually increased to over 300,000. However, since 1946 the number has decreased because of the counter-attraction of secondary industry and mechanization in the gold mines. In 1954 the percentage of Union Africans employed on gold and coal mines was little more than one-third, almost as many coming from Mozambique. The two main recruiting organizations for Africans in the gold mining industry are the Witwatersrand Native Labour Association and the Native Recruiting Corporation Limited, the former recruiting in Nyasaland and Northern Rhodesia, the latter in the High Commission Territories as well.

The effect of this great increase in migrant labour on tribal society has been deplored by many humanitarians and anthropologists concerned at the break-up of family life, and at the decline of agriculture left increasingly to the care of women, owing to the absence of men for long periods away from home. Some industrialists and economists point out the beneficial effects economically in the change from a subsistence to an exchange economy, with increased opportunities and incentives and higher living standards, and emphasize the need for greater freedom of movement and rapid acquisition of technical skills. The effects of the Industrial Revolution in Europe on rural communities were somewhat more gradual than the effects of the mineral revolution in South Africa. The gulf between urban African workers and white employers was far greater than between factory workers and employers in England.

The very rapid change from a pastoral to a capitalist economy in South Africa has been extremely disturbing, and has brought ethnic groups of widely differing characteristics into close proximity to each other with dire political, social and economic consequences.

The economic effects of mineral discoveries on South Africa can only be appreciated fully by studying a wide range of topographical and climatic maps. South Africa was hampered greatly by physical obstacles such as the lack of navigable waterways, poor harbours, the steep plateau edge, the Cape mountains and great distances. Economic development of the

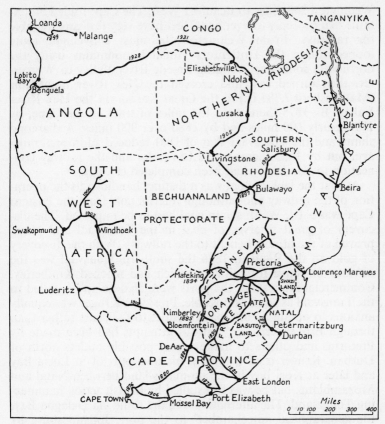

FIG. 42. Railways in Southern Africa with dates of building.

plateau region was virtually impossible without a cheap bulk carrier, as transport costs by ox wagon were high and delivery uncertain. The discovery of diamonds and later gold provided the stimulus for railway construction. Before the mineral age the only railways in South Africa were 65 miles at the Cape and a few miles in Natal (Fig. 42).

In 1872 responsible government was achieved in the Cape, and in 1873 the government bought out the Cape Town Railway and Dock Company and the Wynberg Railway Company and placed them under the Department of Public Works. For reasons of economy a 3-foot 6-inch gauge replaced the 4-foot 8½-inch gauge adopted from England, and was used throughout the country. The first aim in 1873 was to extend the line from

Wellington 240 miles to Beaufort West. The Cape folded mountains rising steeply to over 5,000 feet have very few gaps suitable for railways. From Wellington the most convenient route looped round the Hottentots Holland mountains using the north-west south-east trending Breede River Valley to Worcester, then turned east and crossed the Hex River mountains (Matroosberg 7,385 ft.) to the Great Karoo via the Hex River Valley. By 1875 there were 154 miles of track in the 'Cape, by 1878 nearly 600 miles and by 1880 over 900 miles. A diamond slump and the Transvaal War of 1881 reduced additional mileage, but by 1885 there were 1,654 miles and the railway connection to Kimberley had been completed (Pl. 60).

At first the lack of coal was a distinct handicap to the operation of the railway and, although inferior coal from the Eastern Cape was used, Welsh steam coal had to be imported. The discovery of great reserves of coal in the Transvaal and Natal proved of the utmost benefit to the railways. With the discovery of gold on the Rand in 1886 the southern Transvaal was the obvious objective for railways which had reached Kimberley. Commercial interests at the ports were anxious to be linked to the Transvaal as soon as possible. President Kruger was equally anxious to obtain an alternative outlet to the coast rather than through British territory. Various attempts had been made by Pretorius and others to make use of possible outlets north of Durban. Kruger tried to obtain his own port of St Lucia Bay and later at Kosi Bay in the no-man's-land between Natal and Mozambique, but he was forestalled by British action in annexing Tongaland. The alternative was the route via Delagoa Bay, the geographical antechamber[1] to the port. Johannesburg by rail to Cape Town is 956 miles, to Port Elizabeth 714 miles, to East London 664 miles, to Durban 494 miles, and to Lourenço Marques 397 miles (Pl. 59).

Kruger, therefore, tended to favour the construction of a Rand-Delagoa Bay line rather than railway links with the Cape and Natal. Colonel McMurdo obtained a concession from the Portuguese to build the short Mozambique section of the line from Delagoa Bay to the Rand. Kruger granted the Transvaal concession to a Dutch-German syndicate, the Netherlands South Africa Railway Company. The Cape Government pressed for permission to extend the Cape lines which had reached Kimberley and Colesburg on to the Rand. The Orange

[1] J. Van Der Poel, *Railways and Customs Policies in South Africa*, London, 1933, pp. 3 and 4.

55. A 'face' on the Main Reef, Witwatersrand, showing Johannesburg from the Pioneer Block.

56. Ferreira Gold Mining Company, Johannesburg. Opening a reef by trenching, 1888.

57. Johannesburg suburb, 1898. The use of corrugated iron for roofing is necessary where hail is common.

58. Modern Johannesburg with crushed mine matrix standing in dumps in the background.

Free State Government gave the necessary permission for the lines to cross Free State territory. Kruger, however, hoping to witness the completion of the Delagoa Bay line before the Cape lines, delayed in granting permission for the extension of the Kimberley line. Rhodes, impatient to open up Zambezia, could not wait and decided to push ahead with the construction of a railway to the north through Bechuanaland and not via the Rand. In 1887 he applied for a charter to enable the British South Africa Company to extend the railway northward. The traveller, now wishing to proceed by rail from the Southern Transvaal to Salisbury, has to go far to the west into Bechuanaland before turning north and east into Rhodesia. There should be a more direct route through the northern Transvaal, but the gap in the line of rail between Beit Bridge and West Nicholson has not been closed. The main line to the north still goes through Bechuanaland.[1]

At the end of the 1880s the rival states in South Africa were prosperous and railway expansion was swift. Most of their revenues were made up of customs dues and railway receipts. Unfortunately there was no general control over the direction taken by the railways and many serious gaps in the network have resulted, particularly along the south-east coast. The primary object was to reach the Rand as quickly as possible, and many potentially attractive agricultural areas were by-passed. By 1890 the Lourenço Marques railway had only reached the Transvaal border at Komati Poort 55 miles from Delagoa Bay. The obstacles were great, malaria was serious and the terrain difficult with a forty-mile belt of swampy land to the west of the Bay, the crossing of the Lebombo Mountains and the long haul up to the High Veld of the Transvaal, which presented serious engineering problems. Political factors, however, rather than physical factors delayed the advance of the railways into the Transvaal. Kruger was determined that the Delagoa Bay line should reach the Transvaal first. The Netherlands South Africa Railway soon became involved in serious financial difficulties. The Cape therefore lent the Company nearly £1 million on condition that it built a bridge over the Vaal and a line to Johannesburg and Pretoria linking with the Cape System. As a result of financial stringency Kruger's plan to avoid dependence on British interests was foiled and the Cape Town-Orange Free State railway was the first to reach Johannesburg in September 1892, followed a few months later

---

[1] The 1963 agreement was reached to close the 85 mile gap between Beit Bridge and West Nicholson.

by lines from Port Elizabeth and East London. By June 1892 the N.S.A. Company had pushed on with its line as far as Nelspruit, across broken country beyond the Lebombo Mountains and up the Crocodile River valley, and the Rand was eventually reached in 1895 (Fig. 42).

The Cape suffered from heavy costs of railway construction and the great distance from her ports of Cape Town, Port Elizabeth and East London to the Rand. Added factors were the high cost of coal, sparse population and the lack of suitable return traffic compared to Natal with its strategically placed deposits of coal and far shorter distances to the Rand. Natal was, therefore, determined to exploit her favourable geographical position and capture as much as possible of the Rand traffic. The Cape and the Orange Free State had concluded a customs union, but despite strenuous efforts by the Cape to draw the other two states into the union, the Transvaal and Natal held aloof. For two years the Cape's railways were prosperous and in 1895 had 80 per cent of the Rand's traffic. By 1896 this had dropped to two-thirds and in the early 1900s to only one-eighth, because at the end of 1894 and in 1895, first the Delagoa Bay and then the Durban lines had reached the Transvaal. The Cape railways experienced a period of depression after 1896 that was only relieved temporarily by increased revenues resulting from the Boer War.

The proved wealth in diamonds and gold in South Africa increased interest in the metamorphosed and mineralized rocks of the Archaean shield in the plateau region north of the Limpopo, then occupied by the Matabele and Mashona. The desire to control this territory led to embittered conflict between the Boers and British with the Tswana as catspaw between them. Control rested on the possession of the Great North Road leading to the far interior, which Rhodes described as the Suez Canal to the north. Kimberley, half-way between Cape Town and Matabeleland, was an ideal base from which to operate to the north and Rhodes was able to make excellent use of this springboard in his preparations for the invasion of Mashonaland. He was fired by Ruskin's grandiloquent language on the importance of the British tradition, inspired by his experience of Oxford and influenced by later Victorian imperialism. He thus conceived a major scheme for converting a great stretch of Central Africa into a British domain. Plans for action were hastened when he suspected that Lobengula was discussing the possibility of closer links with Kruger. Rhodes reacted swiftly and persuaded the High Commissioner to conclude an agreement with Lobengula, whereby the latter agreed not to cede any part of his territory without the consent of the High Commissioner. Rhodes sent Rudd and a party including Moffat up to Lobengula's Kraal in 1888 to seek a mineral concession. This was obtained in October of that year in the face of a horde of concession seekers. Gold had just been confirmed in vast amounts in the Transvaal, and it was not doubted that similar discoveries would be made in Matabeleland (Fig. 43).

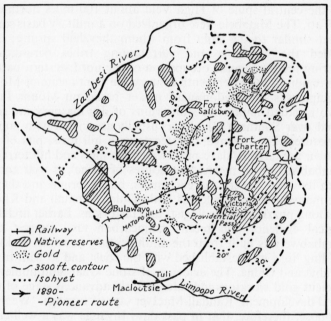

FIG. 43. Pioneer penetration of Southern Rhodesia.

Rhodes immediately took the precious concession to London. But it was only after a year's skilful lobbying that he was able to obtain his charter and establish the British South Africa Company, whose range of activities was very wide, rather on the lines of the Royal Niger and British East Africa Companies. He was granted the rights, among other clauses, of constructing a railway and telegraph line and of colonization and trade. Rhodes was given the mineral rights over a region bounded south, west and east by British Bechuanaland, the Portuguese territories and the Transvaal, but significantly no northern limit was set to its activities. The tenure of the charter was to be twenty-five years.

The great region to the north of the Transvaal, sometimes called Zambezia and later named Rhodesia, was inhabited by a large number of Bantu tribes. There were four Bantu states of some importance, that of the Lozi in Barotseland, the Matabele, the Angoni near Lake Nyasa and the Bemba in what was to become north-eastern Rhodesia. The Matabele lay athwart the route to the north. Lobengula's Great Kraal was at Bulawayo on the central spine of High Veld about 100 miles north-east of Tati. The Matabele were organized on a military basis somewhat similar to the Zulu from whom they had sprung; they raided the Mashona and surrounding tribes periodically. During the Portuguese occupation of the north-eastern part of the region in the seventeenth century the Bantu state of Monomotapa was the predominant power based on Mount Fura. Two hundred impressive stone ruins of dry masonry are scattered over Southern Rhodesia, usually associated with granite exposures. The Inyanga area teems with hill forts, pits of unknown use termed 'slave pits', water channels and hill terraces. Zimbabwe, which means 'the houses of stone', is well known with its walls, towers and enclosures, but its origin and that of the many other ruins such as Dhlo-Dhlo, Nanatali and Khami has long puzzled archaeologists and historians. Earlier archaeological evidence and recent radiocarbon tests suggest that Zimbabwe was built from the ninth century onwards, and that trading links were established with the coast and so with India, Arabia and China. The evidence of stone kraals and numerous ancient gold workings indicates a fairly advanced stage of cultural development. Randall-MacIver says of Inyanga, 'We must suppose, therefore, that in past days Inyanga was a well-cultivated region, inhabited by a large and prosperous agricultural population'.[1] The region had obviously been depopulated by the Zulu raids of the early nineteenth century.

F. Oates describes Matabeleland in 1882, 'out of the level, scantily covered with dry brown grass and with a thick growth of leafless trees . . . rise huge boulders . . . We are in a populous country, strings of people carrying things along the road.'[2] Rhodes wanted to avoid this populous country and so, after imperial sanction had been received in June 1890, a pioneer

---

[1] D. Randall-MacIver, *Medieval Rhodesia*, London, 1906, p. 13.
[2] F. Oates, *Matabeleland and the Victoria Falls*, London, 1881, p. 47.

column was sent to Mashonaland rather than Matabeleland. The party of 179 pioneers, 300 police, a gang of African road builders and 100 wagons set out from Macloutsie in Bechuanaland along a route selected by Selous, the famous big game hunter, and prepared by the Africans. Lobengula's promise to hold back his warriors was kept and the pioneer column was not attacked. The route lay west across the Low Veld to Nuanetsi and then north through the Providential Pass on to the High Veld. The expedition started in late June 1890 during the dry winter season when dangers of flooding were over and perils of sleeping sickness and malaria were reduced.

Two forts were built and garrisoned, Forts Victoria and Charter, before the final halting place near the end of the Gwebi Flats was reached and where Salisbury was built. The pioneers were given 3,000 morgen of land each, in true South African style, and the right to peg fifteen claims anywhere. More prospectors and wagons soon arrived; the first private wagon contained nothing but whisky! Torrential rains in the spring of 1890 turned the site of Salisbury into a swamp, malaria was rife, and for nearly three months flooded rivers prevented communications from being maintained with the south (Fig. 43).

Two campaigns against the Matabele in 1895 and 1896 and one against the Mashona in 1896 were necessary before the great rolling uplands of Matabeleland and Mashonaland were brought under Company control and named Rhodesia in honour of Cecil John Rhodes, a signal honour during a man's lifetime. The circuitous malarial route through the Low Veld was abandoned and the more direct and healthier route along the High Veld was used.

The development of Southern Rhodesia was slow and at the beginning of the twentieth century there were only a few thousand white inhabitants; by 1923 the white population had reached about 34,000. The main reason[1] for this slow growth was the absence of gold on a scale at all comparable with the Transvaal. Gold was the lure that drew the first settlers and prospectors, but owing to the widespread distribution of the small faulted ore-bodies occurring chiefly among the metamorphosed rocks, Southern Rhodesia has been the domain of the individual prospector and the small company. This forms a marked con-

---

[1] There were also difficult physical conditions and problems of agricultural development in an unfamiliar tropical environment isolated by great distances and poor communications from world markets. Describing newspaper criticism from England, Rhodes said: 'Subsequently we were removed from their criticism and they thought the country too bad to say anything about it'.

trast to the mining organization of great companies on the Witwatersrand. The ore in Southern Rhodesia is near the surface and easily mined, and therefore favours the small prospector rather than the large company. About one-quarter of the total gold output has come from over 3,000 small mines (Fig. 4).

Gold became the basis of the country's economy. Until 1903 the Company controlled prospectors and miners by selling their gold and keeping half the profits. A royalty payable to the Company was substituted after 1903. This incentive to production was met by a rapid rise in gold mining by 1905 on the part of the small producer. Production of gold has declined considerably recently because of rising production costs and depletion of auriferous reserves and now is worth about £6 million yearly. Indeed asbestos surpasses gold in value of production, and chrome, coal and copper are other important minerals. Mining industries in 1959 employed over 2,000 Europeans and nearly 60,000 Africans in a total population of about 2,800,000, compared to over 50,000 whites and more than 500,000 Africans in South Africa.

Agriculture also developed slowly, European farms occupying the spine of High Veld, usually above 4,000 feet, and along the railway belt. European farms tended to be on the heavy soils which could not be worked by the Mashona, who cultivated the lighter sandy soils. Nearly half Southern Rhodesia is above 3,500 feet and the climate is temperate, with temperatures ranging from below 60° F. on an average for the coolest months to a little over 70° F. for the hottest months. For much of the year breezes on the High Veld further ameliorate the climate. Nearly three-quarters of the country receives over 25 inches average annual rainfall, while nearly one-tenth has over 35 inches, the highest amounts occurring along the eastern border. The rainfall has a tropical régime and occurs in summer from October to April, the rest of the year being dry. Initially the main emphasis in agriculture was on ranching. The British South Africa Company[1] under the influence of Rhodes carried out experiments in cattle ranching, citrus growing, and sugar and tea planting. African and European land holdings form a mosaic, with the African Reserves located mainly in the Middle Veld below the 3,500-foot contour line. Europeans own about half the land, the average farm in the

[1] The British South Africa Company has done a great deal to aid in the development of Rhodesia and only paid its first dividend in 1923.

beginning being over 6,000 acres in Matabeleland and about 3,000 acres in Mashonaland (Fig. 43).

Bulawayo, or the Place of Killing, established in 1894, was initially larger and more important than Salisbury, which later outranked it. In 1904 the white population was 3,840 and in 1955 it was 40,000. It became the railhead for the line to South Africa. It was built near the site of Lobengula's Great Place. Elisée Reclus[1] describes how the 'royal residence, a house of European construction, crowns a hill in the centre of the village, and is encircled by a number of hive-shaped huts, all comprised within a stout palisade. The dwellings of the traders are scattered over the surrounding plain . . . Both Protestant and Catholic missionaries have also penetrated into the Matabele territory, and to these have now been added the miners, who had *hitherto* long been refused admittance to the country.' The latter is a reference to the Tati mines. Twenty months after Selous had left the ruined kraal he returned to find a European town with many substantial buildings, reservoirs being built, electric light promised and land values going up[2] (Pl. 61).

Salisbury, founded in 1890, grew from two centres, one selected by the pioneer column at the base of a hill, the other selected by the Chartered Company on a nearby slope with a swampy area in between. This was soon drained, and the well-drained site chosen by the Company later developed as the centre of Salisbury, which became a municipality in 1897, a city in 1935 and latterly the capital of the Federation of the Rhodesias and Nyasaland. The following is a description of the town in 1904: 'The town is divided into two portions known as the Causeway and the Kopje, separated by a space some three-quarters of a mile wide, formerly a swamp, but now being gradually built over. The Government Buildings and most of the private residences are in the Causeway, the business portion of the town being at the foot of the Kopje, where the original fort was located in 1890.'[3] In 1904 the white population was 1,726, which had increased to 52,000 by 1955.

Rhodes's railway moved rapidly north from Vryburg and Mafeking to Bulawayo, which it reached by 1897. Rhodes, like Kruger, also sought an ocean outlet in Portuguese territory for his new domains. After attempts to buy Gazaland and

---

[1] Universal Geography, Vol. 13, *South and East Africa*, London, 1888, p. 269.
[2] F. C. Selous, *Sunshine and Storm in Rhodesia*, London, 1896, p. 4.
[3] Union Castle Mail Steamship Company Limited, *The Guide to South Africa*, 1904–5 Edition, p. 348.

Lourenço Marques from the Portuguese had failed he pioneered the use of Beira as a port. By 1899 Salisbury and Umtali were connected with Beira by rail, and by 1902 the link with Bulawayo had been completed. A northward extension from Bulawayo reached the Victoria Falls by 1904 and the Copper Belt of Northern Rhodesia by 1909. The link across Angola to Lobito Bay was not completed until 1931. Constant financial difficulties due to the problems of economic development in an undeveloped region greatly delayed completion of railways in Central Africa. The main railway still consists of only a single track.

The political effects of the Rand gold discoveries were far more widespread than those of the diamond discoveries nearly twenty years before. The diamond fields lay in a debatable triangle of territory where the northern and western borders of the Cape, Transvaal and Orange Free State converged and which was successfully claimed by the Cape. Although the Witwatersrand was a very slightly populated area before the gold discoveries it was well within the oekumene of the Transvaal state, being 70 miles from Potchefstroom, 30 miles from Pretoria and 40 miles from the Vaal River. The great influx of population from the rest of South Africa and oversea caused such a disparity in numbers of Europeans in the Transvaal by the late 1890s, that the Boers were outnumbered by 7 to 3. President Kruger and the Volksraad felt that the political supremacy of the Boers was imperilled by the newcomers. Strict measures were taken to preserve the franchise in 1894, so that no Uitlander could acquire the vote before the age of forty, and only after fourteen years' residence. English was forbidden in courts and schools; monopolies were granted for the sale of commodities like dynamite; heavy taxes were imposed on the mining companies, and there was much bribery and corruption. High railway rates raised the cost of living, and there was a general outcry against Kruger's policy. Uitlander grievances were exploited by Rhodes who, as he had failed to force the Transvaal to a customs union by economic means, now sought to foment dissident elements in the Transvaal. The outcome was the Jameson Raid which occurred at the end of 1895, a foolish and unwise move which sparked off the Boer War and destroyed any hope of achieving a federation of South Africa by peaceful means.

The Boer War or, as it is sometimes called, the Second War of Freedom, was not only a struggle for the unity of South

Africa, but also for supremacy between two different cultures in one state. On the one hand, the war was regarded as a treacherous attack by imperialist and capitalist forces on a poor and defenceless people, on the other hand as an attempt by a ruthless and corrupt Republican foe to impose its will on the rest of South Africa. The Uitlanders turned to the High Commissioner, Sir Alfred Milner, and to Chamberlain for support, while Kruger sought an alliance with the Free State and also tried to enlist German aid. Kruger was re-elected President in 1898 and the stage seemed set for war. In August 1899 a five-year franchise was offered to the Uitlanders by the Transvaal, provided the British dropped the suzerainty clause whereby the British had the right to interfere in the internal affairs of the Transvaal. Chamberlain sent a qualified acceptance couched in such vague terms that Pretoria read it as a refusal. This rebuff, together with the information that 10,000 troops were to be sent from India and the Mediterranean to South Africa, decided the Transvaal to prepare for war.

The war broke out in October 1899, and the Boers attacked British strong points immediately in the hope of achieving a quick victory. Kimberley, Mafeking and Ladysmith situated close to the Republics were invested, and the Boers attempted to force the British away from the High Veld in the east by moving down into Natal and guarding the eastern approaches. The British were pushed back into Ladysmith, but Joubert missed his opportunity of moving quickly towards the sea, and the bulk of the Boer forces became immobilized in besieging the British in Kimberley, Ladysmith and Mafeking. This was a disastrous move, as the strength of the Boers lay in their commando tactics and swift movement of mounted riflemen. They were loosely organized and could move rapidly, but they lacked a unified command and overall strategy. Nevertheless, they could put a far higher proportion of their fighting men into the field than Britain. Estimates vary as to the number of Boer combatants; Lord Kitchener put the number at 95,000; the British Official History of the War at 87,000, of whom nearly half were from the Transvaal. The number of Boers in the field at any time was about 40,000. The British finally had nearly half a million men in the field, so difficult was it to suppress this guerrilla type of warfare (Fig. 44).

The heaviest fighting occurred during the Boer invasion of the Cape and Natal, for it was vital for the Republics that they should prevent the British from reaching the interior plains,

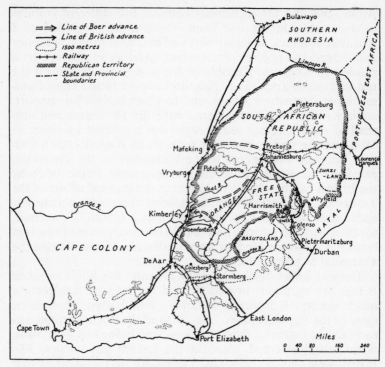

FIG. 44. Lines of advance during the Boer War, 1899–1902.

while it was desirable that the ports should be besieged to prevent the landing of British reinforcements. The British, moving up from the coast with clumsy supply columns, were unable to clear the Stormberg Escarpment of sharpshooters and guerrilla pickets, any more than the burgers could in earlier days deal with the wary Bushmen disputing the High Veld approaches in these same mountains.

In Natal the Boers chose to defend the vital ford over the Tugela River at Colenso. This was done successfully and they gained room to manœuvre below the Natal escarpment in their old territory of the Utrecht Republic and Blood River Territory. At the same time they continued to besiege Lady-smith, a vital point in communications between the coast and the interior. The British tried repeatedly to break through, the battle of Spion Kop in which they were defeated was one such example (Pl. 62).

The turning point in the war came in February 1900 when Lord Roberts, the British Commander-in-Chief, with 30,000 men under command overwhelmed the thin and scattered defences of the Free State. He swept in across the Escarpment, moving up the railway to Kimberley where the siege was lifted and thence pressing on to capture 4,000 Boers at Paardeberg. Seeing their inner defences threatened from the rear the Republicans in Natal fell back to the Escarpment. Ladysmith was relieved, and troops crossed the Escarpment southwards to Bloemfontein which was entered on 13 March 1900. A delay ensued while negotiations were entered into, but these broke down and the British advance continued in May 1900, Mafeking was relieved, Johannesburg entered on 31 May and Pretoria on 5 June, while Laing's Nek, the eastern gate to the Transvaal, had been forced by June. Kruger left the Transvaal to solicit aid in Europe, large numbers of Boers were captured, and by September it was thought that the war was over. Roberts left and Milner was made High Commissioner and empowered to administer the Transvaal and Orange Free State.

The war was, however, by no means over, and entered the second phase of highly mobile commandos, unhampered by baggage trains such as had delayed Cronje near Kimberley, and supplied with food and information from the farmhouses. Botha, De Wet, Smuts and other leaders became more active; Hertzog threatened Malmesbury 40 miles north of Cape Town and Kritzinger the small port of Mossel Bay. The wide untrammelled spaces and even surface of the High Veld, the protection of the broken country of the northern Transvaal, the plateau foreland, and the mountains of the Cape favoured Boer guerrilla tactics. Commandos could be assembled promptly and dispersed quickly, and grazing for horses obtained easily from the veld grasses. The British, encumbered by baggage trains and guns, could be harassed in the mountain passes of the Cape and broken country below the Escarpment, and they were confined to their long lines of communication. The railway lines had to be guarded and great stretches of country to be controlled. The final outcome of the war was not in doubt, as Britain had the resources, manpower and control of sea and land communications, but it was to be nearly two years before the wearing tactics of the Boers were finally to be defeated (Pl. 53).

Kitchener withdrew his detached garrisons and tried a scorched earth policy which did not prove very successful. The country was swept bare of livestock, forage and people, while the farmhouses, which acted as Boer supply bases, were burnt down and women and children placed in camps. To control the sudden movements of the Boers, Kitchener then built a chain of blockhouses, so effectively fencing in areas of the High Veld. Towards the end of 1901 the Boers achieved their last successes; Botha raided Natal, Smuts penetrated the Cape Midlands and De La Rey dominated the western Transvaal. But the British mobile columns, now better briefed, harried the commandos, and matters for the British improved. By 1902 the last phase of the struggle was entered and over sixty mobile columns operated from blockhouse lines in cross-country drives. Peace was finally signed at Vereeniging on 31 May, two and a half years after war had broken out. Peace terms were magnanimous with a promise of early self-government and a loan of £35 million. The question of the native franchise, a thorny problem, was left in abeyance.

Reconstruction was carried out vigorously by Lord Milner as Governor of the Orange River Colony and the Transvaal. Railways were repaired and extended; the amount of track was doubled by 1907; agriculture revived, and gold mining expanded. Some 1,400 British families were settled on the land in the Transvaal and the eastern Orange River Colony in an attempt to increase the number of English in the rural areas of the ex-republics.

The Bloemfontein Customs Conference of 1903 was an important event, which did away with tariff walls between the colonies, Southern Rhodesia and the Protectorates. It adopted two other important resolutions of far-reaching consequence to the newly emerging economy, first that the native question must be treated as a whole, and second that, if native labour could not be obtained from Central Africa, temporary labour should be obtained from Asia. Cheap labour was essential to start the gold mines working again. Milner tried to use the mines to attract more capital and people from oversea who would thus help to create a more cosmopolitan Transvaal, and so pave the way for federation of the South African colonies. A white labour policy was impracticable and by 1905 some 50,000 Chinese coolies had been brought in, but, perhaps fortunately for the future of race relations in South Africa, they were eventually repatriated by March 1910.

Gold output recovered fairly quickly, from £2 million in 1903 to nearly £25 million in 1906, the number of adult males on the Rand increased by nearly a third and the number of Europeans employed on the gold mines rose from 13,000 to 18,000 in two years from 1904 to 1906. In 1908 the total labour force on the gold mines was nearly 19,000 Europeans, 12,000 Chinese and 150,000 Africans. The employment of Chinese labour was made use of politically in Great Britain, where the Liberals under Campbell-Bannerman came to power in 1906 on the cry of Chinese slavery. The two northern colonies were granted self-government, a generous gesture that was appreciated by Boer leaders like Botha and Smuts. As a result Afrikaans political parties, Het Volk in the Transvaal and Orangia Unie in the Orange River Colony, were successful in the elections of 1907.[1]

One of the most striking features of the post-war decade was the rise of the Afrikaans language, and growth of political sentiment. Throughout the nineteenth century Dutch was the language of the Church and of most educated Afrikaners. The bulk of the rural Afrikaans population, however, spoke the 'Taal'. Based on a seventeenth-century dialect of south Holland, Afrikaans had achieved its modern form by the middle of the eighteenth century, barely a hundred years after the foundation of white settlement at the Cape. But it was not until 1875 that *Die Genootskap vir Regte Afrikaners* was founded to translate the Bible into Afrikaans and promote the use of the language.

A new movement for the recognition of Afrikaans arose after the South African War aided by the resurgence of the Afrikaner national spirit in defiance of Lord Milner's policy of Anglicization. The Second Language Campaign proved successful, and Afrikaans rather than Dutch gradually came to be adopted as the cultural language of the Afrikaners. In 1909 the Afrikaanse Akademie was founded and by the 1920s Afrikaans was accepted as an official language which is now widely spoken in South Africa.

The period of mineral discoveries from 1870 to 1910 had a profound effect on South Africa. The pre-mineral age was one of small, widely scattered white communities, isolated from each other, separated by great distances and imperfectly drawn boundaries, and just emerging from a victorious struggle with a more numerous Bantu foe; communities whose economy was still largely subsistence and based on extensive pastoralism. The ensuing mineral age from 1870 to 1910 with the discovery and exploitation of the rich and vast deposits of diamonds and gold brought the primitive communities in the interior of South Africa into violent contact with the outside world and hastened

[1] For details of events leading up to Union in 1910 see Chapter VII.

the transition to a capitalist economy. The political and economic strain caused by the development of the Rand goldfields resulted in the Boer War. The forces of republicanism were defeated temporarily and the union of the four states in 1910 held out a bright hope for the future. It was predicted confidently that Liberal forces from the Cape would prevail and drive back the republican element in the north, but fifty years of Union have proved a sad lesson, and now the tide of republicanism and Afrikaner nationalism is high. The Afrikaners may have lost the Boer War, but they have unquestionably won the struggle for political domination in South Africa. From the Bond of the nineteenth century to the National Party of today their political parties have gone from strength to strength with the rising tide of nationalism and now control the Afrikaans nation and so South Africa.

CHAPTER 7

SEPARATION, CONFEDERATION
AND UNION

IN 1798 the district of Cape Town was one of four administrative areas covering white settlement in the Cape Colony, which by then had already reached the Fish River frontier (Fig. 37). Of these districts, that of Cape Town, placed narrowly along the squat peninsula between the St Helena Bay and False Bay, was the smallest in size but, as the seat of government, the most vital to the Colony. The other three administrative units sprawled across the hinterland of the Cape Fold Belt and the Karoo Basins to the limit of the Colony.

The first of these was the administrative area of Stellenbosch. The people of this district held mostly to the good soils of the Swartland lowland or the well-watered valleys to the windward of the mountain belt. These countrymen, though separated from the Peninsula by the barren Cape Flats or Sand Veld, felt themselves more in sympathy with the people of Cape Town and the Peninsula farmers, than their kinsmen ranging east of the mountain barrier. This allegiance had grown with the passing of the frontier complex. At the end of the seventeenth century the Stellenbosch area holding the majority of Huguenot refugees was strong in its criticism of the unfair practices of the Dutch East India Company's officials.

A century later in the eighteenth century, it was the turn of the magistrates of Swellendam and Graaf Reinet to be restive in face of governmental restrictions. Twice the farmers of Graaf Reinet declared their independence: first from the Batavian Republic in 1795, and next against the British in 1801 when Britain assumed interim control of the Cape on behalf of Holland. The necessary force used by a caretaker government to put down this bid for independence, fired a resentment which burst into open defiance with the second British occupation of the Cape in the Slachter's Nek Rebellion of 1815. The hanging of the rebel leaders which ended this rebellion became a symbol to the Boers of British oppression. Confidence in or liking for the British was never again established. From the Slachter's Nek incident there can be noted a steady growth of national feeling which reached recognition in 1875 with the first self-conscious acclaim of Afrikanerdom with a common history and common purpose.

The acts of independence of these remote communities in the last years of the eighteenth century laid the pattern for the political events of the succeeding century, when Boer republicanism, fostered on the plains of the high interior, persistently challenged British imperialism centred on her coastal colonies, but drawn into the interior periodically in defence of African interests. During the nineteenth century the tussle between republicanism and imperialism acted like a see-saw, the balance coming down now in favour of Boer separation, now on the side of British colonialism under the guise of federalism.

Confederation between the Afrikaner territories and the British colonies was actively explored three times between 1860 and 1874.[1] But the divisions were too deep-seated to allow the Afrikaner spirit, born at Slachter's Nek in 1815, to be submerged by British power, or conversely British interests to be threatened by Afrikaner independence. Conflict finally sharpened to war in 1899: defeat in 1902 brought collapse of the nascent Afrikaner States. This allowed a set of circumstances unlikely to have been realized otherwise, whereby the interior was welded to the coastlands to form the Union of South Africa in 1910.

The paralysing conflict between British and Boer interests, besides the stubborn defence of their land by the Bantu tribes along the borderlands, are among the main reasons why economic progress lagged behind the rest of the Empire, and why Union came so late in comparison with the other British lands. Even the United States of America, or Germany or Italy in Europe were sooner united than was South Africa.

The short-lived republics of Graaf Reinet and Swellendam will serve to demonstrate another aspect of political geography. When these two districts broke away from Cape Town's Government in 1795, the leaders of each district, instead of declaring a union, announced their separate independence. This hiving-off or budding process demonstrated in these separatist

[1] E. A. Walker, *A History of South Africa*, London, 1947, and E. A. Walker, *Historical Atlas of South Africa*, Cape Town, 1922, together give the picture of events leading towards Union.

59. Arrival of the first train at Durban.

60. Arrival of the first train at Kimberley.

61. View of early Bulawayo, date unknown.

62. The South African War, 1899–1902. A Krupp gun used by the Boers.

tendencies, and typical too of tribal organization, became a disruptive feature in the body politic of the Boers. Also, in contrast to New Zealand, Canada or even British parts of South Africa, there were no commercial or artisan classes. The acceptance of absolute equality amongst the Trekkers and the absence of any class distinction, allowed no easy subjection of the group to the undisputed leadership of one man. Had such a leader arisen at the inception of the Great Trek, he might have maintained the cohesion of the Boers as a single political group capable of building a strong state.

Piet Retief, the ablest of the first Trekkers, tried to cement unity amongst the early Trekker parties, by the affirmation of Nine Articles of Association laid down at the Vet River joint Trekker meeting in 1837. Retief's murder by the Zulu in February 1838, and the annexation by the British of Natal along with the Boer capital of Pietermaritzburg, destroyed all hope for the Trekkers of a secure base so necessary to the foundation of even the simplest state. The British annexation of Natal and closure of the sea coast to the Trekkers put an end to the hope of a single republic covering the widely scattered Trekker groups from the High Veld to the coast.

After annexation the Boers from Natal withdrew along the route of entry to join other Trekkers on the High Veld. With Winburg in the Free State and Potchefstroom just across the Vaal as the two main organizing centres, a second attempt was made to define Boer territory. From these negotiations a new sphere of republicanism was envisaged in 1844, which excluded the British-held marginal lands of Natal, but instead stretched south to the Orange, to include the 'old' settled lands of the Free State, and east to Delagoa Bay to ensure an outlet to the landlocked State.

Almost immediately the British annexation of Transorangia in 1848 nullified the effort to lay the foundations of this single republic. The desired secure and settled nucleus might nevertheless have been achieved had the Free Staters fulfilled the leadership expected of them after acquiring independence by the Bloemfontein Convention of 1852. But leadership and positive action by the Free Staters were dissipated in almost continuous warfare. Nor indeed were these 'settled' farmers always kindly disposed to the nomadic type of stock ranger that was found among the Afrikaners north of the Vaal, as later attempts at federation between Transvaalers and Free Staters show.

Instead of the Free State becoming the focus of Boer interests, the Potchefstroom burgers, inheritors of the Matabele lands, assumed the direction of the Boer people. Potchefstroom had a secure base and natural focus on which the State could rest; but between 1836 and 1856, the 'Republic' lacked even the revenue of the Lydenburg hunters, nor could it claim the allegiance of the isolated Zoutpansbergers. While to the south, as already remarked, the old-established Free Staters, having forgone leadership themselves, were not prepared to accept it from the frontiersmen beyond the Vaal.

Hence the bid for leadership by Potchefstroom was more than once opposed, and its attempt in December 1854 to unite all the little Trekker 'states' into one failed and brought about instead separation into independent units. The Trekkers having learned to shake off the authority of Britain by declaring themselves republican, now did so amongst themselves by declaring themselves separate units. By 1856 there were no less than five Boer republics on the plateau, three British colonies along the marginal lands below the escarpment, two Griqua Treaty States bordering the Orange River and four main tribal areas centred on the borderlands of white occupation. In all there were at this date fourteen different territories (Fig. 37).

This balkanization was an expression of the political geography of the period. It demonstrates the reluctance with which Britain shouldered any responsibility for territory outside the need for the protection of the sea route to India. Sectionalism bred of isolation prevailed over unity. None the less, despite the separation of the Boers into independent groups, the intrinsic nationhood of the Afrikaner people was never seriously questioned.

In 1864 Potchefstroom, the most advanced of the three Transvaal republics, brought to the brink of war by Lydenburg, made a sudden show of force and reunited under the name of the South African Republic the three opposed units of Potchefstroom, Lydenburg and Zoutpansberg. This unification excluded the republic of Utrecht in northern Natal (the remnant of Natal that remained to the Trekkers), and was achieved also at the sore cost of relinquishing the Free State with whom Potchefstroom had connived union by the election of M. W. Pretorius in 1860 as President common to both republics.

This unification of the frontier into a single South African Republic, as a territory wholly separate from the Orange Free State, is an expression of geographical difference and change in environmental personality between the Transvaal bankeveld, low veld and bush veld, and the Free State prairie plains. The political boundary between the two is conveniently measured by the Vaal River, though the geographical boundary in fact lies along the axis of the Witwatersrand divide where smooth erosion surfaces give way to broken scarplands and more complex structure and relief.

Once the main Boer republics of the Transvaal and Free State had fully separated after 1864 and the definition of their boundaries had become more precise, the budding process seen in the creation of new little republics became of political importance in those areas where British authority was weak or could be challenged. Of such kind were the republics or independent territories created along the Bechuana borderland of the Kalahari frontier and the Swazi-Zulu border of northern Natal. Such republican annexations were at the expense of already occupied Bantu land. By these practices it was hoped that the Afrikaner sphere of influence, elsewhere frustrated by British intervention, could be unobtrusively expanded. Thus, new republics were declared in 1882 in Stellaland and Goshen on the Bechuana border, while in Natal the Blood River Territory (1875), later to be superseded by a larger New Republic (1884), were proclaimed over considerable parts of Zululand and Swaziland.

These little republics, with scarcely the rudiments of social organization and no actual function of statehood, were too insignificant to carry the authority of Boer expansion. Cecil Rhodes wrote of the Transvaalers, 'They have the pluck of bankrupts, and given the right they would annex up to Egypt tomorrow'.[1]

Despite the kaleidoscope of changing states in the nineteenth century the presence of a thin overall spread of Dutch-speaking people, with a common heritage and fellow feeling, in Afrikaner as well as English-speaking territories, gave a unity to South Africa. The Afrikaner bond was to prove both the strength and the weakness of the country. Undoubtedly Boer ethnic homogeneity allowed the success of Union in 1910 against the suspicions of some that Union would carry with it Afrikaner domination. This fear was realized when the referendum in October 1960 ultimately brought approval for a republic outside the Commonwealth. Separatism can go no further.

If in mid-nineteenth century the Free State failed to provide

---

[1] Hon. Sir Lewis Michell, *The Life of the Rt. Hon. Cecil Rhodes 1853–1902*, London, 1910, Vol. I, p. 159.

the core around which the early Afrikaner State could crystal-
lize, the territory successfully performed the function of passageway between the Cape Colony and the lands beyond the Vaal.
The role of passageway was recognized by Sir George Grey
(1854-61) when he wrote: 'in giving up the Orange River
Sovereignty we gave up the only good line of road which was
at the time known between Her Majesty's several South African
possessions'.[1] Grey seeing South Africa held helpless by the conflicts between territories and peoples set his heart on confederacy. His arrival in 1854 was too late to benefit from Britain's
recent possession of Transorangia, and the year of his becoming
Governor of the Cape in 1854 saw the second abortive Boer
attempt to weld their territories into a single republic.

What were the interests of South Africa as a whole did not
then engage the minds of British statesmen. Each treaty drawn
up with an individual tribal group, as well as the two conventions with the Boer Republics, point to the deliberate British
policy of disengagement from the interior. This 'Little England'
policy was aided by the slackening of influence from the missionary sector in Britain. At that time also Britain was reluctant to be distracted from her maritime interests and the
development of her Indian Empire.

Had the Imperial government permitted the extension of the
boundaries of the Cape Province along with the pioneer fringe,
the problem of federation between the opposing groups would
not have become so complex.

With the advance of the nineteenth century separate group
interests were an increasingly disruptive force in South Africa.
One group despoiled the aspirations of the other, and no two
groups would allow the third to bring unity to the country by
promoting federation. The British group interest is represented
by the Imperial Factor. For the long road to Union the Imperial Factor is most to blame. The wealth, prestige and strong
government of Britain could have imposed unity on the country,
and established British authority might have controlled the
conflict between the frontiersmen and the tribesmen by the
better allotting of land and the proper appointment of administrators. Instead British officials at Whitehall carped at the
continued expenditure on the protection of settlers along the
frontiers. Yet the Governors of the Cape and Natal were
vitally concerned to maintain order, for fear of an African or

[1] E. A. Walker, *A History of South Africa*, London, 1947, p. 279, a quotation
from Sir George Grey's famous despatch on South Africa, No. 216 April, 1860.

Boer onslaught on the coastal bases and English colonial settlements, for which they were responsible while guarding the sea route to India. The limitations of remote control on a rapidly changing and developing local situation were increasingly made manifest.

The alternating British policies of withdrawal from the interior followed by advance into and the annexation of inland territory, allowed the Boers promise of independence without their being able to achieve that liberty for long. Furthermore the reluctance of Britain to assume control of the turbulent borderlands, meant that the Africans lost more land to the settlers than need have been, before their real plight stirred the British Government to action at the earnest plea of the philanthropic and evangelical bodies concerned with African welfare.

The second group interest was that of the Boer. Here the overriding concern was to wrest land from the tribes to meet the insatiable demand for immense farms for each son of a rapidly expanding, exclusively stock-rearing community. It is stated that towards the end of the century, the landless burgers of the Transvaal wanted war in Bechuanaland, since thereby they would come into land through the inevitable dispossession of the weaker tribesmen.[1]

The third group interest was that of the Bantu, who were fighting a rear-guard action against all whites to maintain some hold on their grazing lands. The Africans, awed by the technological superiority of the whites, at first accepted the settlers as guests giving them access to grazing on their spare lands, which appeared to be unoccupied to the European, but were in fact held in reserve for expansion of the tribe or onset of drought. Misunderstandings about alleged purchases and sole ownership of land led to resentment from Africans who still believed themselves hosts to strangers' cattle. Resentment when voiced to the settlers led to the forcible eviction of the tribesmen, and if war followed, then their defeat would mean the eventual withdrawal of the tribal unit from their proper grazing lands to areas beyond the white belt of occupation, possibly into that of a neighbouring tribe.

The British Government in mid-nineteenth century met the pressure exerted by the Cape officials and missionaries to annex troubled areas beyond the Cape frontier by concluding treaties with chiefs or drawing up conventions with the Republics.

[1] J. A. L. Agar-Hamilton, *The Road to the North: South Africa, 1852–1886*, London, 1937, p. 341.

These treaties virtually freed Britain from any direct responsibility in these territories, while binding the signatories to clauses of 'good behaviour'. Nevertheless, pressures, or persuasion, or requests for protection were sometimes sufficient for Britain to advance inland, only too often to recoil again on to the Orange River frontier. Where relinquishment to the Afrikaner was impossible, Britain gave her sovereign rights over such territories to the self-governing Colonies of the Cape and Natal. In this way territories which might have assumed separate individuality, if not independence, were incorporated into the Cape. Thus Griqualand West (1871), British Bechuanaland (1885), Basutoland between 1868 and 1884, and the Transkeian territories, became inseparable parts of the Cape Colony and played no part in the negotiations which led to Union in 1910.

Only at Union was Britain forced to assume undivided responsibility for those African territories which, for want of a unified native policy, were excluded from the terms of reference laid down for the Natal Convention called to discuss Union. In this way the three Protectorates of Bechuanaland (1890), Swaziland (1895) and Basutoland (1884), fell to the care of the Colonial Office. Permissive clauses left the way clear for their absorption into the Union, along with Southern Rhodesia, if circumstances permitted and the African people themselves welcomed inclusion into the Union.

In the nineteenth century lack of cohesion was as marked amongst the British Colonies as it was amongst the Afrikaner territories. If blood and kinship were a supra-national factor binding the peoples of the different Republics, so the Crown served as a link to the British Coastal Colonies. Kinship amongst the Boers and the Crown for the British were more than once invoked in the attempt to bring about confederation in these respective groups. But once responsible Government had been granted to the Cape in 1872 and Natal in 1893, amalgamation of the Colonies was henceforth impossible without the incorporation of the Republics as well in a general Union of all European territories.

Natal welcomed separation from the Cape Colony when she attained Crown Colony status in 1856. It is understandable that Natal, isolated from the Cape by the tribes in Kaffraria on one side of the Basutoland bastion, by the Republics on the High Veld side of those highlands, and Portuguese territory to the north, should feel herself apart, not only from the Cape, but from the Boer communities also. Her subtropical climate, with reliable summer rainfall, her adequate labour, supplied since 1860 by indentured Indians, besides Zulu farm squatters, gave Natal a basis for agricultural advance. Another strong advantage was the security derived from a body of imperial troops sufficient in number to guard the short 'state' axis of 56 miles between Durban the imperial port and Pietermaritzburg the capital. Natal at this period appeared prosperous and was envied by the other territories, both Boer and British.

The great depression of the early 1860s which brought the Republics and the Cape to their knees, only tardily affected Natal, for her cotton and coffee sold well during the American Civil War and sugar continued to command a good price. At length disease in the plantation crops and the collapse of the world market involved Natal also in the depression that engulfed South Africa.

Natal, shut away from the rest and preoccupied with her Zulu problem, kept a weather eye open only to see that the Cape did not impinge upon her insecurely held southern border; and to the north that the Transvaal in the drive towards a coastal outlet, did not obtain a foothold on St Lucia Bay in Zululand.

The personality of Natal is best summed up in the description written of the official caste in the government of Pietermaritzburg who, 'prejudiced against the Dutch, the Cape Colony, responsible Government, soldiers, non-official Natalians, and all outsiders was completely out of touch with the rest of the country'.[1] With the geographical isolation of the order experienced in the coastal area between Durban and Pietermaritzburg, such an attitude of the people and officials might be expected at a time when communications were slow and illestablished.

Between the Drakensberg wall to the west and hostile Zululand, Natal held open a tenuous life-line to the Transvaal. From 1874 onwards, this highway was improved by road and bridge, the better to compete with the Cape for the trade of the interior. With the coming of the railways, tariff war between the British Colonies intensified and acrimony between the ports and the colonies they served, reached ridiculous lengths. At no time was colonial statesmanship big enough to allow the landlocked Republics a share in the substantial revenues obtained from imports.

The most vivid instance of geographical determinism in South Africa in explaining the desire for separation, is that between

[1] Martineau, *Life of Sir Bartle Frere*, II, p. 238, quoted by E. A. Walker, op. cit., p. 31.

the Western and Eastern Provinces of the Cape. The differences between the two regions is sufficiently marked to merit the saying that the Union has five separate provinces, not four. Like British Kaffraria the Eastern Province is a regional unit of distinctive personality, which by historical accident never assumed complete independence. Though Grahamstown is 600 miles from Cape Town, and letters overland then took a week to reach the town, nevertheless Grahamstown was not so remote as to justify direct action by her officials in the affairs of the frontier. Twice the appointment of a commissioner or a lieutenant-governor was found to be unnecessary since direct negotiation with the Governor at Cape Town was often found more time-saving. Yet distance and delay in communication along a frontier where quick decisions were vital, made separation, or at least devolution, of Government an arguable point.

The plea for the separation of the Eastern Province from the Cape had its promoters in the townsmen of Grahamstown and Port Elizabeth. Their ideas were widely publicized after the foundation of the Grahamstown Gazette in December 1831. It is significant that agitation for separation followed so soon after the 1820 Settlers, a group who, made desperate by the harshness of the land allocated to them, demanded a Government sympathetic to their plight.

In 1834 when a Legislative Council was given to the Cape, the Eastern Boer farmers added their weight to a petition asking for an elective *Heemraaden* or Council to deal with the special conditions of the frontier. Instead the question of separation even in this form was allayed by schemes of municipal government granted to the towns of the frontier in 1836.

However, pressure for independence by English settlers was maintained by asking for the capital to be removed to a region where, since the introduction of the merino sheep in 1827, the greatest economic progress in the Colony was taking place. It was stressed also that government centred on Grahamstown (with a population of 3,700 in 1830) would be near the vital events of the border. A capital in the east might serve to check the steady drain on manpower lost through the Trekker movement. In 1835 Governor Sir Benjamin D'Urban did in fact suggest Uitenhage as a suitable new capital; but nothing came of the proposal, since Bathurst, originally planned as the capital of Albany, had already failed to uphold its role.

The supporters of separation for the Eastern Province argued that beyond the Fish River there would be in time further annexation of territory, as had already happened by the incorporation of the Ceded Territory in the earlier history of the Frontier.

When the Province of Queen Adelaide was briefly created in 1835 and later superseded by British Kaffraria (itself to become a Crown Colony in 1860) the Easterners clamoured for independence under the Crown. They held that if freed from the dominance of Cape Town, their thriving wool industry, rising revenues and shorter route to the interior would make them a financially viable Crown Colony.

The Easterners, while benefiting from the rapidly growing wool export trade, organized an inland market for imported goods following the settlement of the Boers in Transorangia. Imperial troops garrisoning the military forts offered a home market. Also the Native levies and friendly tribes were by that time entering the western monetary economy. Like circumstances were to affect Natal in the development of economy in the latter half of the century.

At this period the Eastern Province, because of these trade advantages, was contributing a substantial portion of the Colony's revenue. The Easterners believed their resources were being used to benefit the West, as in the building of the Table Bay Breakwater, while their own Port Elizabeth continued to be served by lighters only.[1] The period of railway building in the latter part of the century increased the agitation that funds raised in the Eastern Province should be used locally and not diverted to the West. Four times in the nineteenth century clamour for separation from Cape Town induced serious political consideration at Government level. Such pressures brought palliatives to local pride by installation of a High Court of two Judges at Grahamstown in 1862, and on that occasion Parliament was called to assemble there.

The calling of Parliament to Grahamstown (which the Western members boycotted) was in honour of a promise made during the drawing up of the Legislative Council in 1852, when the status of a separate constituency was conferred on the Eastern Cape, and the promise made that Parliament could be called to any place named by the Governor.

The Eastern Province leaders achieved neither a shift of the capital to Grahamstown, nor independence from the Western Cape. A geographical interpretation might explain the failure to win these objectives by the transitional nature of the border-

[1] This same argument was put forward in 1962 in Northern Rhodesia in respect of Southern Rhodesia.

land. It is plain the Eastern Province looked beyond the frontier for increase in land to bolster its ambition to become a separate colony. For this project no support came from British Kaffraria, which after attaining the status of Crown Colony, believed its future lay not as part of the Eastern Province, but as an independent self-governing colony to which would be added the lands of Kaffraria proper when once these were absorbed.

Nor did the proposers of separation and independence for the Eastern Province from the Cape, find support from the Dutch-speaking farmers of Graaf Reinet, Colesberg and the Tarkastad areas. These frontiersmen feared to fall under the direction of Jingoist Grahamstown and, not without reason, the separatist movement, itself rallied under the banner of 'The 1820 Party'. Even the Hottentots of Kat River Settlement opposed any move to relax the control of the more liberal men of Cape Town, in whom they had more hope of fairer treatment than from the land-rapacious frontiersmen.

At the realization of responsible self-government for the Cape in 1872, a petition from the Easterners to the Queen asking for separation was rejected, but the plea brought at least equal representation for the Eastern and Western provinces in the new assembly. In deference to the agitation from the Easterners, virtually a federal cabinet was appointed to the new Cape Government. There was carefully selected representation through ministers of important portfolios, not only of men from the Western and Eastern provinces, but from British Kaffraria as well; since this Crown Colony was then incorporated into the Cape Colony.

To put an end to the cry for separation and devolution, the new Prime Minister of the Cape proposed the Seven Circles Act, each area covered by the circle to be a constituency having three representatives. By this novel method regionalism was to be undermined. Also it was hoped such ordering of the constituencies would prevent the older stratum of farmers from being swamped by the townsmen. In this measure there is indication of the increasing division between town and country, based not only on differences between commercial and farming interests, but more fundamentally between English-speaking town dwellers and the Afrikaans-speaking farmers or *plattelanders* as they came to be called.[1]

---

[1] This ethnic and occupational division untimately translated itself into the plateau republics with agrarian economies and British coastal colonies subsisting on their commercial enterprises centred on the ports.

The weighting of the rural vote, in effect the Afrikaner vote, was carried over into Union, permitting an influence on Government which has rarely been equalled in a modern state. The Afrikaner would argue that political loading in favour of the countryman has preserved the South African spirit against the 'Uitlander' or foreign disruptive element which has looked on Europe and more particularly Britain as home. To the Nationalist the true South African is equated with Afrikanerdom, since the language is indigenous to the country and all roots with Europe have been severed.

With this last effort in 1872 to secure separation for the Eastern Province no further attempt was made to break up territorial units already established, though the addition of further territory gained in the Bantu borderlands was by no means at an end.[1]

Consolidation of Boer and British territory had been achieved and the country blocked out into primary independent units. From 1870 onwards it became apparent that no rapid economic progress would be made unless the Republics and Crown Colonies could be brought together under the umbrella of confederation; but with each new political development and the conflicts and jealousies aroused over the borderlands, confederation became increasingly difficult to bring about.

In fact there had been no period more propitious than the decade between 1850 and 1860 for bringing the different white groups together. At that time the Bantu, armed and horsed, were matched in war with the white man. During the same period local intransigence and racial conflicts were douched by a paralysing depression throughout South Africa, made the more acute by a prolonged drought in the latter part of that decade everywhere outside Natal. Common suffering drew the insecure white communities together and enlivened hopes of confederation between the petty states.

The three men at that period most conscious of the value of unity were President Pretorius for the two Republics, Sir George Grey, Governor of the British Colonies, and Moshesh, Chief of the Basuto. Each of these men sought unity, first with their own group, and then looked beyond their own borders for further allegiance to increase the territorial and economic

---

[1] Separation it might be claimed was the last of the legacies left by the Dutch East India Company to the Cape people. In fact the wish for separation and independence was induced by geographic determinism in circumstances where settlement was sporadic and immense distances divided the frontiersmen from the seat of government.

strength of the territory under their care. Each man seeking the benefit of his own interest, destroyed the possibility of federation between conflicting groups or even unity between the same ethnic communities, if interests did not coincide.

Thus when the Free State sought help against the Basuto in 1858 by suggesting union with the South African Republic, the British Governor pointed out that union could invalidate the Conventions on which their independence from Britain rested. Again in another instance, when Moshesh wished to link up with the Xhosa in Kaffraria to give a unified front to white aggression, the same Governor, Sir George Grey, prevented this strategy by the deliberate planting of loyal Tembu, Fingoes and Griqua in Kaffraria between the Basuto and the coastal tribes.

It is evident that the Free State and Basutoland were the pivotal areas in plans for confederation. Basutoland stood a central fortress between all the African groupings and was itself an amalgam of many tribes. Moshesh was in a position to threaten the whole fabric of white settlement. Although Moshesh had never been more evenly matched in arms against the commandos, he knew that ultimately he must give ground. Both the Free State and Basutoland sought help on occasion from their own kin, and at other times when danger really threatened, they asked alliance with or annexation by the Cape Colony and Great Britain. But neither the Cape nor Britain were anxious then to embroil themselves in the defence of the interior. Cape Town in the role of revictualling station for the 200 years of its foundation, remained indifferent to the rest of the country until the discovery of diamonds aroused avarice and desire for control of the interior plateau. Sir George Grey put all the pressure possible on to the Secretary of State to swing him to the opinion that British interests were best served by federation and annexation. He was recalled for his pains; but the British Government showed interest in merging British Kaffraria with the Cape and achieving thereafter a federal union with Natal, thereby reducing imperial expenditure on defence.

In the Sixties initiative in bringing about federation undoubtedly lay with the Crown, but Britain had pursued a policy of non-involvement with the interior ever since the rash venture of annexing Transorangia in 1848. Since that withdrawal no advance of British authority inland had been encouraged.

In the succeeding decade the Cape Colony, self-governing since 1872, should have initiated the moves towards federation.

The prestige of the Colony was at its height between 1865 and 1885. This prestige rested on the basis of the Cape being the oldest Colony, having the largest amount of land (if desert counts for land) and the most population settled in towns served by a road network begun in 1850. The fast-developing ports were linked to the interior by these roads, which from 1870 onwards to the end of the century were slowly superseded by rail. Because the Cape was the mother colony land accretion came to her at the expense of all other territories in South Africa. Before the century ended great stretches of politically and economically vital territory had been added in Bechuanaland, Basutoland and Kaffraria.

With the discovery of diamonds in Griqualand West, Cape indifference to her hinterland immediately disappeared and Whitehall's policy of disengagement from the interior changed to one of active engagement. Because Britain through the Cape still held authority and power, she was able to wrest the diamond fields from the Griqua and Free Staters, and to incorporate within her dominions the Bechuana corridor leading to the supposed Eldorado lying north of the Limpopo. Once commerce and industry were centred on the interior plateau, financed by British and international capital, it was manifestly retrogressive to have coastal colonies in cut-throat competition for the interior trade. Likewise no advance in the Transvaal was possible while revenues of the pastoral republic were expended on trying to circumvent the stranglehold of the British Colonies by seeking a sea outlet via Delagoa Bay. Expediency demanded that there should be some form of confederation. But the Kimberley scheme for federation in 1871 foundered because of the diamond fields dispute. That of Lord Carnarvon, the Colonial Secretary, actively pursued between 1874 and 1881, was also fruitless since the Cape Colony refused to exert leadership for fear that federation would re-open the separatist movement in the Eastern Cape, and that the inclusion of the Republics would necessitate the sharing of the revenues obtained from imports.

The Free State, resentful of her defeat in the diamond fields dispute, secure from Basuto invasion since the annexation of that high land by Britain in 1868, and financially buoyant on the £90,000 paid in compensation for the loss of diamond land, held aloof from the federal movement. Economically she shared with the Cape the prosperity resulting from the rapidly growing diamond industry as well as wool exports. Already by 1871 there was a large urban population in Kimberley ready to be served by the Free State transport riders.

Since the Cape-Free State axis had failed to secure the stable core of United South Africa, the second and potentially the more vital axis between Natal and the Transvaal was examined by Lord Carnarvon in his anxiety to solve the increasingly vexatious question bedevilling South African advance. With the real threat of a general uprising along the Bantu borderlands, a common native policy was also becoming more urgent. There were wide differences in approach towards the indigenous peoples between the Republics and the Cape, the Cape and Natal.

If Natal was now to be the pivot of a confederacy it was as well to realize that her position was one of extreme isolation. Pressed between three of the largest and most cohesive African groups, Natal has always looked seaward to Britain for ultimate support, not to the Cape whom Natal regarded more as a rival than an ally. By the weakly held route to the interior Natal maintained a lifeline to the Transvaal, where lay her proper sphere of influence. In fact Natal in the Seventies harboured expansionist designs on the Transvaal, as is clear by Theophilus Shepstone's annexation of the Transvaal in his desire to thwart the competition that Durban's trade suffered because of the Cape. Natal had cause to fear also that the Transvaal would achieve an independent sea outlet, either through Delagoa Bay in Portuguese territory, or through Kosi Bay in Zululand.

At this period of active talks on Carnarvon's confederation, the Transvaal wavered on the brink of bankruptcy. Such State impoverishment was welcomed by Shepstone, the Natal Minister of Native Affairs, who had been sent to Pretoria to set before the Volksraad the advantage of federation. Shepstone, over-stepping his mandate, annexed the Transvaal in April 1877, thereby annihilating the second axis explored by the Crown in search of a base for general confederation. This enforced annexation, overthrown three years later, so alienated Boer opinion, that total defeat in war of the Republics was necessary to remove the barriers standing now in the way of Federation or Union between Boer and British territory. Thereafter, the initiative towards closer union had to come from the Republics, for no confederation would be possible after the revolt of 1880, unless on the terms of the Afrikaner and under his flag.

Natal, denied her natural hinterland, sank back into isolation and turned with vigour to support the fratricidal war between Durban and the Cape ports for import dues and the trade with the interior. The Free State, no longer threatened by the Basuto, proceeded to carry the railway lines projected from the Cape ports across their grassland corridor to reach the borders of the Transvaal in 1892. The role of passageway still remained the function of the Free State.

The Cape, under Cecil Rhodes, realizing that Republican opinion was hopelessly alienated and embittered, excluded the two Afrikaner territories from the concept of a pan-African union under the British Crown. This is manifest in the placing of the Cape Town-Kimberley railway immediately west of the Orange Free State border. The railway allowed the displacement of the natural grassland route of the Free State corridor westward along the desert margin of the Cape Province and Bechuanaland. The site of Kimberley and the Great North Road were conveniently in line.

The railway made the route possible at all seasons. This displacement and the stimulus of the Tati Goldfield, opened in Matabeleland in 1868, spurred on Rhodes' concept of a possible Federation of all British territory from the Cape Colony north through Bechuanaland to Central and East Africa. A railway from Cape Town to Cairo would link this great central highway of British interest.

With Central Africa as destination in an era of railway expansion, it did appear as if the Transvaal and Natal were outside and peripheral to this scheme planned on continental dimensions. To bring about the highway binding British interests, it was necessary to quash republican aspirations in Bechuanaland, and secure the lands of the Matabele and Mashona, beyond the northern borders of the Bechuana. By acquiring the control of the land named in the Rudd Concession in 1888, Rhodes and his partner Beit, with the money earned on the diamond fields of Griqualand West, established the beginnings of Rhodesia.

Like a plant etiolated by lack of light, Rhodes' empire stretched shakily north without the buttress of continuous white settlement. East of it, the Transvaal remained the true keystone to the South African edifice. Rhodes had mistakenly believed the keystone to be situated in Matabeleland. Indeed he referred to that region as 'the Dominant North'.

In 1886 news of gold ore on the Witwatersrand displaced interest in the placer mines of the valleys of Lydenburg and

Barberton. These goldfields were securely within the republican sphere and could not be wrested from them. Dating from this discovery the abiding leadership of the South African Republic, centred first on Potchefstroom and later on Pretoria, was slowly revealed. The Transvaal after fifty years of impoverishment would soon argue from a position of strength, once the economic centre of South Africa shifted from the coastal ports to the Rand. That the goldfields would endure was at first in question. But after the deep levels had been found accessible in 1894, nothing remained to hamper the rapid development of the Rand, save the intransigent and stubborn reluctance of its Afrikaner farmer government to further what was considered foreign interests inimical to the Afrikaner way of life.

Rhodes with the financial resources drawn from de Beers Diamond Corporation, was one of the founders of the Johannesburg gold mines. After the mines had been proved, Rhodes became impatient of the reluctance of the Transvaal to further commercial development.

It was clear that Boer and British antipathy seeded at Slachter's Nek had fruited in the disputes concerning Griqualand and the control of the Great North Road. Political federation was out of the question but economic federation—a zollverein —could not be to the disadvantage of any group. To achieve this Rhodes forced the issue as Shepstone had done before him. Rhodes therefore initiated the Jameson raid, a political error as grievous as that of Suez in the present day. With the routing of the Jameson raiders, the Transvaal nationalists won further support from their people, for a policy of an independent Boer state freed entirely from British paramountcy.

Several important consequences sprang from that ill-conceived skirmish. Germany anxious to gain a greater foothold in Southern Africa publicly supported the Transvaal, but privately noted that Great Britain would go to considerable lengths to maintain her paramountcy in what she now regarded as her sphere of influence. British policy, so long confined to the sea coast of South Africa, was now engaged fully in the matters affecting the interior.

The Jameson Raid and its aftermath emphasized the importance of the port and harbour of Delagoa Bay, given permanently to Portugal by the Macmahon award of 1875. To the issue of the Bay was linked the future of the African territories bordering on the Transvaal and Natal. The relationship of Swaziland to the Transvaal (the soft under-belly by which the Transvaal hoped to break out of the British hold) was especially important in the situation.

The railway from Delagoa Bay had reached Pretoria in 1894, when the Natal railway was still only at the border. So important did Great Britain regard this escape route of the Transvaalers that she made a show of strength by a warship in Delagoa Bay in 1897 and barred the coast of Zululand as an outlet by annexing Tongaland and Zululand. Swaziland, a pawn in the diplomatic game, of little consequence while Transvaal was occupied by the British, was removed finally from Transvaal supervision and put under a British High Commissioner in 1907.

The audacity of Rhodes' attempt to overthrow the Kruger Government drove the Free State into a binding alliance with the Transvaal. The Free State—the Corridor State—characteristically kept her economic bond to the south in a customs union with the Cape; but now sealed a political alliance with the Transvaal in the north. Burgers, when President of the Transvaal, had said (with forethought) that he wanted no closer union with the Orange Free State, for this would lessen the position of leadership the Transvaal would assume in the ultimate unification of South Africa.

The abortive attempt to overthrow the Kruger régime strengthened the hatred of the Afrikaner nationalist for the British and all British institutions. It inspired in the Afrikaner an increasing pride in race which had grown steadily until then. Among Afrikaners Krugerism had become a yardstick of political behaviour, while the heroism shown in fighting Great Britain became the standard by which all later actions have been measured. Isolation and ostracism hold no fears for the Afrikaner nationalists immolated in a proud exclusiveness. The consequences of the Jameson Raid reach forward to the present.

Rhodes himself suffered a serious political setback. In 1896 when Rhodes ordered the 'Rhodesian' police south to help in the Jameson Raid the Matabele and Mashona rebelled. The chartered lands in Rhodesia nearly slipped from his grasp and British Bechuanaland, earmarked to be incorporated into Rhodesian territory, was placed directly under the protection of Britain.

After the alliance between the Free State and the Transvaal, and following his setback north of the Limpopo, Rhodes began to work for a British federation. To achieve success he had to prepare the ground. He did so by investing money in Natal's sugar industry and priming certain sympathizers to carry the policy of federation forward in the Natal Legislative Assembly to be elected in 1898. In the Cape he worked for a redistribution of seats to ensure greater voice to the federalist group resident in the towns, as against the less reliable Afrikaner Bondsmen of the rural areas who had rallied to the Transvaal cause. His political manœuvring failed, but Natal did join a customs union with the Cape.

Thereafter Rhodes turned to Southern Rhodesia as the lever in his geo-political game. He did know, after a tour in 1894, that Matabeleland would never equal the Vaal borders for mineral wealth, but the development of coal, gold and other small mines along the Rhodesian midriff, made him hopeful that the economic future of his centre-piece in the British mosaic would be assured. Rhodes could not then appreciate that Southern Rhodesia had not yet emerged, as had South Africa, from its pioneer phase. Nor was he to know that Southern Rhodesia would never play the vital role of focal point even in the Federation of its own making. Lying between the continental water divide of the Witwatersrand in the Transvaal, and the Katanga in Northern Rhodesia, it is likely the Rhodesian Charterlands will come to play a role of passageway like that of the Orange Free State.

In 1899, after the Cape had failed to show leadership, Rhodes pressed forward with a plan to federate Southern Rhodesia with the Transvaal. Southern Rhodesia to be the head and the Transvaal the body of the new state. In the Transvaal he recognized that neither the extremism of the 'Uitlander', nor the foreign element agitating for the franchise, nor the Kruger element among the burgers, was the true voice of South Africa. But Rhodes was unable to persuade the Transvaalers that such a federation would maintain their group interests.

The issue was then passed on to Great Britain who took up the cudgels over the franchise of her British subjects in the Transvaal to cover her real concern for the recognition of British paramountcy in an area now regarded as her proper sphere of influence. Kruger offered a qualified franchise to foreigners in the Transvaal in return for free access to the eastern seaboard across Swaziland. Deadlock ensued.

Retrenchment in expenditure on the mines and death by *rinderpest* disease amongst Boer cattle brought the Transvaal to the edge of bankruptcy. The ultimatum of September 26th 1899 seemed to some a welcome event in the face of the political impasse, and the virtual collapse of the economy. Appropriately the first shots of the Boer war were fired on the Great North Road in the upstart republic of Goshen, which stood defiantly athwart the highway established (in Rhodes's mind) to link British Africa from Cape to Cairo.

The war was virtually over in 1900, and in May of that year Great Britain annexed the Free State as the Orange River Colony. The Transvaal fell the following September. In the two years that remained to guerrilla operations there was constant talk of a federation of all the colonies in South Africa. It had been implied in such discussions that war would reassert British dominion, which, while in this ascendancy, could direct the country as a whole towards unity.

Lord Milner, presupposing the shift of economic and political gravity to the Rand, as the most active centre of development, had the High Commissioner's office removed there along with the Court of Appeal. Milner failed in getting the British Government to suspend the Cape Parliament which he thought necessary before all the Colonies could be properly reassembled as a single political unit.

Failure to suspend the Cape Parliament and the death of Rhodes in 1902 put an end to an early federation following hard on a peace settlement. Thereafter only a scheme for greater union under the aegis of the Afrikaner people was likely to succeed. But Milner did achieve the economic federation that Cecil Rhodes sought before his death. This took the shape of a customs union bolstered by rail tariff agreements, not only between the colonies of South Africa, but also between them, Southern Rhodesia and the British Protectorates. There were besides reciprocity clauses covering trade with the United Kingdom and other countries of the Empire. South Africa for the first time was acting as a unit in Commonwealth trade.

In the years that followed the Peace Treaty of Vereeniging in 1902 means to political union were constantly advocated.[1] And in the events leading ultimately to union in 1910, the four self-governing Colonies played parts which the political geography of each might seem to indicate as the most likely. The impulses towards closer union came from opposing elements in South African society, Afrikaners, English speaking colonists and the British officials. Each element believed that unity, first

[1] L. M. Thompson, *The Unification of South Africa* 1902–1910, Oxford, 1960. This book forms the basis for the ensuing geographical interpretation leading to union.

considered in terms of federation, would serve the aspirations and advance the status of their particular group. Fifty years before, group interests had worked against close union and wrecked schemes towards federation.

The Afrikaner view, as voiced by General Smuts, believed that united South Africa would at last exclude the Imperial Factor from the internal affairs of the country. British officials foresaw that continued disunion would bring Great Britain into increasing disfavour, for her arbitration would be sought in the tariff war that showed signs of beginning between the States since the completion of two new railway lines in 1906. By manipulating South Africa as a unit within the framework of the British Empire it was believed its value to the imperial structure would increase. It was held also that a united South would offer a stable base on which there would be a natural accretion, as territories to the north of the Limpopo became eligible for absorption. The Rand would be the workshop for the development of this hinterland, and the economic stability accruing therefrom would attract a steady flow of British immigrants to offset the numerical superiority of the Afrikaner people. More especially union must be achieved under the British flag before war broke out in Europe.

The English-speaking colonists, concentrated in the towns and dominant nowhere but in Natal, believed that in a mixed Parliament the English viewpoint would be made known throughout South Africa. Moreover, predominantly concerned in commerce, the English knew their interests were inextricably bound to the fortunes of the two ex-Republics.

In the anxiety that federation would not be achieved, partial union along old axes was invoked. Thus it was suggested the Cape Colony should unite with the Orange Free State, and Natal suggested partnership with the Transvaal; then, a real threat to the coastal colonies, the unification of the Afrikaner states was declared a possibility. This last amalgam would have brought the British coastal colonies to ruin, for the Afrikaner self-governing colonies would have set up a customs barrier to British ports and concentrated on Delagoa Bay.

The importance of the inland trade to the British ports can be gauged from the fact that in the financial year ending in June 1903, 32 per cent of the Cape Colony's revenue and 24 per cent of the revenue of Natal was derived from customs dues; while the railways contributed 48 per cent to the Cape Colony's coffers and 53 per cent to those of Natal. Trade was vital to the life of the coastal states and competition for it a constant source of friction, which was likely to intensify with the announcement that the Transvaal intended to withdraw from the Customs Union and seek new agreements at an inter-colonial conference in 1908. The threat was the more serious, in as much as the years following the Boer war were ones of acute depression in the coastal colonies. The presence of 200,000 British soldiery gave a prosperity to the towns and a ready market to the farmers supplying food and fodder to the imperial army. The departure of the troops brought collapse to the home market. So sharp was the economic decline that the white population in Natal fell rapidly from 97,109 in 1904 to 91,443 in 1908, from which date recovery once again was noticeable. In the Cape Colony there was stagnation rather than outright loss as the slow rise from 579,741 white persons in 1904 to 582,377 in 1911 shows.

The collapse of the diamond market following a financial crisis in Europe brought further hardship to the Cape in 1907; while at the same date Natal became alarmed for the safety of the whites with the sudden revolt of the Zulu in the poll-tax uprising of 1906. A punitive expedition to Zululand in concert with Transvaalers in 1907 brought further unease.

Natal faced total economic eclipse if the Transvaal turned to the Delagoa Bay outlet as the cheapest route of communication between Europe and the interior. Already in 1898 40 per cent of the Transvaal trade went by that gateway, while Durban received 30 per cent and the Cape ports between them shared the remaining 30 per cent of trade. The Transvaal stood to gain if she brought the greater part of her trade across Portuguese territory, for by a *modus vivendi* clause the Portuguese allowed two-thirds of the mine labour to be recruited in their territory.[1]

Meanwhile in the post-war phase, Great Britain was rehabilitating the devastated rural economy of the Boer lands and money and men were being concentrated on the Rand to resuscitate the mining industry from which the revenues for reconstruction and economic recovery were expected to be secured. Johannesburg was the centre of the reconstruction schemes. Population in the Transvaal increased by over 100,000 white persons to 420,562 by 1911—a considerable addition where density of persons was so low. The Transvaal showed a buoyant budget while the Cape and Natal tabled an accumulating deficit as the depression worsened.

The population in the Orange Free State increased less

[1] Thompson, op. cit., p. 55.

startlingly; but the Free State drew to itself, as the pure source of Afrikaner culture, many dispossessed Boers, besides the British farming population which had been set along the Basuto border where land lay vacant.

The new Liberal Government in Britain hastened to make amends for the Boer War and were quick to grant the Afrikaner colonies self-government—in 1906 in the case of the Transvaal and in 1907 in the Orange Free State. In the first elections the Afrikaners in both colonies emerged in supporting monolithic parties, since they were racially and culturally so homogeneous. The British in the Transvaal, divided then as now by religion, class and occupation, split their votes among several parties while still showing allegiance to the Crown.

In 1908 the Cape Colony elected to power the South African Party on Afrikaner support, though under the leadership of the anti-imperialist Z. X. Merriman. Thus in three of the four self-governing colonies the Government was now in the hands of men seeking a common destiny for the whole of South Africa. The leaders would collaborate to that end rather than undermine efforts towards closer union, as had been done when Great Britain had attempted to foster federation.

Nevertheless, it was through the High Commissioner, Lord Selborne, that a memorandum setting out the necessity of Union was first put forward and later debated in the Cape Parliament. Once before the public the members in the separate Parliaments became the mouthpieces for the expression of regional feeling on this most important issue.

The Transvaal, as the emerging focus or heartland of South Africa, was in a strong position to dictate procedure and aims of union. This was done under the clever guidance of Smuts when the Union Convention was eventually called. Meanwhile, within the Transvaal, rural Afrikaners evinced a strong reversion to isolationism, and protectionism also became manifest. The resurgence of the economic strength of the Transvaal, supported by the open gateway to Delagoa Bay, gave substance to the desire for exclusive self-reliance. A strong English element in the gold mining area balanced the Afrikaner centripetal attitude, by encouraging extra-territorial contacts in mining, trade and industry.

The Transvaal leaders, Generals Botha and Smuts, attempted to weld the two conflicting forces in promoting a conciliatory policy with the aim of one united nation of Boer and Briton. Such a policy was proper to a state which knew itself to be the mainspring of the South African economy and the host of a developing industrial society which attracted to it workers from every cultural group, black or white, in the southern half of the continent.

From the premise that a South African nation could spring from the basis of a common Teutonic origin and Protestant belief came the plan to press for a unitary system of government, rather than a federal system. With both cultural groups spread evenly throughout most of the territory, a federal system would do little towards protecting a minority group.

The Transvaal leaders were well aware that their territory might in the future be the nucleus on to which the British lands north of the Limpopo would in time be welded. Such an expansion northward had always been part of the Transvaalers dream of greater dominion. The jockeying for position in Bechuanaland on the Great North Road had been part of this unfinished saga. Also plans for the British Empire northward had occupied Cecil Rhodes' last year and the plan was still actively pursued in the post-war years, when it was believed a great industrial empire based on mineral wealth would extend to the heart of Africa. Johannesburg, it was assumed, would be the natural capital of this great British dominion.

The leaders in the Transvaal and Cape Colony, both British and Boer, vigorously pursued the policy of closer union from 1906 onwards. Expression of opinion in the Cape Colony in that period seemed proper to a territory which boasted the oldest political organization amongst the Boers in the Bond founded as early as 1881.

The Afrikaner people of the Cape Peninsula and immediate hinterland, unaffected by frontier hysteria, nor prejudiced against alien miners, had been able to mould a society happy in their own language and culture, yet fully at ease with the English speakers and their language and customs. The English in the Cape had in turn become imbued with the South African spirit which resents dictate from home-born British, and above all the interference of the Colonial Office in what were considered internal and domestic affairs.

In the immediate post-war years there was a strong anti-imperialist feeling in the Cape which drew the South African English towards those Afrikaners, like the Bondsmen, who advocated a federal dominion with full self-government under the umbrella of the Union Jack.

The Orange Free State was the avenue of contact and communication between the two forceful states to the north and south of it. But on the remote farms of the Free State was nursed that Afrikaner nationalism which burst into a consuming fire with the election of the Nationalist Government in 1948. The Free State, so long an avenue of physical movement north and south, became also the avenue of Afrikaner nationalism, which found response throughout South Africa. Ex-President Steyn, in the guise of prophet, gave his views on closer union and believed thereby that the Afrikaners once united in a single state, would the more effectively move towards full national independence. This aspiration was in fact achieved with the proclamation of the South African Nationalist Republic in 1961. A Christian national system of education and the political premise that South Africa should have two white peoples developing separately, but equally, were also the Free State contribution towards the concept of Afrikaner nationalism.

Natal was left ignorant of these early investigations into the possibilities of Union. J. X. Merriman, Prime Minister of the Cape Assembly, writing to ex-President Steyn of the Free State, remarks, 'I think in the present juncture all our energies should be concentrated on getting the Governments in the Cape, Orange River Colony and the Transvaal—Natal is past praying for—then we may proceed to a national convention on elected lines to consider this great and complicated question'.[1] At no point in the preliminary negotiations was Natal formally consulted. Indeed after the punitive campaign against the Zulu in 1907, described by General Smuts as 'loot and rapine', Natal was considered politically too immature even to merit the self-government given her in 1893. From that date Natal has been managed by groups from the rival centres of Durban or Pietermaritzburg. There was rivalry also between the coastal plantation farmers and the mixed farms of the interior plateaux. It was suggested that Natal could be bought into Union by the offer of the Utrecht or New Republic territory, which indeed was added to Natal at Union.

Natal knew she had no adequate defence once the imperial forces were withdrawn. Hence the need to gain security by partnership with the Transvaal was greater than the desire to maintain a characteristically British colony.

The pride of having Durban chosen as the centre in which the Inter-Colonial Convention was to meet to discuss Union,

[1] Steyn Papers, 21 June 1907, quoted by L. M. Thompson: *The Unification of South Africa*, 1902–1910, Oxford, 1960, p. 75.

allayed much of the resentment of being ignored by the other Governments. Natal favoured federation—the only state to do so at the conference—but in the face of the Transvaal argument her ill-prepared thesis fell away, and Natal thereafter supported the Transvaal.

Union all but floundered on the questions of the franchise of the non-European and the Native policy to be adopted by South Africa as a whole. Rather than have unification set aside, these controversial matters were left in abeyance, and each province continued to administer their non-European sector of the population as before. Since Britain was also involved in these questions in the Protected Territories, it was decided to leave these outside the terms of Union, with this proviso that they be absorbed 'as a matter of course' into Union when these matters were finally resolved.

During the preliminary exploration of closer union in the Transvaal Assembly views had been expressed by Ministers that steps should be taken to include the province of Mozambique within the projected Federation. Such an impractical proposal illustrates the Afrikaner sentiment, that expansion into or inclusion of any African territory is the obvious course if Afrikaner people or their interests are involved. Such an attitude is at present strongly felt in relation to South West Africa, despite its mandatory position.

Southern Rhodesia was felt to be insufficiently developed for the newly fledged Union to bear the burden of its defence and exploitation. It was believed it would be a matter of time before Southern Rhodesia (like the Protectorates) would be absorbed into the Union.

In June 1907 the Transvaal Government announced their withdrawal from the Customs Union set up after the war, and asked for an inter-colonial conference to discuss future tariffs. This was the Conference which Smuts hoped would be 'the starting-point of a united South Africa'. Thereafter events led to the Convention at Durban, where the political map of the Union of South Africa was blocked out, leaving aside the anomaly of British protected African land within the body politic of the newly founded state. Another issue which all but brought the Union Conference to a standstill was the choice of a national capital. In this minor issue regional jealousies and sectional interests became quite clear. Natal, standing outside the inner deliberations, was offered monetary compensation for the loss of the national capital. Ultimately it became necessary to divide the functions of capital between the regional capitals of the other three Colonies.

Johannesburg was the obvious centre for an entirely new capital, save that Afrikaner sentiment would not accept a city founded by the English and for purposes outside their mode of life. However, with the present mobility of communication Johannesburg, the financial centre of the Union, is only an hour's journey from Pretoria. Continued urban growth will shortly see the two cities physically joined, when the functions of administration and finance proper to a capital will be within the one metropolis. If, as is hinted, the Legislature is brought from Cape Town to new parliament buildings in Pretoria, then the full expression of a capital city will be realized.

Johannesburg, to which place the High Commissioner removed his office from Cape Town following on the liberation of the City in 1900, became the unrecognized capital city for the English-speaking people of the interior. The establishment of the Anglican Cathedral and the largest English-speaking University, along with financial dominance, gave a three-fold basis to the city's claim to leadership.

Thus Pretoria and Johannesburg each enjoys the esteem delegated to a capital, but by different sections of the population. The Africans, Indians and Coloureds so long associated with the city and its development would claim it as a capital city proper to a plural society. But like the country of which it is a microcosm, the conurbation now developing on the Rand is built of cells, each developing separately. When fusion ultimately takes place, then South Africa may be free to call itself United South Africa, with a capital city composed of all sections of that multiple society.

BIBLIOGRAPHY

ACOCKS, J. P. H., *Veld Types of South Africa*, Memoir of the Union Botanical Survey, No. 28, 1953.

AGAR-HAMILTON, J. A. L., *The Road to the North*, South Africa, 1852–1886, London, 1937.

A Guide to the Cape of Good Hope, London, 1819.

An Ecological Survey of the Mountain Area of Basutoland, Crown Agents, 1938.

BACKHOUSE, J., *A Narrative of a Visit to the Mauritius and South Africa*, London, 1844.

BARNARD, Lady Anne, *South Africa a Century Ago*, ed. by W. H. Wilkins, London, 1901.

BARROW, J., *Travels into the Interior of Southern Africa*, London, 1806.

BROOKS, H., MANN, R. J., *Natal*, London, 1876.

BRYANT, A.T., *The Zulu People*, Pietermaritzburg, 1949.

BRYCE, J., *Impressions of South Africa*, London, 1899.

BUCHANAN, K. M., PUGH, J. C., *Land and People in Nigeria*, London, 1955.

BURCHELL, W. J., *Travels in the Interior of Southern Africa*, 1822–4 (Reprint 1953, Glasgow), Vol. II.

CAMPBELL, J., *Travels in South Africa*, London, 1815.

COLE, M., *South Africa*, London, 1961.

COLLINS, W. W., *Free Statia*, Bloemfontein, 1907.

CORNISH, Vaughan, *The Great Capitals*, London, 1923.

CORY, G. E., *The Rise of South Africa*, London, 1913, Vol. II.

DAVIDSON, B., *Old Africa Rediscovered*, London, 1961.

DE KIEWIET, C. W., *A History of South Africa*, Oxford, 1941.

DE KIEWIET, C. W., *British Colonial Policy and the South African Republics 1848–72*, Imperial Studies No. 3, 1929.

DE KOCK, M. H., *The Economic Development of South Africa*, London, 1936.

DE KOCK, M. H., *The Economic History of South Africa*, Cape Town, 1924.

DUFF GORDON, Lady, *Letters from the Cape*, ed. by J. Purves, London, 1921.

DUFFY, J., *Portuguese Africa*, Cambridge, Massachusetts, 1959.

DU TOIT, A. E., 'The Cape Frontier: A Study of Native Policy with Special Reference to the years 1847–66', *Archives Year Book for South African History*, 1951, Vol. I.

EDWARDS, I. E., *The 1820 Settlers in South Africa*, A Study in British Colonial Policy, Imperial Studies No. 9, London, 1934.

ELLIS, W., *Three Visits to Madagascar*, London, 1858.

FAGE, J. D., *An Atlas of African History*, 1958.

FAIRBRIDGE, D., *Historic Houses of South Africa*, London, 1922.

FLEURE, H. J., *Some Problems of Society and Environment*, The Institute of British Geographers, Pub. No. 12, London, 1947.

FRANKEL, S. H., *Capital Investment in Africa*, London, 1938.

GREEN, L. P., FAIR, T. J. D., *Development in Africa*, Johannesburg, 1962.

HAILEY, Lord, *An African Survey*, Revised 1956, Oxford, 1957.

HARRIS, W. C., *Narrative of an Expedition into Southern Africa*, Bombay, 1838.

HATTERSLEY, A. F., *More Annals of Natal*, London, 1936.

HOCKLEY, H. E., *The Story of the British Settlers of 1820 in South Africa*, Cape Town, 1957.

INGRAMS, H., *Uganda*, London, 1960.

KEANE, A. H., *The Boer States*, London, 1900.

KEPPEL-JONES, A., *South Africa*, London (N.D. Hutchinson's Univ. Library, No. 3).

LE VAILLANT, *Travels in Africa*, London, 1796.

LICHTENSTEIN, H., *Travels in Southern Africa*, Van Riebeeck Society, Cape Town, 1928, Vol. I.

MACKENZIE, J., *Ten Years North of the Orange River*, Edinburgh, 1871.

MACKINDER, Sir Halford, *Democratic Ideals and Reality*, 1909.

MARAIS, J. S., *The Cape Coloured People, 1652–1937*, London, 1939.

MATHERS, E. P., *Gold Fields of South Africa*, Reprinted from *Natal Mercury*, Durban, 1884.

MAUD, J. P. R., *City Government*, Oxford, 1938.

MENTZEL, O. F., *Description of the Cape*, Van Riebeeck Society, Cape Town, 1944.

MICHELL, Hon. Sir Lewis, *The Life of the Rt. Hon. Cecil Rhodes, 1853–1902*, London, 1910.

MOODIE, D., *The Record Papers on the Native Tribes of South Africa*, Cape Town, 1838.

MULLER, H. P. N., *Oude Tyden in den Oranje-Vrystaat*, Leiden, 1907.

NATHAN, M., *Paul Kruger*, Durban, 1944.

NEUMARK, S. D., *Economic Influences on the South African Frontier 1652–1836*, Stanford, 1957.

OATES, F., *Matabeleland and the Victoria Falls*, London, 1881.

PERCIVAL, R., *An Account of the Cape of Good Hope*, London, 1804.

Précis of Information Concerning the Transvaal Territory, London, 1881.

RANDALL-MACIVER, D., *Medieval Rhodesia*, London, 1906.

RECLUS, Elisée, *The Universal Geography*, London, Vol. XIII.

Report of the Transvaal Indigency Commission, 1906–8, Pretoria, 1908.

REUNERT, T., *Diamonds and Gold in South Africa*, London, 1893.

SANDERSON, J., *Memoranda of a Trading Trip into the Orange River Free State, and the Country of the Transvaal Boers, 1851–2*.

Scenes and Occurrences in Albany and Cafferland, London, 1827.

SCHAPERA, I., *Western Civilisation and the Natives of South Africa*, London, 1934.

SCHAPERA, I., *The Cambridge History of the British Empire*, Cambridge, 1936, Vol. VIII.

SELOUS, F. C., *Sunshine and Storm in Rhodesia*, London, 1896.

S. W. Silver and Co.'s Handbook to the Transvaal, London, 1877.

STOW, G. W., *The Native Races of South Africa*, London, 1910.

TABLER, E. C., *The Far Interior*, Cape Town, 1955.

THEAL, G. M., *Chronicles of Cape Commanders*, Cape, 1882.

THEAL, G. M., *Compendium of the History and Geography of South Africa*, London, 1878.

THEAL, G. M., *History of South Africa*, London, 1897.

THEAL, G. M., *History of South Africa since 1795*, London, 1908, Vol. I.

THOMPSON, L. M., *The Unification of South Africa 1902–10*, Oxford, 1960.

TROLLOPE, A., *South Africa*, London, 1878, Vol. II.

WALKER, E. A., *A History of South Africa*, London, 1947.

WALKER, E. A., *A History of Southern Africa*, London, 1959.

WALKER, E. A., *Historical Atlas of South Africa*, Oxford, 1922.

WALTON, J., *Homesteads and Villages of South Africa*, Pretoria, 1952.

WELLINGTON, J., *Southern Africa*, Cambridge, 1955, Vols. I and II.

234   BIBLIOGRAPHY

WHITING SPILHAUS, M., *The First South Africans,* Cape Town, 1949.

WILLIAMS, B., *Cecil Rhodes,* London, 1938.

VAN DER POEL, J., *Railways and Customs Policies in South Africa,* London, 1933.

VAN RIEBEECK SOCIETY, *Collectanea,* Cape Town, 1924.

INDEX